Strategic Management

For my parents
Anthony and Elizabeth

Strategic Management

A PC-based approach

Patrick B. McNamee

BUTTERWORTH
HEINEMANN

Butterworth-Heinemann Ltd
Linacre House, Jordan Hill, Oxford OX2 8DP

 PART OF REED INTERNATIONAL BOOKS

OXFORD   LONDON   BOSTON
MUNICH   NEW DELHI   SINGAPORE   SYDNEY
TOKYO   TORONTO   WELLINGTON

First published 1992

© Patrick B. McNamee 1992

British Library Cataloguing in Publication Data
McNamee, Patrick B.
  Strategic Management: A PC-based approach
  I. Title
  658.400285

ISBN 0 7506 0505 7

Library of Congress Cataloguing in Publication Data
McNamee, Patrick B.
  Strategic management: a PC-based approach/Patrick B. McNamee.
  p. cm.
  Includes bibliographical references and index.
  ISBN 0 7506 0505 7
  1. Strategic planning.   2. Strategic planning – Data processing.
  I. Title.
  HD30.28.M3854
  658.4'012'02855365–dc20   92–7296
                                                                CIP

Photoset, printed and bound in Great Britain by
Redwood Press Limited, Melksham, Wiltshire

Contents

Preface

Although the concept of strategic management is now well recognized in many companies, its practice is still not prevalent. This book aims to make its practice more widespread. The book has been written for managers who wish to increase their knowledge of strategic management and how it can be implemented on a personal computer. More specifically it is aimed at the manager who is perhaps developing and writing strategic plans for the first time, and the book can be regarded as a manual for developing such plans. Indeed the final chapter – Chapter 16: 'Developing and Writing a Strategic Plan' – provides a template for a formal planning document that managers may tailor to their own particular requirements.

A feature of the book is the inclusion of a computer disk that will carry out all the calculations in the text. This disk runs on a 'cut down' version of Javelin Software, and shows the reader how suitable this software is for strategic planning, financial analysis and market planning. Readers are advised to use the models as provided until they become familiar with them, and they should then attempt to construct their own models.

The book has been designed so that it is an integrated text, irrespective of whether the computer disk is used or not. So readers who do not wish to use the software may skip those chapters that are computer-orientated, and the remaining chapters will still be a complete text on strategic management.

After reading this book readers should be familiar with the core concepts in strategic management, have a good knowledge of the register of the language of strategy and have the computing skills to develop planning models.

Although the book has been written with managers in mind, it should also be of interest to MBA and final level Business Studies, Accounting and Marketing students.

Finally there are many people that I must thank for helping me in this task. By far the most important and helpful influence has been my family – Brid, David and Stephen. Of the many other people who have been of immense help and encouragement, I would like to single out in particular: Charles Carroll of the Irish Management Institute for the many ideas of his that I have included in this book; Stephen Hurrell of Information Resources for his assistance with the software; James Lancaster, James Leonard, David

Keen and Ian MacFarlane of TM Group for the feedback they provided; Gavin McWhinney of the University of Ulster for his encouragement; and finally the students at the University of Ulster for all their help and patience.

Patrick B. McNamee
University of Ulster

Figures

Tables

1 Strategic management: the concept and a model

THE QUESTION OF STRATEGY

Strategy is now a key word in the register of top management language. One hears of company strategy, strategic management, strategic issues, corporate strategy, international strategy, and information technology strategy. Indeed the usage of this word is now so common that, through familiarity, its true meaning may have become lost or at least somewhat blurred. This book is concerned with clarifying the meaning of the concept. It is concerned with helping readers to develop a clear conception of what strategy is, what it is that distinguishes the issue of strategy from other issues in business, and finally how they can become more effective in their strategic management.

Consider the performance of the following companies:

Canada: International Thompson Organisation; *France*: LVMH Moet Hennessy; *Great Britain*: Hanson Trust: *Holland*: Unilever NV; *Ireland*: Smurfit Group; *Japan*: Toyota Motor; *Sweden*: L.M. Ericsson; *Switzerland*: Nestle; *US*: Coca Cola; *West Germany*: Bayer Company.

Each company is from a different country. Each company is in a different industry. Each company is outstandingly successful. Each company's success is durable and is seen to have been sustained over many years. Each company's success seems almost independent of economic conditions. In other words, it really doesn't seem to matter whether the world economy or the company's national economy is stable, is in recession or is growing, or to which industrial sector the company belongs, each of these companies continues to outperform rivals. They are consistent winners.

Although each of the above companies is a major international player, similar observations can be made about local or regional small businesses. In most of the economically developed regions of the world there are local firms in all industrial sectors that are consistent outperformers.

Why should this be so? Why is it that for some companies, irrespective of their size, location or industry, success seems so certain?

The suggested answer is that these enduringly successful companies have achieved this status because they have been so effective in their *strategic management*, where strategic management is defined as that type of management through which *the company obtains a sustainable long-term excellent fit with its environment*, and the quality of this fit is reflected in repeated superior performance. Strategic management therefore is concerned with those long-run, fundamental and often irreversible decisions about the company's mission, scale of operations and spread of activities. This concept of strategic management implies that it is distinguished from other types of management by the following characteristics.

Characteristics of successful strategy

Time scale

The time scale for strategic decisions is many years. It is concerned with the long-run nature of the company and its activities. An extreme example of this perspective is provided by the very successful Japanese Matsushita Corporation's strategic plan for 1932. This plan had a 250-year time span!

> On the fifth of May 1932, the fourteenth anniversary of the company's founding, Konosuke Matsushita assembled his 162 employees and announced his business philosophy and a 250 year corporate plan, broken up into ten 25 year sections. 'I, myself, and you assembled here are to carry out the first 25 years. Our successors will carry on exactly the same for another 25 years, and so on.'[1]

Scope

The scope of strategic decisions is company-wide. It is concerned with the totality of the company rather than individual parts. For example, the strategic decision of the US conglomerate ITT in the late 1980s to withdraw from the European electronics/computer business had major implications for all parts of the company and not just for the electronics/computer divisions. This was a strategic decision.

Reversibility

Strategic decisions normally will be extremely difficult if not impossible to reverse. Thus the decision taken by the United Kingdom government in the 1950s to rely on nuclear power for electricity generation has in recent years appeared to have been a rather expensive one. However, changing from nuclear to non-nuclear sources is extremely difficult. The decision to rely on nuclear energy was strategic and consequently very difficult to reverse.

Level

Strategic decisions are normally taken by the top management of companies. Thus the decision of Asea of Sweden to merge with BBC of Switzerland was a decision of immense strategic importance, which was taken by the top management of both companies with a great deal of reported stimulation from the Chief Executive Officer, Percy Barnevik. 'Percy Barnevik is determined to shape ABB into what he believes is the model European company of the future.'[2]

Importance

The importance of strategic decisions cannot really be over-emphasized. An incorrect strategic decision may ruin a company, whereas incorrect operating or administrative decisions may usually be weathered. For example, the decision of multinational media company News International to enter the United Kingdom satellite broadcasting business in the late 1980s was of major importance to the company's future, reflected in relatively poor performance by the group in 1990. In contrast to this, a decision concerning, say, an increase in the number of staff in a particular department in the company – normally an administrative decision – is not of such great significance.

Thus effective strategic managers ought to have the knowledge, the skills and the vision necessary to:

- *Understand the total company*, i.e. its mission, its goals, or objectives, its culture, its strategies, both higher and lower level, and the activities of the different functional areas and the resources available.
- *Understand the environment* in which the company is operating, with particular reference to the opportunities and the threats that are, or will be, present.
- *Develop strategies* that are appropriate to the company and its environment.
- *Implement chosen strategies.*
- *Control, evaluate and amend* as appropriate, the strategies that have been selected.

This brief description is the core of the model of strategic management that will be employed in this book, and is the framework upon which the book's computer model of strategy (see Chapter 3) is built.

A MODEL FOR STRATEGIC MANAGEMENT

Figure 1 shows, schematically, the model of strategic management that will be used in this book. It is concerned with developing a framework to achieve long-term success. Although each element in the model is set out sequentially, in practice this neat delineation and sequencing will not usually occur – many of the elements are overlapping and their analyses will be conducted

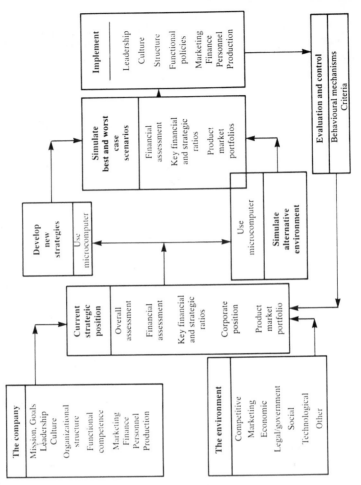

Figure 1   A model of strategic management

simultaneously, and the process of strategic management will be one that is integrated and iterative. However, for the purposes of exposition, each element will be treated separately and will comprise a single chapter in this book. In order to provide an overview, each of the elements is now introduced and briefly discussed.

ANALYSING THE COMPANY

It is suggested that the first step in the strategic management process is analysing and then understanding the nature of the company. More specifically the starting point for the process is understanding the company's mission, goals, aspirations, strategies and structure.

Chapter 4 will develop a methodology for doing this, and it is assumed that the following are the principal determinants of any company's profile.

Mission and goals

Understanding the mission and the goals of the company is the fundamental starting point of strategic analysis – an examination of who the top decision-makers and stakeholders in a company are and what are the value systems that drive them. The top managers tend to set the corporate strategic goals and it is from these that all the company's activities flow.

Leadership

Leadership is usually a fundamental determinant of the success or failure of a company. Effective leadership can take many forms, from coercive and autocratic at one end of the spectrum to participative and democratic at the other. Leadership, in strategic management, is assessed not according to style, but according to its appropriateness and consequent effectiveness.

Culture

The culture of a company is assumed to be that somewhat nebulous but nonetheless real set of values and attitudes that somehow pervades all companies and binds (or in some cases fails to bind) their people together. For example, companies in traditional industries such as banking and insurance tend to have rather conservative cultures, while less traditional industries, such as information technology and advertising, tend to promote a much more dynamic image. Neither of these cultures is superior; rather, each is appropriate for its industry.

Organizational structure

The formal structure of a company can have profound effects upon its performance, all other things being equal. For example, the decision to combine Ford of Germany and Ford of Britain and form a new structure – Ford of Europe – in 1967 had profoundly beneficial effects upon the long-run performance of that company. This section of the analysis will be concerned with establishing the appropriateness of a company's structure to its strategy.

Functional composition

Finally a methodology for assessing the relative strengths and weaknesses in the principal functions that most companies have, i.e. finance and account-

ing, marketing, production and personnel, is set out. In passing, it is important to note that although it is frequently maintained that it is important to
have balanced functional strength, this is not necessarily always true. Thus
during the start-up stage of a business, it may be more important to have
relative strength in the marketing function, as it is likely to promote *growth*,
than to have strength in, say, the finance and accounting function, which is
more likely to promote *control*. In contrast to this situation, during a period
of retrenchment, when *control* is likely to be required, it may be more
important to have relative strength in the finance and accounting function.

An analysis of all the above elements will be used to provide a picture of the
strategic health and potential of the company.

ANALYSING THE ENVIRONMENT

Understanding the environment faced by a company is of immense importance: *successful strategies are ones where the company adapts to its environment*. Those companies that fail to adapt to their environment will not in the
long run survive, but will, like dinosaurs, disappear.
   An example of this type of failure is provided by the demise of the UK
motor-cycle industry, which failed because it did not mount an effective
strategic reaction to a major environmental change – namely, the emergence
of the Japanese motor-cycle industry. The Japanese producers planned and
managed their motor-cycle industry on a world basis, i.e. they built factories
that were designed to serve the world and not just their home market. Such a
development was a major competitive innovation to which the UK
companies, with their much less automated production facilities and their
more parochial visions of their markets, were unable to respond effectively.
   The shortcomings of their response is shown by the selected production
figures shown in Table 1.

Table 1   Productivity in the motor-cycle industry[3]

Company	Unit output per year	Units/man per year
NTV	20,000	15
Honda	2,000,000	174
Yamaha	1,000,000	200
Suzuki	800,000	114
BMW	25,000	20
R & D manpower		
NTV	100	
Honda	1,300	

The process of environmental analysis presents the strategic planner with a dilemma – if all those environmental elements that *could* have some influence on the company are included, then the analysis becomes extremely complex and unwieldy, with the constituent elements being analysed to a relatively low level of resolution. Alternatively, if, in the interests of reducing the level of complexity, certain environmental elements are omitted, then, although the resolution should be higher, certain crucial environmental forces may be omitted from the analysis. In practice deciding upon the appropriate balance between the width of the environmental analysis and its depth is frequently a function of the nature of the industry, and requires knowledge, experience and judgement on the part of the strategic planner.

Chapter 6 will examine the environment in detail. It will set out a methodology for understanding the total environment in which a company operates, and then identifying and analysing those elements or forces that will either be *opportunities* for the company to exploit or *threats* to its existence that ought to be counteracted. It is suggested that the environment can be segmented into the broad forces set out below, which have been found frequently by strategists to be the most crucial.

Market forces

The market forces determine whether the products or services offered by a company will be ultimately purchased, at an acceptable price, by consumers. Among the more important market forces are:

- The size and affluence of the market.
- The number of competitors and their sizes.
- The growth rate of the market.
- The influences on buying decisions – prices, product features, methods of distribution, and methods of promotion.
- Market position relative to competitors.

Competitive forces

Closely related to the market forces are the competitive forces.[4] These buffet all companies to a varying degree, and effective strategic planning requires that they be recognized and counteracted. They are normally grouped under the following headings:

- The threat of new entrants.
- The threat from substitutes.
- The power of buyers.
- The power of suppliers.
- The degree of rivalry.

Economic forces

Here the economic context – global and national – in which the company operates is examined and its impact assessed.

Legal / government forces

Frequently a company's current and future operations are affected by legislation over which it has very little control. Increasingly the legislative forces are becoming international rather than just national. For example, the implementation of the Single European Act in 1992 will have profound effects upon companies within and outside Europe.

Social trends

This element is concerned with assessing how social trends affect or will affect the company. For example, in the late 1970s and 1980s in many developed Western countries society in general became very concerned about health, diet and fitness. This social change provided market opportunities for industries and companies that were aware of the change. Thus the growth in the sales of running and jogging equipment reflects a major social change.

Technological change

In many industries technological change has fundamental influences, and in such industries, in order to survive, companies must be cognisant of such changes and keep abreast of them. For example desk-top publishing has revolutionalized the ability of authors to publish books without using established publishers.

Geographical location

With the development of almost instant global information communication systems and the decreasing costs of physical transport, industry has in general become less restricted in its choice of manufacturing location. Many industries are no longer tied to natural factor endowments such as sources of raw materials, or cheap labour, nor are they forced to be close to their markets. Instead industry's location is increasingly determined by a whole range of factors of competitive advantage or necessity, which vary from industry to industry but which in advanced industries, according to Porter, frequently include 'human resources with particular skills, resident scientific infrastructure of appropriate types and access to sophisticated suppliers'.[5]

Other forces

This is really a 'catch-all' category for any relevant environmental forces (should there be any) that are not captured in any of the other categories.

In summary, analysing the environment is concerned with isolating, understanding and then measuring the prevailing fundamental environmental forces and trends that affect a particular company, and then estimating their future likely impact.

THE CURRENT STRATEGIC POSITION

In Chapter 8 a methodology for assessing the current strategic position of a company will be developed. In this part of the strategic process the company appraisal (Chapter 4) is married to the environmental appraisal (Chapter 6) to provide a strategic locus for the company, as shown on p. 137.

This assessment is considered from four major complementary perspectives:

- *An overall assessment*, which presents a qualitative perspective of the company's strategic position.
- *The financial analysis*, provided through the use of common financial statements – income statements, cash-flow statement, balance sheets, funds-flow statements and ratio analysis statements.
- *Key strategic ratios*, which show the company's performance and its competitive position.
- *Corporate portfolio position*, which shows how a strategic business unit (see Chapter 2) or division is performing from a corporate perspective.
- *Product market portfolio*, which shows the balance of the portfolio of products a company has (see Chapter 10).

DEVELOPING STRATEGIES

This could be regarded as the most creative part of the strategic management process. Here, building upon the company's current strategic position, a future strategy is formulated. A crucial element in the development of a future strategy is the quality of the planner's judgement about the future. The approach advocated is that accurate quantitative forecasts are extremely difficult to make, and consequently an approach that favours using micro-computer-based models to simulate alternative future scenarios, and their likely consequences, is recommended.

Although there is an infinite variety of strategies that a company can develop, a two-stage methodology that covers all possible strategies is provided in Chapter 12. Figure 53 on p. 190 illustrates the stages.

Stage 1: The fundamental strategy

This decision will be determined by the company's goals, its current strategic position and its competitive prospects. It is assumed that there are just five fundamental strategies:

1 Conservative growth.
2 High growth.
3 Neutral.
4 Recovery.
5 Reduction.

Once a fundamental strategy has been selected, it can then be further refined into more precise functional sub-strategies.

Stage 2: The generic strategy

Porter[6] suggests that there are just three generic strategies that will enable a company to gain competitive advantage. These are:

1 *High volume / low cost.* This strategy seeks to gain competitive advantage through having lower costs and higher volumes than competitors. Companies that have successfully adopted this approach include Black and Decker power tools and Toyota motor cars.
2 *Product differentiation.* This strategy seeks to gain competitive advantage through differentiating the product from lower priced offerings on the basis of some non-price factor such as quality. For example, BMW has very successfully differentiated its cars from others on the basis of quality and performance.
3 *Focus.* This strategy seeks to gain competitive advantage through a company concentrating on serving just one very narrow customer group or market segment and not attempting to serve any others. The competitive advantage arises out of tailoring one's strategy to the requirements of a relatively small niche in the market.

STRATEGY IMPLEMENTATION

In many companies it is the case that the words of a strategy are more the reality than its implementation, i.e. although the company *says* that it intends to move in a particular direction, its *actions* don't show this movement. Chapter 14 will develop an approach that tries to ensure that the words of a strategy are turned into action. Implementation takes place when sentiments are translated into actions. For example, if the fundamental strategy of a company is 'to have real sales growth of 10 per cent per annum for the next 3 years', then action will need to be taken to ensure that in the company:

1 The leaders are seen to be in agreement.
2 The leaders have the ability to achieve the specified targets.
3 Adequate resources are provided for all areas affected by the target.
4 The structure is capable of supporting this target.

The methodology for achieving implementation can be broken down into the following related elements.

- *Leadership and implementation.* How appropriate is the current leadership for implementing the new strategy? More specifically, does it have the sufficient power, influence, and knowledge to ensure this?
- *Culture and implementation.* Is the culture that prevails in the company capable of implementing the strategy?
- *Structure and implementation.* Does the current structure of the company match the goals and strategies that are to be implemented?
- *Implementation of functional policies.* Have company strategies been translated into effective and feasible functional policies, targets and precisely delineated programmes and operations?
- *Resources.* Are there sufficient resources at all levels to ensure that strategies can be translated into actions?
- *Information systems and procedures.* Are the company's information systems sufficient to ensure that the strategy can be implemented, monitored, and amended if necessary?

In summary, implementation is concerned with ensuring that verbal or written strategic aspirations, which are often formulated by those at the apex of the company's hierarchy and which are frequently couched in broad financial or marketing terms, are transformed into effective material and measurable programmes for action at all levels throughout the company.

EVALUATION AND CONTROL

This is the final element in the model, and it is concerned with two issues: first, how effectively the chosen strategy has been implemented and, second, triggering appropriate actions if the company is failing to meet the goals of the chosen strategy. This will call for a consideration of:

1   The behavioural aspects of the need to monitor.
2   Mechanisms for ensuring objectivity, speed and accuracy in feedback.
3   Criteria for the assessment of the success of operations.
4   Mechanisms to ensure action on deviations from strategic targets.

SUMMARY OF THE MODEL OF STRATEGIC MANAGEMENT

This model of strategic management provides a comprehensive integrated methodology for:

1   Analysing the strategic position of a company in terms of its strengths and weaknesses and in terms of the threats and opportunities in its environment.
2   Formulating future strategies.
3   Implementing, monitoring and evaluating those chosen strategies.

As Figure 1 shows, the model is a closed loop, and strategic management should therefore be regarded not as an activity that takes place at a certain specified time in the business calendar, but rather as a continuous process that is iterative and should be self-correcting.

THE STRATEGIC MANAGEMENT COMPUTER MODEL

The computer model accompanying this book – THE CLASSIC GROUP – attempts to capture the main elements in strategic management that have been summarized in this chapter. It is suggested that readers should now run the model to obtain an overview of its operation and also to try to relate it to this chapter. Details on the model and instructions for running it are given in Chapter 3.

References

1 Ghoshal, S. and Oullet, R., *Matsushita Electric Industrial Co. Ltd (MEI)*, Case Clearing House, Cranfield, 1987.
2 *Business Week*, 23 July 1990, p. 34.
3 Source: Boston Consulting Group, 'Strategic Alternatives for the British Motor Cycle Industry': A report prepared for the Secretary of State for Industry, 30 July 1975.

4 Porter, M. E., *Competitive Strategy: Techniques for Analyzing Industries and Competitors*, Collier-Macmillan Publishers, London, 1980.
5 Porter, M. E., 'The Industrial Competitiveness of Nations: Beyond Comparative Advantage,' Address to Irish Management Institute, Dublin, June 1986.
6 Porter, *Competitive Strategy, op. cit.*

2 Factors affecting strategy development

INTRODUCTION

This chapter examines a number of concepts that have been found to be of core importance in strategic management and the construction of strategy models. These topics are the following: the relationship between a company's structure and its strategic planning system, the product life cycle, a classification of decision-making in companies, and finally strategic decision-making versus functional decision-making.

THE RELATIONSHIP BETWEEN A COMPANY'S STRUCTURE AND ITS STRATEGIC PLANNING SYSTEM

For effective strategic planning the system adopted must match the structure and needs of the company in which it is being employed. This means that strategic planning systems can range from the unwritten verbal plans of an entrepreneur to the large and detailed planning volumes of a multinational corporation. Neither of these systems is naturally superior; the important thing is that each system should be appropriate. The importance of having an appropriate structure is exemplified by the recent history of the Dutch electronics group Philips. In 1989 Philips posted its largest loss ever: $1.06 billion dollars. Many analysts attributed the company's failure to its bureaucratic structure and resultant culture:

> Although the 57 year old Timmer (the Chief Executive Officer) is noted for taking tough decisions, there's growing doubt that even this tough company veteran can win against Philips' vast headquarters bureaucracy. 'The culture and huge central staff in Eindhoven remain untouched', commented Bill Coleman, an analyst from James Capel & Co. in London.[1]

Analysts regarded the structure as wholly inappropriate for many of the fast moving areas of electronics in which Philips was engaged. 'While the computer unit produced minis, its bureaucrats didn't realise customers were changing to PCs.'[2]

The Philips structure is in direct contrast to the top management structure of the highly successful ABB Asea Brown Boveri. This company has a rather slim central staff, comprising the Chief Executive Officer and twelve top aides (six Swedes, three Swiss and three Germans).

Although the selection of a planning system should not just be the mechanical matching of a system to a company, there are nonetheless fundamental differences in planning systems, which are a direct function of company structure. The main forms of company structure and their associated planning systems are set out below.

Simple or small business structure

This is the most basic type of organizational structure and is shown in Figure 2. This type of structure tends to have an owner or a manager who has a small number of employees that produce a limited range of products for a limited range of market segments. This structure is also known as 'entrepreneurial', as it is often employed at the start-up phase of a business.

In this type of structure strategic management tends to be informal and takes place at two levels:

1   At the *business* level the owner or manager devises strategies for the business.
2   At the *operational* (or *functional*) level the employees, under the owner's or manager's supervision, implement these strategies.

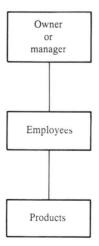

Figure 2   Simple or small business structure

Normally the products, technology, markets and the set of competitors are fairly fixed, and the principal concern of strategic planning is competing effectively against rivals in existing, or extensions of existing, product lines. Thus the business is 'given' and the *major strategic issue is how to succeed in that given business*. An example of this type of business would be a local bakery, where the range of products is limited, the customers are from the locality, and the set and nature of competitors is fairly static.

This structure is really only effective for the smallest type of business, and normally, as businesses grow – through increasing the range of products manufactured and the number of personnel – specialization becomes possible and the small business structure tends to evolve into a functional business structure.

Functional business structure

As a company develops, the structure is frequently changed in order to enable it to handle the increased complexity of expanding the range of activities, and to reap the economic benefits that additional size should bring. Figure 3 gives a schematic representation of a functional business structure, in which personnel are grouped into departments according to the function that the department carries out. Traditionally these functions are marketing, accounting and finance, production, personnel, and research and development. Each of these departments has a manager, who, as well as having the tasks of managing the department and promoting co-ordination between departments, also acts as a two-way co-ordinating link to the board of directors, which will frequently comprise the owners of the company plus the heads of the functional departments.

Strategic planning is devised by the board of directors, and is implemented largely by the functional managers. Therefore, as in the small business structure, planning takes place at two levels – the business level and the functional level.

Thus at the business level it is assumed that the business area is given, i.e. the products, technologies, markets and set of competitors are already in existence and the major task of the strategic planner at this level is to plan how the business can succeed against competitors who are in the same or similar businesses. In most cases the company will have a range of products and a range of markets, and strategic planners will therefore have discretion about altering the balance of the portfolio of products manufactured and also the range of markets in which the company competes, in order to achieve strategic goals.

At the functional level the major task is to implement the business level strategies. Strategic planning in this type of structure is thus simply an extension of strategic planning in the small business structure.

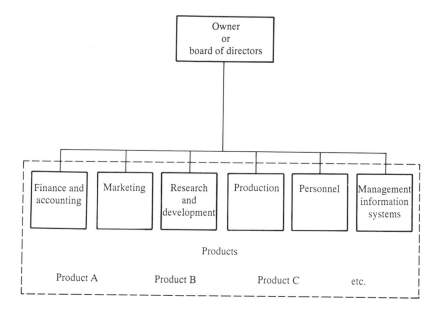

Figure 3 Functional business structure

The divisional structure

Frequently, as a company grows, the functional structure becomes inadequate for its range of activities or inappropriate to its goals. This can be seen particularly clearly when a company develops discrete ranges of products that are not directly related to each other. For example, a motor vehicle manufacturer may have three discrete ranges of vehicles – specialist sports cars, volume cars and commercial vehicles. Although the ranges are related, there are clear distinctions between the nature of the products in each range, the market segments at which each range is aimed and the nature of the competition each range faces. Because of these differences in products, markets and competitors, different levels of resources, different skills and different business performance expectations apply to each range.

Frequently it is logical to structure such a company to reflect these differences. This type of structure is known as a divisional structure, and in the above case the divisions could be known as Specialist Sports Car Division, Volume Car Division and Commercial Vehicle Division. A schematic representation of a divisional business structure is shown in Figure 4.

A well known company that attributes its success partly to being organized on this basis is the UK luxury consumer goods manufacturer Dunhill. Its structure is shown in Figure 5.

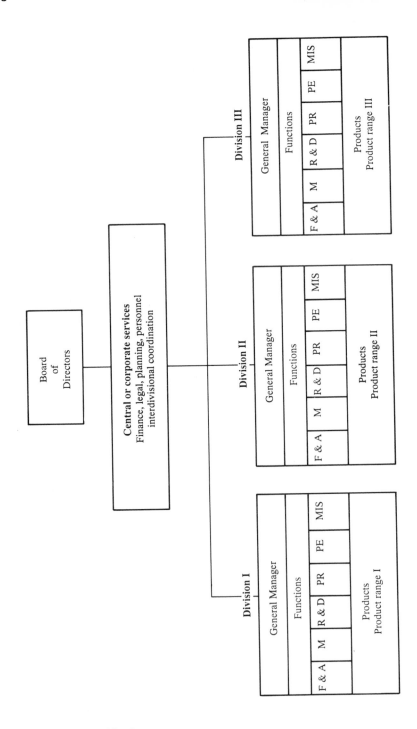

Figure 4 Divisional business structure

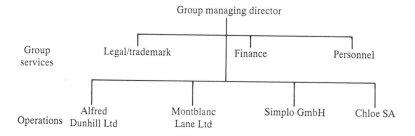

Figure 5   Group structure of Dunhill Holdings Plc[3]

As can be seen, Dunhill operates in four distinct product market segments:

- *Alfred Dunhill Ltd,* which is in the business of merchandising and marketing luxury consumer products for men.
- *Montblanc Lane Ltd,* which is engaged in the manufacture and distribution of tobacco and smokers' products in the USA.
- *Simplo GmbH,* which is engaged in the manufacture and marketing of writing instruments.
- *Chloe SA,* which is engaged in merchandising and marketing of luxury fashion products for women.

Each of these divisions is run fairly independently within corporate parameters.

In a divisionally structured company strategic planning is a conceptually different process from strategic planning in either the small business structure or the functional business structure. In the divisional business structure strategic planning takes place hierarchically at three levels:

1   The corporate level.
2   The business level.
3   The functional level.

The planning process for the business and functional levels is as previously described. However, at the corporate level, strategic planning is concerned with the issue of deciding 'In what businesses should the company be engaged?' Thus this type of strategic planning is conceptually different from strategic planning for the small business structure and the functional business structure, where the set of businesses is given and the issue is *how* to compete in the given businesses rather than the issue of what is the optimal *portfolio of businesses* the company as a whole should have. Although the definition of just what constitutes optimality will vary from company to company, in general this level of strategic planning will be concerned with developing a balanced portfolio of businesses through expansion of existing businesses, acquisition of new businesses, or the disposal of businesses. The question of what constitutes a balanced portfolio will be discussed in the section 'The Concept of the SBU' (p. 24).

In a divisional business structure it is normally the case that the various divisions are managed, as largely independent businesses by division managers, within certain corporate parameters and with support from corporate services as required. Indeed it was considered by many that the strict adherence to this concept of 'hands-off' management by Tony Greener during his chairmanship of Dunhill was a major influence in determining the increase in sales of that company from £98 million in 1975 to £525 million in 1987.

The board of directors in this type of divisionalized company structure will frequently comprise the owners of the business, top corporate managers and the managing directors of the various divisions.

Matrix structure

In companies where there are two (or more) dominant criteria for success it is important that these criteria are reflected in the organizational and power structures. For example, it may be the case that for a multinational food company to succeed it must have both effective *product* management and also be sensitive to the preferences of the various markets or *areas* in which it sells. In other words, the company will not succeed if, firstly, it does not manufacture effectively and, secondly, if it is not sensitive to local preferences. In such situations matrix structures have been developed.

A schematic representation of a matrix structure is shown in Figure 6. This example illustrates the structure for a multinational company that manufactures three sets of product ranges – Product I, Product II and Product III – and sells the products in three areas – Area A, Area B and Area C. Effective product management and sensitivity to each area market are considered crucial to this company. Therefore the company is structured in a two-dimensional matrix form with the axes of the matrix being 'product' and 'area'.

Along the 'product' axis there are three product managers, one for each product, while along the 'area' axis there are three area managers, one for each area. The product managers and the area managers are of equal status and power in the company, and each pair of product and area managers (for example, Product I Manager and Area A Manager) reports to a Product and Area Manager who has responsibility for both aspects of the business. Thus the structure explicitly recognizes the importance of both effective production and sensitivity to local tastes.

In this type of structure, as in the divisional structure, strategic planning takes place at three levels:

1 *The corporate level*, concerned with the portfolio of businesses and carried out by board of directors and corporate staff.

2 *The business level*, concerned with the portfolio of products and markets and carried out by the product and area managers.
3 *The functional level*, concerned with implementation and carried out by functional managers.

In the matrix structure there are two or more command systems, which in theory have equal weight. For example, in the above food company example there would be an equally strong command and information link from the manager of Product I and Area A to the Area A manager and to the Product I

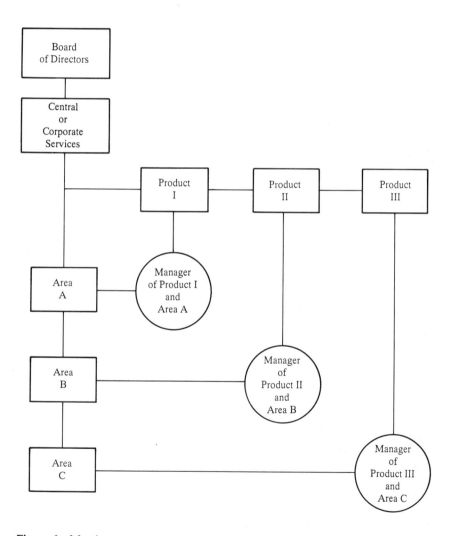

Figure 6   Matrix structure

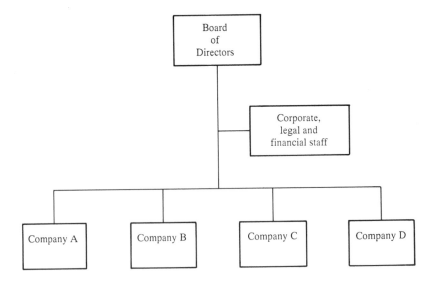

Figure 7   Holding company structure

manager. In practice, however, it is normally the case that one of the dimensions of the matrix is more important than the other.

Holding company structure

Figure 7 illustrates a holding company structure, which is in many ways similar to the divisional structure. The fundamental difference is the degree of independence exercised by the constituent companies. The holding company is really just a collection of separate companies that are held together by a financial control system. The management and strategic decision-making of the constituent companies is carried out with minimal corporate interference or influence, for the relation between the constituent companies and the corporate headquarters is mainly financial, and there also tends to be minimal co-ordination among the various businesses in the company.

In this type of structure strategic planning tends to be a lesser feature of the total company than in other structures, as the main corporate concern is financial management. However, it could be argued that strategic planning takes place at three levels in this structure:

1   *Corporate level*, mainly financial decisions, carried out by corporate staff.
2   *Business level*, as before, carried out by the top management within each separate business.
3   *Functional level*, as before, carried out by the functional managers in each separate business.

Although it has been argued that the holding company structure grew out of

Table 2 The recent performance of BTR

	1982	1983	1984	1985	1986	1987	1988	1989	1990
Sales (£m)	725	1970	3487	3881	4019	4194	5472	7025	6742*
Profit before tax (£)	107	171	284	362	505	590	820	1080	966
Earnings per share (pence)	6.3	8.5	12.2	16.0	21.2	23.6	28.7	36.1	31.8

* Change in accounting policy re exchange rates. Had the new policy applied in 1989 turnover would have been £6904 Mn. Source: Extel.

the divisional structure, i.e. as a divisional company developed, there also developed increasing independence between the divisions, which led ultimately to the much looser holding company structure.

A good example of an effective use of this type of structure is afforded by the British conglomerate BTR. As shown in Table 2, BTR has had a phenomenonally successful history, and it attributes its success, in part, to having an appropriate structure.

It is reported:

BTR divides its activities into three geographic regions
  – Europe
  – the West (which includes the US)

and into five business areas

  – construction
  – energy and electrical
  – industrial
  – consumer related
  – and transportation

Within these the group now has over 300 operating companies, each of which has enormous autonomy in terms of day-to-day and strategic decision-making. The only constraints imposed from the centre are financial ones. Managers have to meet certain profit targets and adhere to certain financial ratios imposed by one of the three geographic head offices. These central offices are like small banks. They will not, for example, normally sanction capital expenditure if the payback period is likely to be more than five years. But their obvious difference from real banks is that they are run on a shoe string.

The chairman and group chief executive, Sir Owen Green commented in the 1981 Annual Report:

[This] basic structure pioneered by us many years ago, which may be described as in the shape of an inverted saucer, continues to serve our lively organisation well and has required little change. Having withstood the tests of time and tide, it is in fine fettle and on sound foundations.[4]

Implications of company structure for modelling

The influence of company structure is fundamental to the strategic modelling process. Any strategic model should explicitly reflect the structure of the company for which it has been developed. Therefore in strategy models the hierarchical nature of the strategic process should be clearly seen. This is a feature of the Classic Group model, which is set up as a conventional corporate headquarters–division–product line structure, as shown in Figure 14.

THE CONCEPT OF THE STRATEGIC BUSINESS UNIT OR SBU

Do the following companies compete?

British Aerospace – Boeing – Ford Motor Company

At first glance it may appear that just the aircraft companies, British Aerospace and Boeing, compete with each other, and the motor vehicle company, Ford, is not a rival to either.

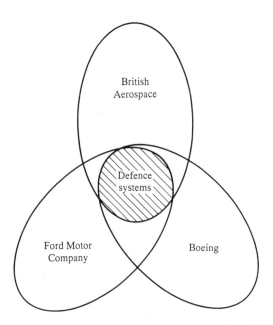

Figure 8 One way in which British Aerospace, Boeing and Ford Motor Company compete

Table 3   The main business areas of three diversified companies[5]

BRITISH AEROSPACE	Commercial aircraft; motor vehicles; defence systems; property, including retailing and leisure parks; and space communications.
BOEING	Commercial transportation products and services; military transportation products and related systems; and missiles and space.
FORD MOTOR COMPANY	Electronics; glass; plastic castings; climate control; leasing; rental; space technology; defence; satellites; land development.

However, this view is too narrow. There is a greater degree of competition among these companies than their names imply and it takes place in a very large number of product-market configurations. Thus when the activities of each company are analysed, as shown in Table 3, it can be seen that they all engage in a considerable number of discrete business areas, and that the competition between them takes place in a variety of unique arenas.

From Table 3 it should be clear that competition between companies does not, in general, take place at the corporate level; rather it is conducted at the product–market–customer level. From this it follows that if the strategist wishes to understand the nature of the market in which his company is competing, then he must have detailed knowledge of the discrete product–market–customer segments that make up the company. Thus for the above companies their most public areas of competition are revealed through where the sets representing them intersect, i.e. the set intersections yield the units of the companies that compete.

One of the most effective ways so far developed of perceiving the true competitive units that comprise any company is to break down the company into its component strategic business units (SBUs). Indeed it could be argued that one of the most important components in developing a superior business strategy is to reconfigure the company into new and innovative strategic business units.

The concept of the SBU

An SBU could be described as a 'natural strategic grouping' within a company. Such a grouping is one in which the company's activities are configured into a number of groups that will:

1   Pinpoint where strategic effort should be made.
2   Form a basis for resource allocation.
3   Provide strategically useful performance measures.

Normally an SBU will have the following characteristics:

- It is managed by an SBU manager, largely as an independent unit. The SBU manager also acts as a link between the SBU and the board of directors.
- It has its own set of goals and strategies, which, within broad parameters, are largely set by the corporate board of directors (or corporate planners).
- It embraces all phases of business, i.e. design, research and development, manufacturing, marketing, selling and distribution.
- It has a range of related products that share similar technologies or production processes, and its products are sold in similar or related market segments to fairly homogeneous sets of customers against well-defined sets of competitors.
- In any given company SBUs are, as far as practicable, similar in size.
- Each SBU in a particular company should be able to operate independently of any other SBU.

DEFINING SBUS

There are no hard and fast rules for objectively disaggregating a company into its constituent SBUs. However, the Strategic Planning Institute, SPI, has the SBU as the core planning unit upon which its studies are built, and consequently it has devoted considerable attention to the process of how companies can be divided into SBUs. A summary of some of their guidelines is set out below.

Overview of defining SBUs: segment and cluster

The decisions upon which a company's SBU configuration is based are determined by creatively segmenting the company into its constituent products, markets and customers and then iteratively clustering these segments into unique combinations until an optimal configuration is developed.

Segmenting the company

Although a company may be segmented along a multitude of dimensions, the SPI has suggested that the following approach is likely to lead to strategically effective configurations. Start at the most aggregate level possible and then segment the company according to its natural segments. These will normally include segmentation according to:

1   Product families.
2   Common technologies.

3 End-user groups.
4 Sales and distribution channels.
5 Geography.

Decide if the resultant segments should be the company's SBUs

When the segmentation has been completed, ask the following question: 'Logically should these various segments be kept separate, or should they be combined?' Generally if the units that the initial segmentation has yielded demand different strategies, then they should be kept separate. However, if the units the initial segmentation has yielded demand strategies that coincide, then they should be combined.

Deciding upon significant differences

The SPI has suggested that the following yardsticks are the crucial determinants of whether or not a unit requires to be separately defined. Do the units yielded by segmentation:

1 Require different marketing skills?
2 Employ different basic technologies?
3 Exist at different maturity stages of the life cycle? (See p. 32.)
4 Occupy different competitive positions?
5 Permit sensible accounting allocations to be made?

Finally, the SPI suggests that, in general, for the above questions, when the number of 'Yeses' exceeds the number of 'Nos', then the units should be separated and vice versa.

SBUS AND PORTFOLIO MANAGEMENT

Dividing a company into its constituent SBUs permits corporate management to engage in the practice of *portfolio management* in addition to its other, usually financial, concerns.

Portfolio management is concerned with the achievement of corporate objectives through taking appropriate cognisance of each SBU's strategic position in relation to its life cycle and its cash contribution, and also in terms of its position in relation to the portfolio of the corporation. In addition, portfolio management is often necessary because of the difficulties in analysing, assimilating and integrating into a unified strategic plan the huge amounts of diverse information that large companies generate.

These problems are frequently manifested in the failure of corporate staff to provide appropriate resources for those businesses that are likely to grow, and in failing to withdraw resources from those businesses that are likely to be unsuccessful. In other words, there is a failure at the top of the company to provide the guidance that will lead to the development of a balanced portfolio of businesses, which in turn will lead to a corporate portfolio that is superior to competitors and will consequently provide enduringly superior results for the company's stakeholders. This is the essence of portfolio management.

Although the balance of a portfolio can be assessed along many dimensions, the more frequent ones used are:

1   *Growth*. Has the company a portfolio of SBUs that are at different stages of growth, i.e. are there:

    - SBUs at the development stage that are likely to be net absorbers of cash today but may be cash contributors in perhaps 3 years' time?
    - SBUs at the growth stage that are currently cash neutral but should be net cash generators in the immediate future?
    - SBUs at the mature stage and likely to be net generators of cash for some time to come?
    - SBUs at the senile stage that are currently absorbers of cash and likely to remain so as long as they are supported?

2   *Cash flow and profitability*. Is the combined flow of funds from the businesses in the portfolio in balance, and are the stakeholders in the company satisfied with their returns?
3   *Risk*. Is the spread of businesses such that it offsets risks, thus minimizing the overall risk of the portfolio? The principal dimensions of risk are economic, marketing, financial, geographical and political. The SBU is an invaluable device for engaging in this type of strategic management.

THE SBU AS AN INTEGRATIVE DEVICE

The SBU also serves as an intermediate device for effectively linking corporate management with SBU (i.e. divisional), functional or product managers. Thus it enables corporate management to apply a corporate perspective and resolve such corporate issues as:

1   What are the goals of this company and are they being fulfilled?
2   Are the company's stakeholders being satisfied?

3   In what businesses is the company operating?
4   Why is the company in these businesses?
5   What businesses ought the company to be in in 5 years' time?
6   Is the company's portfolio of businesses balanced?

Corporate management can then set guidelines within which SBU managers must operate. Thus the corporate planners at the apex of the company hierarchy do not take part in the day to day management of an SBU, but are rather concerned with seeing how the individual SBUs, when consolidated, constitute a corporation that fits together to form a balanced portfolio of businesses. Frequently the main numeraire used to ensure that SBUs comply with corporate guidelines is corporate cash.

Thus through portfolio management SBU managers are able to concentrate on strategies at the business level that will enable their particular business unit to succeed against competitors, success being measured by the parameters given by the corporate planners. Consequently SBU managers will often have discretion over all the functions necessary to operate a full business, and are thus much more than just managers of a manufacturing unit: they are strategic decision-makers. Figure 9 gives a schematic representation of a company structured on an SBU basis.

In summary the SBU type of organizational structure helps overcome some of the problems associated with size and diversity by breaking strategic planning into three levels:

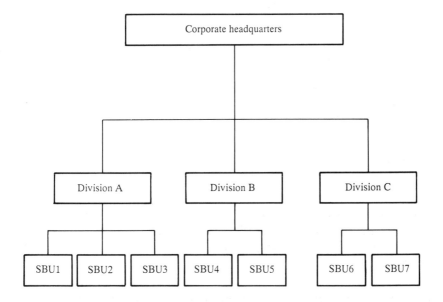

Figure 9   A company structured on an SBU basis

1   *The corporate level.* At this level the fundamental task is to develop a
    balanced portfolio of businesses that will achieve the goals of the corpor-
    ation and satisfy its stakeholders.
2   *The SBU level.* At this level the business, or set of activities, is a given, and
    the main considerations for the strategic planner are how the business will
    succeed against competitors and also satisfy corporate success criteria.
3   *The functional level.* This is as described on p. 16 for the functional
    business structure.

SBUs could therefore be said, in a structural sense, to provide the best of
both worlds. On the one hand, through interaction with corporate strategists
the SBU managers are aware of corporate goals and strategies, while, on the
other hand, because they have almost complete control of their unit, they are
free to pursue the strategies they believe are optimal for their unit with
minimal corporate interference.

It should be noted that although the concept of the SBU and the concept of
the division are very similar and are treated similarly in a strategic planning
context, they are not necessarily identical concepts. Thus an SBU may include
more than one division. However, for the purposes of this book they will be
treated as interchangeable concepts.

A GENERALIZATION OF THE SBU CONCEPT

The SBU was developed originally in the General Electric Company in the
United States in order to break the company down into 'manageable chunks'.
Indeed in the description of 'the SBU' above it was set mainly in the context of
a large diversified corporation. This need not be the case: the SBU may be
usefully employed in a much wider spectrum of organizations, ranging from
small business to the public sector.

Employing the SBU concept in a small business context

It can be extremely fruitful for a small or medium-sized business to question,
using the guidelines on pp. 26–27, the appropriateness of its structural
configuration. Such a questioning will either confirm the appropriateness of
the existing structure or else it will yield a new and superior configuration,
which could:

1   Confer competitive advantage upon the company.
2   Make the business more easily manageable.
3   Provide greater insights into the contributions of particular products and
    particular markets.

Table 4 A proforma to help a small business question its structure

	Product line 1		Product line 2		Product line 3		Product line 4	
Market segment 1	LC	Tech.						
	CP	Dist.						
Market segment 2			LC	Tech.				
			CP	Dist.				
Market segment 3			LC	Tech.	LC	Tech.	LC	Tech.
			CP	Dist.	CP	Dist.	CP	Dist.
Market segment 4			LC	Tech.				
			CP	Dist.				

Note: LC = Stage in life cycle
Tech. = Technology
CP = Competitive position
Dist. = Distribution method

The exercise can be carried out by means of a proforma similar to that shown in Table 4.

In Table 4 the business managers complete those squares in which their actual products and markets intersect, and then ascertain whether the current structure is appropriate or whether advantage would be gained if new clusters were developed.

Employing the SBU concept in a public sector context

Increasingly, in the United Kingdom anyway, there has been a seemingly inexorable tendency towards making public sector organizations 'more accountable' or striving to make them provide 'value for money'. The phrase value for money suggests that for every £1.00 invested in any public sector organization there ought to be a measurable return. (This return will not always be measured in monetary terms. It could be, for example, 'quality of service'.) This implies accountability and investment selectivity, i.e. investments will be made in those areas where returns are likely to be greatest. The SBU concept can be tailored to the public sector to provide a device that will:

1 Help give strategic direction to the organization.
2 Provide a balanced portfolio of activities.
3 Permit the 'business units' within a public sector organization to function most effectively.

Employing the SBU concept in strategic modelling

The Classic Group is structured on an SBU basis. As Figure 13 shows, the group is engaged in three discrete areas of business: Bacchus in brewing, Midas in financial services, and Perseus in transport.

THE PRODUCT LIFE CYCLE AND ITS ROLE IN STRATEGIC MANAGEMENT

Introduction

In spite of having been the subject of considerable criticism for many years, the product life cycle is still widely regarded as a fundamental tool of marketing and strategic management. In its simplest form this concept maintains that all commercial products have a certain life and that during it they pass through a series of discrete stages that, when taken together, form 'The Product Life Cycle'. Additionally, the stage at which a product is in its particular life cycle has major strategic implications.

The theory asserts that the 'life' of a product can be divided into four distinct stages: development, growth, maturity and decline, as shown in Figure 10.

Development stage

This is the stage when a new product is introduced on to the market. Typically, at this time, there will be a single pioneering company or a small number of pioneers, prices of the product will tend to be high and sales volumes will be low. The introduction of the product will tend to be regarded as 'risky' for a number of reasons:

- As the product is new, there is no certainty that consumers will purchase it in the required volumes and at the required price. This fate befell the video disk when it was marketed as a rival to the video cassette recorder.
- The novelty of the product may mean that the competitive rules for success in the industry have not been established, and consequently the fundamentals of potentially winning strategies have not yet emerged. For example, the winning strategies in the personal computer market have changed remarkably since the product was introduced. Initially personal computers were regarded as toys with limited memory and very limited capabilities, and lacking a wide range of proven software. Their appeal was primarily to children and to people with a technical interest or disposition. However, today the principal market is for serious business

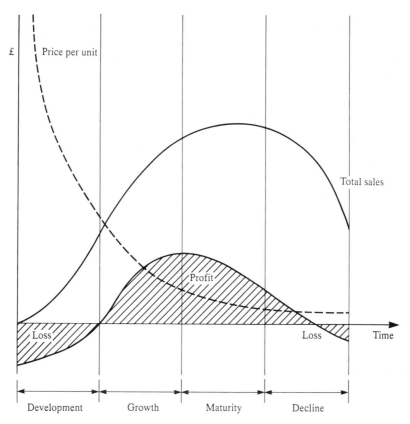

Figure 10 The product life cycle

use, with the games aspect of the business playing a relatively minor role. The competitive rules of the game have changed as the product has matured.

- Production facilities must be constructed.
- Personnel must be recruited and trained.

Generally at the development stage competitors tend to have two fundamental pricing strategies available, which are the following.

A skimming price strategy

Here the objective is to maximize the returns to the company as quickly as possible through setting a high price for the product. Such a pricing strategy makes it appealing to the purchaser who is willing to pay a premium price for a novel or original product. The major benefit of this type of strategy is that super profits may be earned and the return on the investment will be maximized extremely quickly. However, such a strategy has the drawback that it will make participation in the industry a very attractive proposition to potential new entrants, i.e. companies who are not manufacturing the product will be tempted to do so by the lure of the large profits that are being seen to be earned by the 'price skimmer(s)'.

A penetration pricing strategy

A company following this strategy sets the price of its product at a fixed percentage above its cost and then continues to reduce price at the same rate as costs decline. The rationale is that market demand for the product will be strongly stimulated because of the relatively low price, and also new entrants will be discouraged because the profits being earned are modest and the investments required by new entrants in order to be effective competitors are substantial.

Growth stage

At this stage the product has been accepted by the market, and a very rapid increase in market size is likely. New companies (imitators who have seen the success of the pioneers) will enter the now less risky market with similar products. Complementing the accelerating increase in sales, there is a rapid decrease in price levels, which is caused by two major factors:

1   In order to gain market share, the increased number of firms engage in price competition.
2   Because of the increases in the volume of production that successful firms are enjoying, there are cost reductions, effected through economies of scale.

Additionally at this stage, in order to serve the rapidly expanding market, promotion and distribution require increased resources. Finally it is in this stage that profits tend to reach a peak.

Maturity

At this stage, although sales may be continuing to increase, they are increasing at a slower rate, while prices and profits are declining. The importance of promotion also tends to decline, as consumers usually have, at this stage, adopted particular brands and tend not to switch.

The number of competitors may decline as some companies leave the industry for brighter prospects elsewhere. Alternatively, takeovers or mergers may occur.

As the maturity stage continues and growth continues to decline, consumer saturation develops; this further increases the downward pressures on prices as the competition among the remaining competitors intensifies in their efforts to maintain acceptable market shares. This competitive pressure is further exacerbated by those competitors who wish to increase their share of the market – as there is no growth in the market the only source of growth is to take market share from an existing competitor.

An industry that appears to have entered this phase is the commercial vehicle industry, especially in Western Europe and the United States.

> Commercial vehicle makers and in particular the truck producers, face harsh challenges.
>
> Demand in Europe is slipping from the record levels of the previous two years; some important markets are already in recession. Several North American and western European manufacturers have fallen into losses and renewed pressures on margins and mounting investment needs are leading to another wave of restructuring in Europe.[6]

Decline

At this stage saturation of the market has occurred and absolute sales of the product decline. (On occasions demand for the product will even disappear completely, as has happened with the demand for hand-held LED calculators and LED digital watches.) Because of the ensuing overcapacity in the industry, there is strong competitive warfare, which is manifested in severe promotion battles (using price competition and advertising), declining profits and withdrawal from the industry by the less successful competitors. This phase is also frequently described as the shakeout phase and is characterized by an increasing concentration of competitors as they form alliances in the hope of making some profit.

A good example of an industry that appears to have entered this phase is the European domestic appliance industry:

> The 300-odd European companies fighting for increased shares of a stagnant market are already in the throes of a shakeout. On present trends, after the process of absorption and extermination now under way, there will be four to five major international companies left in Europe with perhaps the same number of 'niche' producers in each country producing for local or specialist needs.
>
> Those with the nerve to bet on the outcome suggest that the international survivors – despite many difficulties, not all of which are connected with appliances – will be Electrolux-Zanussi, representing Italy, Philips-Bauknecht in a Dutch-West German combine, Thomson-Brandt of France, and the Bosch-Siemens joint production company with AEG-Telefunken representing West Germany...
>
> ... Most industry leaders suggest that Europe will follow the U.S. where the number of washing machine makers has fallen from 60 to five in the past 25 years.[7]

Table 5 The basic strategic and functional implications of the product life cycle

		Development	Growth	Maturity	Decline
BASIC STRATEGY		Invest	Invest	Hold	Divest
FINANCE	LIQUIDITY	Low	Improving	Improving	High
	PROFITABILITY	Losses	Greatest	Decreasing	Decreasing–loss
	CASH FLOW	Negative	Improving	Improving	Large–negative
	LEVERAGE	High	High	Decreasing	Low
	DIVIDENDS	None	Small–increasing	Increasing	Large–none
MARKETING	NO. OF COMPETITORS	Few	Increasing	Decreasing	Fewer
	MARKET SIZE	Small	Growing	Stable	Declining
	MARKET SHARE	Small	Growing	Stable	Declining
	PRICE	High	High	Falling	Low
	EXPENSES	High	High	Falling	Low
	RESEARCH	Intense	Reducing	Minimal	None
PRODUCTION	VOLUME	Low	Increasing	Stable	Declining
	COSTS	High	Falling	Falling	Stable–low
	DEVELOPMENT	Continuing	Slowing	Minimal	None
	TECHNOLOGY	New	New	Established	Obsolete
PERSONNEL	NUMBERS	Increasing	Increasing	Fewer	Fewer
	SKILLS	Being developed	Developed	Developed	Developed
RISK IMPLICATION		Very high	Decreasing	Low	Low

FUNCTIONAL IMPLICATION

These are the major stages of the product life cycle and a summary of its basic strategic and functional implications is given in Table 5.

LIMITATIONS OF THE PRODUCT LIFE CYCLE

Although the product life cycle is an attractive aid to making strategic decisions, its use should take account of the many criticisms it has received. Prominent among the criticisms are the following.

The shape of the PLC

There is no one universal curve that applies to all products. Various studies have shown that many products simply do not pass through the four classic stages. For example, certain products, frequently 'necessities of life' such as beer, soap and vehicles, have been purchased in large volumes for decades. They seem to be set permanently in the mature stage of the life cycle and show no signs of ever going into a decline phase. By way of contrast, other products, such as skateboards, seem to just go through two stages – explosive growth and then rapid decline.

The level of aggregation

There is controversy about the level or levels of aggregation at which the product life cycle applies. Some authorities take the view that the concept can apply at the industry level, i.e. all industries go through these stages. Others maintain that the concept has some validity at the product class level, when classes of products go through these stages, e.g. denim jeans; but it has almost no validity at the brand level, i.e. branded products such as Levi jeans or Wrangler jeans do not follow product life cycles.

The PLC as a predictive tool

There is no evidence to suggest that the technique has any predictive power. Its chief power seems to be in the analysis of historical situations. Thus because there is no single curve, it is impossible to know exactly what stage a product is at at any particular time, and therefore the PLC offers little strategic guidance. For example, if a product that, it is accepted, is in the mature stage experiences a decline in growth, it is impossible to know, at that time, if this is signalling the onslaught of the decline stage or is merely a temporary hiccup in a continuation of the growth stage.

Companies can alter the shape of the life cycle of their products

The product life cycle is not a law. It is a phenomenon that is frequently observed with the benefit of hindsight. Many companies have been able to influence the shape of a life cycle through such devices as product innovation and effective advertising and promotion. Japanese companies have been very adroit in wringing the maximum economic life out of products through extending their life cycles.

Conclusions on the PLC

The product life cycle can be a useful vehicle for understanding the stages that products are likely to pass through in their lives and the implications that these stages have for resource requirements and performance expectations. It also helps strategic planners to see the age relationships that exist in a company's portfolio of products and to see how their company's products are relating to market developments.

However, it must be remembered that there is no single unique curve that fits all products, and this lack of rigour or universality makes the PLC's predictive powers minimal. A consequence of this is that strategists should be aware of the concept and integrate the information it provides with other sources of information and models, but they should be wary of basing firm strategic decisions on this type of analysis alone.

CLASSIFYING ORGANIZATIONAL DECISIONS

Although there are many axes along which organizational decisions can be classified, here the classification is structured hierarchically into four levels: corporate, strategic, administrative and operational.

Corporate decisions

These types of decision are made by the top corporate management in a company that is structured on an SBU type of basis. These are the major long-run decisions (i.e. the time frame is many years) of the company and are often concerned with issues such as:

- The company's mission, goals, targets, corporate strategies.
- The portfolio of businesses the company intends to have in order to achieve its corporate goals.
- The balance of the portfolio in terms of risk, growth, cash use and returns.

- The core strategies, i.e. grow, hold, harvest, divest, for individual SBUs.
- The control and evaluation of the company as a whole and the scrutiny of the performance of individual SBUs.

For all companies the consequences of decisions on the areas outlined above are immense and the effects of the decision are likely to affect the company for many years if not for the rest of its existence. A company that has given public expression to the importance of corporate and strategic decisions is the UK chemicals giant ICI:

> The challenge within a large complex company such as ICI is to allow the development of individual businesses while maintaining the coherence of the Group. A profit crisis arising from problems in the external environment led to a reassessment of the short-term objectives and long-term strategy, and brought about fundamental changes in the company's management style and direction. The broad strategy was to achieve two major thrusts: to improve competitiveness, in terms of both costs and added value, and to change Group shape in respect of both products and territorial spread...
>
> The Planning Department has the dual role of developing corporate and business strategies and assessing changes in the external environment and their implications including the activities of competitors.[8]

Strategic decisions

These decisions are made by top management. These are the major decisions of the company, are long run, i.e. 3 years or longer, and are concerned with such fundamental issues as:

- The company's mission, goals, targets, strategies.
- The portfolio of products the company intends to have in order to achieve its goals.
- The balance of the company's portfolio of products in terms of risk, growth, cash use and returns.
- The core strategies, i.e. grow, hold, harvest, divest, for individual products.
- The control and evaluation of the company as a whole and the scrutiny of the performance of individual products. In addition, if the company is structured on an SBU basis, an additional concern is the SBUs' relationship with the total company in general and corporate headquarters in particular.

Administrative decisions

These decisions are at the next level in the hierarchy, tend to be taken by middle managers, and frequently do not require top level endorsement or

Table 6 Classification of organizational decisions

Decision type characteristics	Operational	Administrative	Strategic	Corporate
Time span	Short-run	Intermediate	Long-run	Long-run
Risk level	Low	Intermediate	High	High
Nature	Highly repetitive	Repetitive	Unique	Unique
Programmability	Programmable	Programmable	Not programmable	Not programmable
Frequency	Very frequent	Frequent	Infrequent	Infrequent
Reversibility	Easily reversed	Reversible	Not reversible	Not reversible

approval. Typically these decisions are shorter-run than strategic decisions, and are concerned with functional issues such as:

- How should the finance department be organized so that it can provide the required information at the appropriate speed and cost?
- What additional resources should the marketing department receive over the coming year so that it can meet the increase in sales volume that has been set.

Operational decisions

These decisions are short-run, low risk and frequent. They will often be made and implemented with minimal senior management approval. These are the routine day to day decisions in running any business and are concerned with issues such as:

- Daily/weekly/monthly reports on the meeting of targets.
- Decisions about the hiring of additional casual labour to meet a surge in demand.

Finally, Table 6 gives a summary of the four types of decision and their characteristics.

STRATEGIC DECISION-MAKING VERSUS FUNCTIONAL DECISION-MAKING

There is an important distinction to be made between the nature of decision-making from a strategic perspective and a functional perspective.

When decisions are made in the context of a functional perspective, such decisions will tend to reflect, and will be sustained by, the cultural context of the functional area. For example, decisions taken by accountants will tend to reflect concern about issues such as prudence, control and evaluation, while those taken by marketing personnel will tend to reflect concern with issues such as growth of sales, market share, customer satisfaction, quality, price, etc. If left to their own devices, especially in large companies, each function would, increasingly, pursue strategies that would be in the interests of itself but not likely to be optimal for the company as a whole.

Ideally strategic decision-making should transcend functional bias, and so strategic decision-makers should be able to:

1   Draw upon each functional area.
2   Synthesize their contributions.
3   See patterns and recognize threats and opportunities that a narrower perspective would not reveal.
4   Take decisions that are in the best interests of the total organization rather than just a single function.

It is this wider set of perspectives that gives strategic decision-making its currency, and such an approach should make the company more assuredly effective in the long run. In other words, strategic perspectives should help free the planners from the natural bias engendered by their functional specialization, and help them see the opportunities for their organization and the threats against it in a new and more creative light. The element of creativity is becoming an increasingly important aspect of strategic management, as the following quotation shows:

> More organizations evolve naturally toward specialization. An organization of specialized people is more efficient, easier to direct, and easier to control than one in which everybody tries to do everything. Yet, specialization puts information into channels that eliminate the ability to see new patterns, and hence organizational intuition.
>
> The organizational separation of research, marketing, engineering and manufacturing, for example, is a classic – and obvious – block to the ability to generate new products that fill a consumer need, that are priced to sell, and that are engineered for proper manufacturing costs. Each of these functions pursued on its own to optimize its individual priorities will never see the tradeoffs implicit between them. They cannot create something new that optimizes the system, rather than the elements.
>
> Organizational intuition requires integration of organizational elements and is the essence of the creative enterprise.[9]

References

1 *Business Week*, 16 July 1990, p. 68.
2 *Ibid.*
3 *Source*: White J., *Dunhill Holdings Plc*, The Case Clearing House, Cranfield, 1987.

4 *BTR*, The Case Clearing House, Cranfield.
5 Extel.
6 *Financial Times*, Commercial Vehicles Survey, 1990.
7 Parkes, C., 'Why just a few will survive', *Financial Times*, 18 July 1985, p. 26.
8 *Financial Times*.
9 Boston Consulting Group.

3 A Javelin-based strategic management computer model: the Classic Group and Bacchus Beer

INTRODUCTION

The model the *Classic Group* is the kernel of this book, and is the organizational and strategic framework within which it is assumed that typical complex corporate planning decisions are made. The objective of the model is to enable planners to see how diverse or related changes in strategies and in the environment can affect a divisionalized company.

Figure 11   Companies must adapt their shape to the environment

The starting point of the model is the assumption that a company can only have sustained success if it adapts its shape to the environment. This is shown schematically in Figure 11. More precisely, the model assumes that there is a divisionalized company called The Classic Group and it is adapting its shape through *strategies* so that it obtains an optimal fit with its *competitive environments*. This is shown schematically in Figure 12.

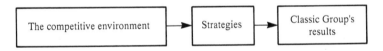

Figure 12   The core of the model: how the Classic Group adjusts to its environment

A BROAD OVERVIEW OF THE CLASSIC GROUP AND ITS APPROACH TO STRATEGIC PLANNING

The Classic Group is a small divisionalized company that is split into three strategic business units (SBUs), and strategic planning is assumed to take place at two levels: the corporate level and the SBU level.

STRATEGIC PLANNING IN THE CLASSIC GROUP AT THE CORPORATE LEVEL

The Classic Group's three strategic business units are Bacchus Beer, which is engaged in the brewing business; Perseus Transport, which is engaged in transport and distribution; and Midas Financial Services, which is engaged in finance. This structure is shown schematically in Figure 13.

Each SBU has a number of product or service lines. For example, Bacchus Beer has Super Beer, Premium Beer and Standard Beer. How products, SBUs and Corporate Headquarters are linked is shown in Figure 14.

Planning at the corporate level is undertaken by a small team at corporate headquarters that does not concern itself with shorter-term SBU issues. Rather, corporate headquarters has the view that its function is to set broad corporate parameters, usually in the areas of finance and marketing, within which it expects the SBUs to operate. Indeed corporate headquarters will only take part in planning at the SBU level if its assistance is specifically requested by an SBU, or if an SBU is failing to meet corporate parameters.

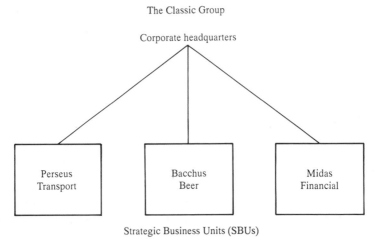

Figure 13   The organizational structure of the Classic Group, with particular reference to the corporate and the SBU levels

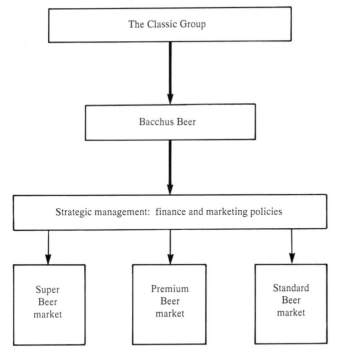

Figure 14 How products, SBUs and corporate headquarters are linked in the Classic Group

The main corporate planning functions undertaken are:

- The setting of corporate objectives and the development of long-run plans that will enable these objectives to be achieved.
- The implementation of these plans.
- The subsequent control and evaluation of the effectiveness of these plans in meeting corporate objectives.

More specifically, strategic planning at the group level has the following major financial and marketing concerns.

Financial

1 The primary financial objective is the achievement of satisfactory returns and growth for its shareholders and stakeholders through the consolidated operations of its SBUs.
2 The achievement of a balanced financial structure through appropriate corporate financing, investment, dividend, and cash management

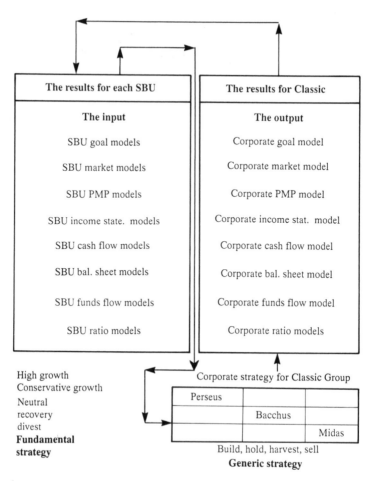

Figure 15 Strategic planning at Classic Group, with particular reference to the corporate and SBU levels

policies. It should be noted that the Classic Group does not have the usual centralized policies and procedure for shares, dividends and tax payments: each SBU is assumed to have autonomy (within corporate parameters) for these decisions. A consequence of this is that corporate shareholdings, corporate dividends and corporate tax payments are simply the consolidations of the decisions of the individual SBUs. The classic Group has been structured in this fashion for didactic reasons: it is to enable users of the model greater freedom to make major strategic decisions even when they are using the model at the SBU rather than the group level. Once the user is familiar with the model, however, it is relatively easy to restructure it to have these decisions taken centrally and to convert the SBUs into investment centres, profit centres, or cost centres.

Marketing

The primary marketing objective is the achievement and maintenance of a balanced portfolio of SBUs which will ensure that the primary corporate marketing and financial objectives continue to be achieved. Finally Figure 15 shows how corporate planning takes place in Classic Group with particular reference to the corporate level. As can be seen, the major input for the corporate decisions are the results of the SBUs.

STRATEGIC PLANNING IN THE CLASSIC GROUP AT THE SBU LEVEL

Each SBU is managed fairly independently within the broad corporate parameters set out above, and strategic planning within each SBU is carried out

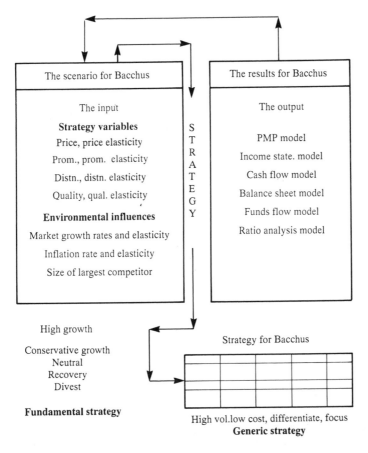

Figure 16 Strategic planning in the Classic Group with particular attention to the SBU level

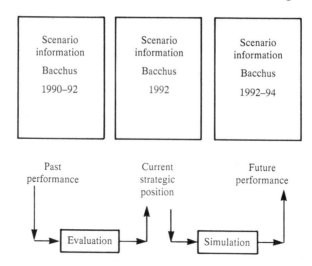

Figure 17   How the model operates

by the SBU's managing director and its top management. The main strategic planning functions are:

- The setting of SBU objectives and the development of long-run plans for the SBU with reference to given corporate parameters.
- The implementation of these strategic plans.
- The subsequent control and evaluation of the effectiveness of these plans in meeting SBU objectives.

SBUs are delineated according to the product–market group that they serve, as set out above. In fact each SBU has a range of three products or services and associated markets. Figure 16 shows schematically the structure of the Classic Group with particular reference to the SBU level.

THE OPERATION OF THE MODEL

The model pivots on the year 1992. Classic Group's results for the years 1990 to 1992 are available, and the purpose of the planning exercise is to decide upon alternative environmental scenarios and alternative strategies for the group for the next 3 years, then to assess the implications of following alternative strategies, and finally to decide upon a preferred strategy. This is shown schematically in Figure 17.

CONCLUSION AND COMMENTS

The Classic Group is the core of this approach to modelling, and this brief exposition has been provided at this stage so that readers may have a

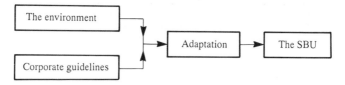

Figure 18   How SBUs must adapt their shape to the environment and corporate guidelines

structural and strategic context in which to view the detailed sub-corporate models upon which the Classic Group is built. On the accompanying disk, because of space limitations, just one typical SBU – Bacchus Beer – has been included. An overview of the operation of this SBU is provided next.

BACCHUS BEER: AN INTRODUCTION

The objective of this model is to enable planners to see how changes in strategies and in the environment affect a strategic business unit: Bacchus Beer. It should be noted that although this model has been couched in terms of a strategic business unit, the principles can be applied easily in a small or medium-sized business or in a public sector organization.

The starting point of the model is the assumption that an SBU (Bacchus Beer) can only have sustained success if it adapts its shape to fit its environments and also conform with corporate (Classic Group) guidelines. This is shown schematically in Figure 18.

DETAILS ABOUT BACCHUS BEER

The planning process in Bacchus Beer

Bacchus Beer undertakes its own strategic planning under guidelines from the Classic Group, and it is carried out by the Bacchus Beer's managing director and top management. The main strategic planning functions are:

- The setting of SBU objectives and the development of long-run plans for the SBU with reference to given corporate parameters.
- The implementation of these strategic plans.
- The subsequent control and evaluation of the effectiveness of these plans in meeting SBU and corporate objectives.

Bacchus Beer's activities

Bacchus Beer has three product lines – Super Beer, Premium Beer and Standard Beer – each of which sells in a separate and unique market segment.

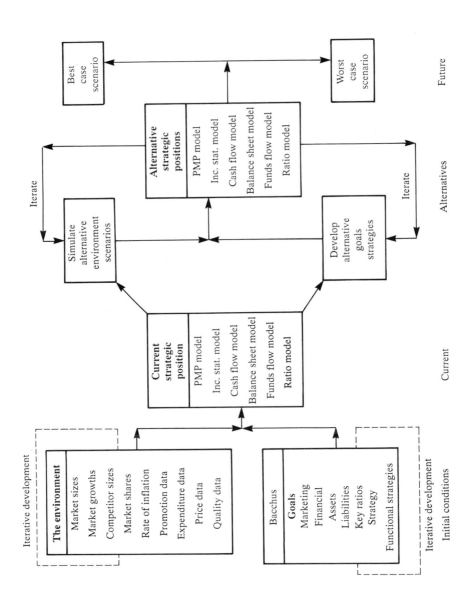

Figure 19   Bacchus Beer's strategic planning model

Figure 14 shows schematically these relationships and also the relationship between Bacchus Beer and corporate headquarters.

The strategic planning model employed by Bacchus Beer

In order to help with its strategic planning, Bacchus Beer has a strategic planning model, which is shown schematically in Figure 19. This model attempts to capture many of the essential elements required for strategic planning, and also allows the planners to simulate the effects of alternative future strategies under alternative environmental conditions.

THE OPERATION OF THE MODEL

As with the group model Classic, the time at which this model is set is 1992. Bacchus Beer's results for the years 1990 to 1992 are available and the purpose of the planning exercise is to decide upon strategies that the SBU ought to follow for the next 3 years. See the implications at, firstly, the SBU level and then the group level of following these strategies, with the initial assumptions continuing to hold. This is shown schematically in Figure 20.

This model is a fundamental building block in the total corporate model. Starting here, the user should ultimately be able to trace the consequences of strategies for individual products, firstly, upon the performance of the SBU and, finally, upon the performance of the group. The details of the constituent models of Bacchus Beer are considered next.

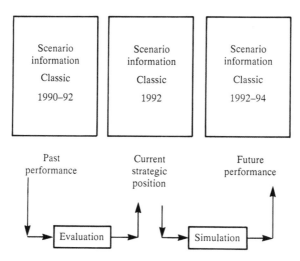

Figure 20   How the model operates

A NOTE ON RUNNING THE MODEL

One of the features of the model, and all the other models, is that all the instructions needed to run it are provided on the screen, so it is suggested that you follow the process of strategic planning in Bacchus Beer through running the total planning model now to obtain an overview. Each of the constituent models will be considered in greater detail in later chapters.

To obtain an overview proceed as follows:

1   Place the disk in drive A and close the drive. Then
      Type A:
      Type Intro
2   Follow all instructions on the screen until you return to the Intro model.

4 Analysing the company

INTRODUCTION

A fundamental assertion made in Chapter 1 was that the primary function of strategic management was the company 'obtaining a sustainable long-term excellent fit with its environment'. This chapter develops a methodology for disaggregating any company into its constituent elements in a manner that will enable the planner to form a judgement about its internal strategic posture. This approach relies upon a three-stage methodology, the stages being:

Stage 1: Division of the company. The first stage is to divide the company into a limited number of sections that tend to be important for most companies.

Stage 2: Analysis of the sections. The second stage is to analyse in detail each section and to make an assessment of its strengths or weaknesses.

Stage 3: Attributing weights to each section. The third stage is to attribute a weight to each section that will reflect its strength or weakness.

In this analysis the process must be tailored to the company. For example, if the company were in the business of manufacturing bricks, the analysis would be biased towards considering elements such as production efficiency, control and costs, while the analysis of a company engaged in, for example, high-class fashion clothes would be focused more on areas such as design and marketing.

STAGE 1: DIVISION OF THE COMPANY

A diagrammatic representation of how any company may be divided and then analysed is shown in Figure 21.

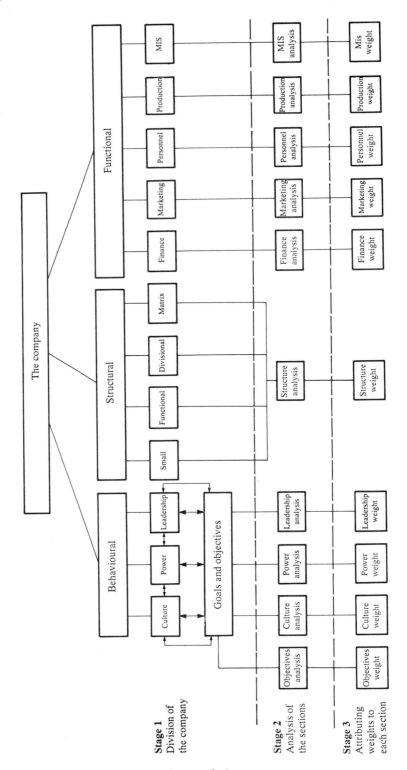

Figure 21 A three-stage approach to analysing a company

STAGE 2: ANALYSIS OF THE SECTIONS

The behavioural analysis: culture, power and leadership

The behavioural analysis is considered first because there seems to be evidence to show that to understand any company it is necessary first of all to understand the behaviour of the people in it. This behaviour can be conveniently considered under the headings culture, power and leadership. Each of these is now considered.

Culture

Ackoff[1] has shown that in their strategic behaviour managers strive not just for results but also for a certain style of behaviour. For example, it is not unusual for family-owned businesses to have the, usually unstated, goal that the business should always remain in family control. Indeed this cultural influence is so strong that it is relatively common for the owners of such businesses to allow them to fail rather than surrender family ownership or control. The powerful influence of culture is not always negative, however. For example, the American high-tech company Hewlett-Packard has always had the cultural stamp of its founders Hewlett and Packard strongly visible on its products and its activities. Thus the company has the cultural attitude that makes it a 'people orientated company with management policies that encourage individual creativity, initiative, and contribution throughout the organisation.'[2]

Although it is difficult to define the culture of a company, it can be considered to be that common set of dominant values, traditions and behaviour patterns that displays the 'attitude' of the company. These 'attitudes' can range from companies that are considered 'dynamic' at one end of the spectrum to companies considered 'stodgy' at the other end.

Company culture can be considered at two major levels: the overall corporate culture and the sub-cultures within companies.

Overall corporate culture

Many companies display an overall culture. For example, companies in advertising tend to exhibit an image of extroversion, dynamism, 'trendiness', and progressiveness; while companies in banking tend to exhibit an image of conservatism, prudence and stability.

There is no universal correct culture for a company to have; rather the culture will be a reflection of the industry and the value systems of the top managers in the company. So the culture of banks as described above is likely to be the correct one in that such a culture is likely to engender a sense of trust in depositors.

Sub-cultures within companies

In many companies, particularly those that are large and diversified, it is often the case that there is not a single homogeneous culture. Instead there exists a variety of cultures that reflect the activities and aspirations of the various sub-divisions. For example, in an SBU-structured company it would be surprising if the culture of a low growth, low technology, low profitability SBU was similar to that of a high growth, high technology, highly profitable SBU.

Below the SBU level, i.e. at the functional level, further sub-cultures also exist. Thus it is not unusual for the culture in, say, the accounting department to be substantially different from that of the production department or the marketing department. Although each of these departments will generally consider its particular cultural perspective to be the crucial one for the company's success, this is rarely the case, and indeed the unbalanced dominance of a single set of functional cultural values can be disastrous, as was shown by the collapse of Rolls-Royce in 1971:

> While strongly rejecting the theory that Rolls-Royce failed because of poor accounting information, they (the inspectors) do agree that, as with many companies, the information system was deficient. In particular, the board were given two documents at each meeting, a green folder and a red folder. The green folder contained all the important matters to be discussed and was compulsory reading for all directors. All the financial data – masses of it in great detail – were in the red folder, i.e. the voluntary one, which few of the directors would have had time to absorb. The other reason was that 'the personalities on the financial side were out-gunned and out-numbered by those on the engineering side'. (For example, in 1969 the Derby Engine Division board had 22 members of whom only one was not an engineer.)[3]

Power

The case of Rolls-Royce well illustrates the importance of power in the behavioural analysis, and understanding the power structure and the power process is fundamental to understanding a company. Power could be considered to be the ability of an individual or a group to influence other individuals or groups. Although it is not normal for power to be explicitly defined in most companies (except through an organization chart), its presence is real and its effects are significant. Consequently a consideration of power is essential in any comprehensive strategic analysis.

In any company power can accrue to or be accumulated by individuals or groups either through official or unofficial means. The important consideration in any analysis of the power structure and process is not whether it is official or unofficial but what is the practice that prevails. Thus when a company has an official power structure – as expressed by its organization chart – which is not followed, and an unofficial set of power relationships that is followed, it is the unofficial power structure that should be analysed.

In general in most companies power can be acquired officially or unofficially from the following main sources.

Power over resources

Individuals or groups who exercise power over resources that are scarce and important tend to accumulate power. Traditionally the most important resource in Western companies has been money, and this has led to a predominance of managers with a financial background becoming the most powerful group in Western companies. This is seen particularly clearly in the case of General Motors. Table 7 shows the chairmen of General Motors since 1917 and their functional backgrounds. Clearly finance has been the dominant function.

In contrast to the dominant influence of finance in Western companies, Japanese companies tend to regard money or finance as just one of the many critical resources necessary for success. Consequently the composition of their decision-making boards tends to be functionally much broader than their Western equivalents, reflecting the power accorded to each of the functions.

The power of knowledge or skills

Those managers who possess knowledge or skills that are crucial to the company tend to accumulate power. This is particularly noticeable in new high-tech companies, where viability is largely determined by the technocrats.

The power of reward or punishment

Those individuals or groups who are in a position to offer rewards or deal out punishments tend to accumulate power, as their influence is usually considered by other groups to be a fundamental determinant of career advancement.

Table 7 Functional backgrounds of the chairmen of General Motors[4]

Name	Years	Background
P. S. Du Pont	1917–29	Finance
L. Du Pont	1929–37	Engineering/finance
A. P. Sloan	1937–56	Finance
A. Bradley	1956–58	Finance
F. G. Donner	1958–67	Finance
J. M. Roche	1967–72	Operations/engineering
R. C. Gerstenberg	1972–75	Finance
T. A. Murphy	1975–	Finance

Table 8   Reported characteristics of effective political actors[5]

Characteristic	Per cent of respondents mentioning
Articulate	29.9
Sensitive	29.9
Socially adept	19.5
Competent	17.2
Popular	16.1
Extrovert	16.1
Self-confident	16.1
Aggressive	16.1
Ambitious	16.1
Devious	16.1
'Organization man'	12.6
Highly intelligent	11.5
Logical	10.3

The power of personality

The personality or charisma of an individual can have fundamental power effects. Those individuals who have the ability and skills to exercise the type of power can and do have material effects upon the directions taken by companies. For example, the influence of Ross Johnston in RJR-Nabisco seemed to be based largely upon personality.[6] The personal characteristics which a survey of managers believe are most important for gaining power are given in Table 8.

Pfeffer[7] has claimed that there are four main personal characteristics that determine the power of an individual in an organization:

1   Verbal skills and articulateness.
2   Diagnostic skills.
3   Understanding the rules of the organization.
4   Personal belief in oneself.

Power configurations

Companies exhibit different power configurations, ranging from the highly autocratic centralized power structure, where, typically, great power is concentrated in the hand of the chairman or managing director, to distributed power structures. The type of power configuration that a company ought to have is a function of the industry and the goals, culture and traditions of the company. Generally those companies that are in stable environments and are most homogeneous in their work will have centralized power structures, while those that are in the most dynamic environments and have the greatest heterogeneity in their work will tend to have the most distributed power structures.

The exercise of power

The way power is exercised in a company is a function of the nature of the industry and the company's traditions and culture. Generally power is exercised in one of three ways: consensus, trade-off and autocratic:

1 *Consensus*. The benefit that can accrue to a company through having a consensual approach is well illustrated by the success of Japanese companies. In the main, Japanese companies seek, at all levels, to have strategies and operations implemented by the power of consensus. The rationale behind this approach is that when power is exercised in such a way, it helps build a very high commitment to the strategy adopted, and this commitment is reflected ultimately in superior performance. The principal drawback to the consensual approach is that it can be extremely time-consuming.
2 *Trade-off*. This occurs when there are a variety of individuals or groups who all have positions of power so that no single individual or group is dominant. In this situation political trade-offs are negotiated among the various power-holders and compromise agreements reflecting the power configuration of the groups are adopted.
3 *Autocratic*. This approach tends to be employed when companies are strongly centralized and power is held at the centre. It is particularly appropriate where the work of the company is relatively homogeneous and where decisions need to be taken relatively quickly. Although this approach suffers from the drawback that it is coercive and therefore not likely to command the same commitment that a consensual approach would, it does have the attribute of speed of response.

Power shifts

Changing the existing power structure in any company is extremely difficult – the existing power-holders have a vested interest in retaining their status and usually will be most unwilling to surrender it. Ansoff[8] asserts that major shifts of power can only occur when a company faces a crisis so severe that its very survival is threatened. Under such conditions the various power groups will unite in their common goal of saving the company. The old leaders, because they have failed, will be dismissed and a new leader (the 'Saviour') will be brought in. This new leader will enjoy a honeymoon period in which he will be granted, by most power groups, the right to behave autocratically, and impose previously unacceptable strategies in the interests of the company's survival. A good example of this happening is provided by the UK electronics company Thorn EMI:

A fully-blown crisis hit Thorn EMI last summer when the once cash-rich business built on the pillars of TV rental and lighting began to run out of money. Peter Laister, chairman and chief executive, resigned and Sir Graham Wilkins,

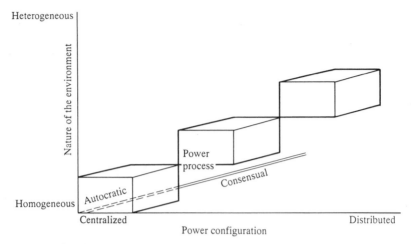

Figure 22   The relationship between the power process, the power configuration and the time required for an adequate response

> Thorn's deputy chairman and former chairman of the Beecham Group, immediately took over and announced a substantial reorganization of its two biggest trouble spots, Inmos, which makes microchips, and Ferguson, the television manufacturing subsidiary...[9]

Assessment of power in a company

There is no single appropriate power configuration or process. Rather the way in which power is distributed and exercised is a function of the industry and the company's goals and cultural climate. Figure 22 shows diagrammatically possible power configurations.

Leadership

The importance of good strategic leadership is not really questioned. However, the nature of just what good leadership actually consists of is a more complex issue. Broadly speaking, the views as to what constitutes good leadership polarize into two main camps – the 'task view' of leadership and the 'people view'.

The task view stems from the work of Taylor,[10] and it suggests that the most effective leaders are those who have the qualities necessary to achieve the tasks facing the company in the most efficient way. Thus this view asserts that the primary concern of leadership is with efficiency; consequently the human problems that may be generated in achieving high levels of efficiency are given secondary attention. In other words, the people in a company are just a factor of production and should be used as efficiently as possible.

The alternative view, which stems mainly from the work of Mayo,[11] asserts that the way for a company to achieve its goals is through the commitment of the people who comprise it. Therefore a leader's primary purpose is not the efficient carrying out of tasks, but the *motivation* of groups of people to carry out the tasks. In other words, when people are sufficiently motivated, they will wish to, and indeed will, carry out the tasks efficiently.

Although there is no checklist of the attributes necessary for good leadership, some or all of the attributes listed below are frequent requirements.

Vision

At the senior management level perhaps the most important attribute that leaders can have is that of vision. Leaders with vision have the dual ability to see the company as a whole and to develop and implement strategies that will be in the long-term interests of the total company. It is not unusual for such visionary leaders to have a view of the future that is at variance with that held by most other contemporary observers.

Personality or charisma

Frequently good leaders exude an exceptional personality or aura of charisma. Such leaders are often able to influence others to adopt their views, and are usually extremely adept at communicating their ideas and infecting others with their own enthusiasm.

Intellect

Leadership can often be based on knowledge. This type of leadership is particularly evident in knowledge-based industries such as high technology and the professions.

Legitimacy

Leaders can only continue to lead as long as they are regarded as 'legitimate' by the people in the company. This legitimacy, which can be manifested in terms of vision, charisma, intellect, performance, dedication, etc., is most frequently questioned after failure. If after failure the general view prevails that the leader no longer has the qualities necessary for leadership, then the leader loses legitimacy and will be changed.

Leadership in a survival crisis

As stated above, when a company faces a crisis so severe that its survival is threatened, frequently there will be a power shift and a change of leadership. When a new leader is installed in such circumstances, the quality of the leadership faces its most severe test. If the new leader successfully resolves the crisis and the company also perceives the crisis to be over, there will then be attempts to return the company into its old pre-crisis behaviour patterns and strategies. Resisting these forces is a major leadership test. Finally, if the new leader fails to resolve the crisis, he too will be replaced, and this will continue until the crisis is resolved or until the company fails.

The behavioural analysis: missions, goals, objectives and operating plans

At the core of each person are beliefs and attitudes to life. These behavioural parameters largely determine, within resource constraints, how an individual will lead his life. Similarly, it is a fundamental assertion of this book that behavioural parameters, again within resource constraints, largely determine how a company will structure its operations and activities. These behavioural parameters can be considered to be a company's mission, goals and objectives.

Missions

The key and superordinate determinant of a company's behavioural and operational complexion is its *mission*. The word mission is an entirely appropriate one. If the word is considered in terms of its traditional usage – the Christian drive to set the spiritual agenda for people's lives – it should be clear that this meaning implies that missionary activity was concerned with setting up value systems to which converts would subscribe, and that these value systems would determine the behaviour and actions of converts in all aspects of their lives. The mission of a company can be thought of in analogous terms. A company's mission, or mission statement, ought to set out the *raison d'être* for its existence; it should be reflected in the company's strategies, products, services and customers. Although many companies do not have an explicit mission statement or, if they do, it is difficult to unravel its true meaning, it does not mean that no mission exists. Usually, even in companies that claim to pay no regard to having a mission at all, there will often be some aspiration, or hidden agenda, after which the company strives. Discovering this agenda is a prerequisite to understanding the current and likely future behaviour of the company. For how to ascertain what the true mission of a company is likely to be, see p. 66. However, many companies' missions are quite clear.

Thus the UK publishing house Virago has the fundamental mission of disseminating 'women's views' on life through the publication of books by women for women. Consequently books selected by Virago for publication are based on their currency as well-written literary vehicles of 'women's views' rather than their market potential – a somewhat different mission from that followed by the publishers of cheap, mass-market paperback books.

Similarly the BMW company's mission is not concerned just with the manufacture of automobiles. Rather this company is concerned with the manufacture of a particular type of car for particular types of customers.

In a similar vein Matsushita Electric, the giant Japanese electrical and electronics company, has stated that:

> The company Creed expresses the basic business philosophy of Matsushita Electric which defines the direction of the company. The Creed translates as follows: 'Through our industrial activities, we strive to foster progress, to promote the general welfare of society and to devote ourselves to furthering the development of world culture.'[12]

Thus the mission of a company is essentially a long-term view of its fundamental reasons for existence, and it sets out usually in fairly broad terms its central driving beliefs. It maps, in general terms, the future terrain of its operations.

Goals and objectives

There is in the literature of strategic management considerable disagreement on the distinction between goals and objectives. There are writers who claim that goals determine objectives and others who claim that objectives determine goals. In this book the nomenclature used by Mintzberg,[13] who has researched and written very extensively in this area, will be adopted. According to Mintzberg goals and objectives can be distinguished in the following way.

> A company's goals are the intentions behind its decisions or actions. Goals will frequently never be achieved and may be incapable of being measured. Thus, for example, it is difficult to be sure that the Matsushita corporate structure goal will always be realized: 'Our goal is the creation of a corporate structure so strong that it will enable Matsushita Electric to achieve long-term earnings growth regardless of the external climate.'[14]

Thus, although goals are more specific than a mission statement and tend to have a shorter number of years in their time scales, they tend not to be precise measures of performance.

Objectives are goals expressed in a form in which they can be measured. Thus, a *goal* of increasing sales could lead to an *objective* of increasing sales by 17 per cent in the next year.

The goals that companies follow can be analysed along a number of axes and the principal ones are now considered.

Single goal versus multiple goals

In traditional economic theory the role of goals can be understood quickly and easily, for it is assumed that the rational economic man who controls a business has a single goal – profit maximization – and he resolutely pursues this goal to the exclusion of all others. Unfortunately for economists, there is considerable evidence to show[15] that, generally, this does not accord with reality.

Even in the smallest and most entrepreneurial businesses, where it would be thought that profit maximization would be most likely to prevail, there is evidence to show that the classic 'economist's entrepreneur' may pursue goals other than profit maximization, and that his goals may change over time. Thus it is not unusual to find that entrepreneurs have, in addition to the profit goal, such goals as 'feelings of autonomy', and 'feelings of achievement', 'outlet for skills', etc. In more complex companies, where frequently there is more than one top decision-influencer, the case for the single goal profit-maximizing model of business becomes even more untenable.

Therefore in this book all companies are assumed to have multiple goals that they strive to reach. However, multiple goal companies normally will not be able to reach all goals simultaneously. (For example, the multiple goals of increasing marketing expenditure and reducing costs are often mutually exclusive.) So the process by which such companies reach, or fail to reach, their goals becomes important. One method for understanding the process has been put forward by Cyert and March.[16]

They have asserted that companies really consist of a coalition of different groups, with each group having its own preferences and beliefs, and that goal incompatibility is resolved through trade-offs, based on power relationships, among the various interest groups. They assert that it is often the case that goals are reached sequentially and that the order of the sequence will change over time. When this is the case, then, in the longer term, no one goal is maximized, but instead a series of goals are maximized. For example, most companies are affected by business cycles, i.e. there are times of growth and times of consolidation, and it seems likely that the goals that are maximized are a function of the stage in the cycle, with goals such as 'sales maximization' being dominant in the growth stage of the cycle and goals such as 'control of costs' being dominant in the trough of the cycle.

The sources of companies' goals

Similarly structured companies in the same industry often display considerable differences in the goals that they pursue. For example in the field of retailing, although it could be argued that the well-known UK retailers Marks & Spencer, British Home Stores and Sainsbury's are all in similar businesses, each of these companies had enunciated goals that are clearly different. Why should this be so? Research shows that the goals that companies follow derive from three main sources: the people who comprise the company, the company itself and the environment.

Source 1: The people who comprise the company

Cyert and March[17] have asserted that companies are not inanimate structures. Rather, they are composed of people, and people have personalities, needs, aspirations, loves, hates, insecurities, egos, etc. This human aspect of companies is the major source of a company's goals.

People in companies are grouped together according to many criteria, such as status, function, location, age, etc., and therefore it may be more correct not to regard a company as a single entity but to regard it as a coalition of interest groups. Each of these interest groups will tend to strive after the goals that are most important to its particular value system. Therefore the corporate goals a company follows develop out of the trade-offs between the different groups that comprise the coalition. The interest groups will use such devices as power, politics, status, and tradition to impose their value systems and goals upon the company.

The interest group that will normally, though not always, be the dominant group in the formulation of goals will be the top management, i.e. the group responsible for the strategic decisions of the company. (In practice the influential set of values could come from just one person in the group (the leader) or from a sub-group or faction within the top group.) Consequently, understanding the value systems of the top group and the influences that motivate them are often crucial prerequisites to understanding the strategic behaviour of the company. An example of the influence of one person on a company's goals is provided by Dr Edward Land, the founder of the instant photograph company Polaroid.

In the 1960s the Polaroid company sought technical help from Kodak (the world's largest photographic company) to develop colour instant film. However, Polaroid lost its monopoly in the instant photographic market when, in 1976, Kodak launched its first instant photograph camera. Six days after the Kodak camera was available in the shops Polaroid sued Kodak on the grounds that during the years of their co-operation Kodak had stolen Polaroid's proprietary secrets and infringed their patents. The dispute between the two companies cost Polaroid $10 million in legal fees, lasted for 10 years and was finally settled, in Polaroid's favour, in January 1986. A major factor influencing Polaroid's decision to fight the much larger Kodak so tenaciously was the value system of Dr Land. Land was 'a near-fanatic in protecting Polaroid's intellectual property' and was outraged by Kodak's actions. A goal of the company became the return of the intellectual property.[18]

Polaroid had the goal of commitment to excellence through innovation implanted in its culture by Dr Land.

Source 2: The company

Not only do the people who comprise a company have goals they bring to their companies, but the companies themselves have goals they transmit to their employees. That is, the company can be regarded as having a 'life of its own', and it influences the people who work there. The power of companies to transmit its goals to its people is well illustrated by reference to IBM. In spite of heterogeneity before employment in IBM, their staff, after some time in the company, often tend to be regarded as homogeneous in their business attitudes and appearance. They absorb the company's value systems and goals and are often recognized, by people they have never met, as IBM people – they have absorbed part of the company.

Source 3: The environment

Goal formulation in companies is influenced by the power that the environment exerts. In general the stronger the external influences are on a company, the more influential outside forces are likely to be. Thus, before its privatization, British Airways was a government-owned airline enjoying monopolies on many domestic routes. Its public status and monopoly position effectively insulated it from many competitive realities on these routes, and the goals that were pursued reflected this privileged position. With the deregulation of domestic air routes in the early 1980s and its subsequent privatisation, BA became more dependent on its external competitive environment, and this change of dependency was reflected in the goals that were then pursued. Perhaps the most noticeable of the changes was the goal of becoming more competitive through giving priority to the passengers, manifested in improvements in the areas of punctuality of flights, the provision of in-flight meals and refreshments and a more flexible fare structure.

Recognizing a company's goals

Recognizing just what the goals of a company are is not always an easy task in that the goals which are stated by a company to be its 'official' goals may not, in practice, be the ones it actually pursues. To return again to the example of Matsushita: 'The Creed translates as follows: "Through our industrial activities, we strive to foster progress, to promote the general welfare of society and to devote ourselves to furthering the development of world culture"'.[19] From this it would appear that the company is only interested in promoting world welfare through its activities, and the commercial consequences of this activity is secondary. Thus in trying to ascertain what the goals of a company are a dilemma may arise if there is a discrepancy between its official and its unofficial goals. Which set of goals – the official or the unofficial – is the true set of goals of the company?

The true goals of any company are those ones which in practice are followed whether they are official or unofficial and the test of which goals are being followed is the willingness of the company to devote resources to them.

Once again Matsushita provides a clear example. This company had the goal of becoming the world's largest manufacturer of video recorders. Although it lost money on this product for 20 years, it still continued to devote substantial resources to it:

> Although the twenty years of losses created pressures within the profit-driven Matsushita system, the company commitment to the product never flagged. The losses were 'tuition fees' as one manager described them, helping Matsushita refine its development and manufacturing capabilities, by responding to market feedback'.[20]

The goals that companies actually follow

In spite of the wide diversity in the goals that companies have and how they measure them, there are certain classes of goals – generic goals – that appear to have some influence on all companies. Although the goals set out below can be envisaged most easily at the SBU level, they apply equally strongly, although at a different level of aggregation, at the corporate level.

Growth

For many companies growth appears to be a naturally sought after generic goal. Perhaps this is because growth, apart from the material benefits it bestows upon the stakeholders of a company, also facilitates solving difficult management problems. Thus when there is growth, managers who are successful can be rewarded through promotion and increased benefits and managers who are relatively unsuccessful can be 'moved sideways'. However, in times of stagnation managerial frustrations develop in the successful managers, since their efforts do not appear to them to be receiving adequate recognition, and the relatively unsuccessful managers may be fired – an action that tends to cause general fear and discontent. In short, growth helps companies cope with strain.

Survival

A fundamental generic goal appears to be survival. The importance of this goal is demonstrated in periods of severe crisis, when all other goals are temporarily discarded and all strategies and actions are directed to weathering the storm. Examples of this are provided by the dramatic changes in strategy that occurred in the Australian company the Bond Corporation as its survival became threatened and then it collapsed having to service extremely high levels of debt.

Control and efficiency

Most companies place some emphasis on these related goals. Perhaps the goals are best seen in Japanese companies. Mikami has asserted that a fundamental reason for the outstanding success of Japanese business has been the goal of efficiency. 'Of the top ten management strategies selected by Japanese managers as being of great importance over the next five years, rationalization, labor saving, and energy-saving problems related to increased productivity ranked second.'[21] At the same time, Japanese managers expressed the intention of strengthening those activities in the years ahead.

Setting goals and objectives

From the above it follows that the goals and objectives in a company are set by the dominant power group (or coalition of groups) and Ansoff[22] has suggested that this is done in a hierarchical fashion. That is, the primary goals and objectives are set by the dominant power group and then these goals and objectives 'cascade' down through the company, with progressively more precision being added as they percolate to the lowest levels in the company. For example, a diversified holding company that had the *mission* of 'increasing the wealth of its shareholders' could have, as its primary *goal*, the achievement of a satisfactory return on investment (ROI). This could then be refined into an *objective* of an ROI of 16 per cent, and then further refined, at a functional level, into 'a net profit to sales' ratio of 4 per cent and a 'sales to assets' ratio of 4. These ratios could be still further refined into *operating targets*, i.e. value of assets, prices, costs and sales targets necessary to achieve these results. These 'operating targets' could then be turned into budgets and targets for departments and individuals.

In summary this method of setting goals and objectives suggests a filtering through the company, as shown in Figure 23, with a progressive refinement, a shortening of the time scale and less discretion for deviation as the aspiration cascades down the company structure.

Characteristics of goals

When official goals are effective, they are followed. Some of the general characteristics which help goals to be effective are set out below.

Consistency

Goals ought to be consistent both vertically and horizontally. Thus in the hierarchy of mission, goals, objectives and operating targets there should be a vertical consistency so that each level in the hierarchy dovetails with the other levels. Similarly, in any stratum in this hierarchy, there should be horizontal consistency such that the targets or goals can co-exist. For example, if three

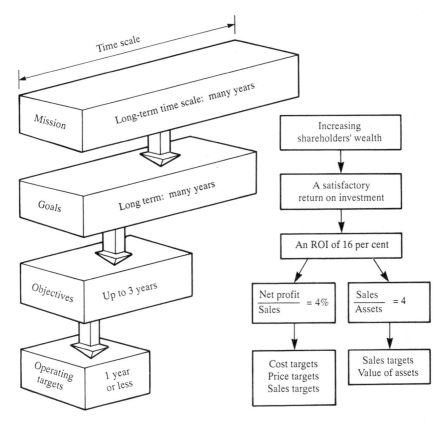

Figure 23 How operating targets derive from a mission statement

goals of a company are lifetime employment for all employees, the introduction of the latest labour-saving technology and the improvement of return on investment, it is unlikely that these goals will all be simultaneously achievable without very great expansion of sales. Such a set of goals may well be inconsistent and unrealizable.

Feasibility

Any goals that are followed by any company should be feasible; otherwise they will not be taken seriously in the company and will become meaningless paper sentiments or, even worse, may lead to disaster. Carroll[23] has shown that small companies that have the goal of being a leading world force in high tech industries in which there already are major competitors are unlikely ever to realize this goal. His research shows that the goal is not feasible because the small company is not of sufficient size, and therefore lacks the resources, to engage in the degree of research and development and marketing necessary to be competitive and profitable. Most companies who have these characteristics will fail to realize this goal because it is not feasible.

Understandability

For goals to be implemented they must be understood by those who are responsible for their implementation. Therefore when goals are enunciated, whether verbally or in writing, they must be capable of being understood and, as a corollary, be effectively communicated.

Acceptability

Goals must be acceptable to those groups in a company whose power of veto would cause them not to be realized. For example, the goal of many Fleet Street newspaper proprietors of introducing new printing technology in the 1980s was denied by the power of the craft-print trade unions until their power was removed by the activities of Rupert Murdoch (the proprietor of News International).

Capable of measurement

At the level of objectives and below, in the hierarchy, it should be possible to measure the achievement of objectives. Failure to have some measure means that it is impossible to say if an objective is being achieved. An objective of a 'return on sales of 4 per cent' is clearly measurable, whereas an objective of a 'satisfactory return on sales' is much more subjective.

The functions of goals

There are several main reasons why companies set goals and objectives, the main ones being the following.

To define the business

When the goals of a company are known, the business is more easily defined. Thus if a business explicitly sets goals in terms of its desired financial perform-ance, products, markets, personnel policies, and reasearch and development activities, then it is easier for employees of the company and external stake-holders to have a true conception of the nature of the business in which the company is engaged. Explicit goals define the business for interested parties.

As signals to outside stakeholders

Explicitly stated objectives are used by companies to send signals of their intentions to outside stakeholders. Thus when package tour holiday companies declare a goal of 'providing the lowest cost foreign holidays ever', this is a signal to potential customers that they will obtain excellent value-for-money holidays from this company, and it is also a signal to competitors that the competitive instrument this company will use will be price.

To give direction

Goals help give a company a sense of direction. Thus when Nabisco Inc., the international food company, states that it 'will be the lowest cost producer while maintaining its reputation of high quality products', this statement helps give a direction to the strategies and operations that the various personnel in the company ought to follow.

To knit the company together

When goals are consistent and effectively communicated, they should have the effect of unifying the company behind common purposes. This 'knitting' should take place in a vertical and a horizontal direction.

To set targets

As well as giving directions, goals and objectives also have the effect that they present targets for all levels in the company so that success and failure can be measured.

Conclusion on mission, goals and objectives

Understanding the mission, goals, goal structure, and objectives is a fundamental first step in understanding why a company is following particular strategies. An understanding of a company's goals should also reveal what it is likely to do in the future. Goals are essentially of the future and not the present or the past, and so they are targets at which the company will be aiming; they could be described as the driving forces which cause the company to go in a particular direction or directions.

The functional analysis

This section is concerned with analysing the functional strengths and weaknesses that a company has, and assessing how well it is performing at this level.

In the functional analysis it is *relative* strengths and weaknesses that are important, not absolute measures of performance. Thus the analysis is concerned with ascertaining the functional strength of the company in relation to its existing and potential competitors.

For example, in the vodka industry, where the technology is well-known and generally available, the primary functional requirement is 'strength in marketing': most vodkas are not clearly characterized on the basis of taste or strength, so vodka manufacturers often devote significant resources to differentiating their product and developing brand loyalty. By way of contrast, in the missile industry one of the crucial requirements is technology and the resources necessary to support the very high development costs. Thus in appraising the functional strengths or weaknesses of a company regard must be paid to the drivers of its market / industrial sector.

For the purposes of functional appraisal it is assumed that all companies can be divided into the following functional areas: marketing, finance, production and personnel, and the strengths or weaknesses of each of these areas can be assessed under the following headings:

1 *Resources.* What are the total resources that the company has allocated to it?
2 *Efficiency.* How efficiently is it managed?
3 *Measures.* What measures can be used to indicate the quality of the performance?
4 *Control.* Is control exercised effectively?
5 *Balance.* Within each functional area is there internal consistency, and is there consistency with the other activities of the company?

Marketing

In this book marketing is considered a fundamental aspect of strategic planning, and because of its importance it is considered here in terms of assessing a company's internal marketing strength. It is also considered in Chapter 6, when assessing the marketing environment and in Chapter 7, when the Bacchus Beer marketing model Bacmar is considered. Consequently this section should be read jointly with pp. 99–113 in Chapter 6 and Chapter 7.

The marketing function has the goal of ensuring that the company's products or services meet the needs and wants of customers in a manner that enables the company to realize its goals. The marketing function pursues these goals through the following strategies:

1 *Market identification,* i.e. effectiveness in identifying markets that it is, or will be, exploiting.
2 *Market segmentation,* i.e. effectiveness in dividing markets into segments in which it outperforms rivals.
3 *Product positioning,* i.e. effectiveness in positioning its products in its segments.
4 *Marketing mix strategies,* i.e. effectiveness in its product, distribution, pricing and promotion strategies.

The marketing function is now considered under the headings given above.

Resources

1 What is the total marketing budget?
2 How many people are employed in the marketing area and what is their quality?

Costs and efficiency

1 What are the total costs of marketing?
2 What percentage of sales is contributed by each product?
3 What are the margins that are realized on each product?
4 What is the extent and quality of the distribution network?
5 What is the spread of sales by region?
6 What is the spread of sales by customer type and size?
7 What are the margins that are realized on each channel of distribution?
8 What are the margins that are realized in each geographical market served?
9 What are the margins realized from each customer type?

Control

1 What is the reporting system?
2 What is its speed and accuracy?
3 What is the quality of the sales and market data?
4 What are the procedures which are used when variances arise?

Balance

1 Are the marketing activities consistent with company goals?
2 Are the marketing activities internally consistent within the marketing function?

Table 9 Measures and marketing strategy

Measure	Core marketing strategy
Total sales volume* Total sales value* Sales per employee* Total gross profit margin* Total contribution margin*	Overall marketing effectiveness
Total net profit margin* Promotion costs as a percentage of sales* Selling and distribution costs as a percentage of sales*	Promotion and distribution effectiveness

* It should be noted that these measures are given either in the Bacmar or the Bacrat models.

3 Are the marketing activities consistent with the activities of other functional areas?

Measures of performance

The main, and most easily extracted measures of marketing performance are given in Table 9. Other more specific measures are given below.

Specific areas of marketing performance

1 For each product line
   (a) Gross contribution margin.
   (b) Profitability by product line (see note under Table 9).
   (c) Product controllable margin to sales.
2 For each channel of distribution
   (a) Gross contribution margin.
   (b) Profitability by channel of distribution.
   (c) Product controllable margin to sales.
3 For each sales region
   (a) Gross contribution margin.
   (b) Profitability by sales region.
   (c) Product controllable margin to sales.

Finance

Traditionally the finance function has as its primary goal the maximization of shareholders' wealth, subject to such constraints as scarce resources and risk minimization. The finance function pursues this goal through three main and interrelated sets of strategies:

1 *The investment strategies*, i.e. deciding which new investments should be undertaken and how the current portfolio of investments in fixed and current assets should be managed.
2 *The financing strategies*, i.e. determining the optimal mix of finance through activities such as capital budgeting (raising finance), capital structure (determining the mix of debt and equity), and working capital management (determining the levels of working capital, debtors, creditors and inventories).
3 *The dividend strategies*, i.e. determining the optimal levels of dividends.

Thus the finance function is concerned with developing optimal strategies for the above and integrating them into the strategy of the company.

The finance function is now considered in greater detail under the headings given on p. 72.

Resources

1 What are the total financial resources, long-term and short-term?
2 How many people are employed in the finance area, and what is their quality?

Costs and efficiency

1 What are the sources of funds available and their costs?
2 What is the capital structure, and is it optimal?
3 What is the level of working capital, and is it optimal?
4 What are the levels of debtors and creditors, and are these optimal?
5 What is the level of dividend payments, and are they appropriate?
6 What is the tax position?

Control

1 What is the reporting system?
2 What is its speed and accuracy?
3 What procedures are employed when variances arise?

Balance

1 Are the financial activities consistent with company goals?
2 Are the financial activities internally consistent?
3 Are the financial activities consistent with the activities of other functional areas?

Measures of performance

The more frequently used measures and the core financial strategies to which they most closely relate are given in Table 10.

Table 10   Measures and financial strategy

Measure	Core financial strategy
Return on investment Return on capital employed	Investment
Debt to equity ratio Creditors ratio Debtors ratio	Financing
Return on equity Payout ratio	Dividend
Current ratio Quick ratio	Liquidity

It should be noted that each of these ratios is provided in the Bacchus Beer Ratio model Bacrat.

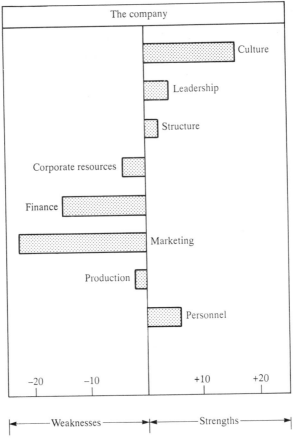

Figure 24 A company assessment diagram

Production

The production function attempts to satisfy company goals through producing the highest quality goods at the lowest possible costs. This is often
pursued through the following production strategies:

1 *Cost reduction strategies*, i.e. arranging the production facilities so that
   the products are produced at the lowest possible cost.
2 *Quality maximization*, i.e. ensuring that the relative product quality[24] is
   as high as possible.
3 *Capacity flexibility*, i.e. ensuring that the plant and equipment have
   optimal capacity utilization.

The production function is now considered under the headings given on
p. 72.

Resources

1 What is value of the facilities and equipment?
2 What is the age of the facilities and equipment?
3 What is the production capacity and is there flexibility?
4 Are the facilities locations optimal?
5 Is there good access to raw materials or supplies?
6 What is the degree of vertical integration?
7 How many people are employed in the production area and what is their quality?

Costs and efficiency

1 What are the unit costs?
2 What are the raw material costs?
3 What are the inventory costs?
4 What is the level of capacity utilization?
5 How good is quality control?

Control

1 What is the reporting system?
2 What is the quality of the production data?
3 What are the wastage / reject rates?
4 What is the level of quality?
5 What are the inventory levels?
6 What are the procedures which are used when variances arise?

Balance

1 Are the production activities consistent with company goals?
2 Are the production activities internally consistent?
3 Are the production activities consistent with the activities of other functional areas?

Measures of performance

The principal measures of performance are shown in Table 11.

Personnel

The personnel, or human relations, function has the task of contributing to corporate goals through providing appropriate people. It is therefore primarily concerned with strategies in the following areas.

Table 11   Measures and production strategy

Measure	Core Production Strategy
Unit costs* Capacity utilization	} Cost reduction
Investment intensity* Fixed assets to total assets* Sales to net current assets	} Cost reduction/flexibility
Inventory turnover ratio* Relative product quality Reject rates Wastage rates	} Quality

* These ratios are provided in the Bacchus Beer ratio model Bacrat.

1 *Recruitment and training strategies*, i.e. ensuring that the company has the appropriate numbers of personnel with the appropriate skills.
2 *Compensation strategies*, i.e. ensuring that there are patterns of career development that will make personnel maximize their efforts on the company's behalf.

The personnel function is now considered under the headings given on p. 72.

Resources

1 Does the company have high quality staff?
2 How many people are employed in the personnel area, what is their quality?
3 Does the company have appropriate training and development programmes?
4 Does the company have a motivating career planning and compensation system?

Costs and efficiency

1 What are the unit labour costs?
2 What is the level of productivity?
3 What is the rate of labour turn-over?
4 What is the level of absenteeism?
5 What is the attitude towards change and flexibility?

Control

1 What is the reporting system?
2 What are the staff evaluation procedures?
3 What are the staff development procedures?
4 What are the speed and accuracy of the system?
5 What are the procedures used when variances arise?

Balance

1 Are the personnel activities consistent with company goals?
2 Are the personnel activities internally consistent?
3 Are the personnel activities consistent with the activities of other functional areas?

Measures of performance

Some of the leading measures which can be used to assess the effectiveness of the personnel function are given in Table 12.

STAGE 3: ATTRIBUTING WEIGHTS TO EACH SECTION

In this stage the various sections that have been selected in Stage 1 and analysed in Stage 2 are given weights that reflect their strength or weakness.

The *importance* of each section that has been analysed is ranked on an ordinal scale running from 0 to 5. Thus if strength in a certain section is considered to be of crucial importance to the company, then this section merits a score of 5; if it is considered to be of average importance, it merits a score of 3; and if it is considered to be of no importance at all, it scores zero. For example, in the vodka industry the functional segment of 'marketing' is of crucial importance and would probably score 5, while for a company in the 'missile' industry the marketing segment would be relatively less important and therefore likely to score less than 5.

Once the importance of each section has been determined, then the *strength* of each section is then ranked on an ordinal scale from −5 to +5, where −5 indicates that this section is likely to have as strong a negative influence on the company as possible. For example, if a company needs great expertise in the marketing function yet it does not develop or intend to develop such expertise, then a high negative number could be assigned to this

Table 12 Measures and personnel strategy

Measure	Core personnel strategy
Unit labour costs	
Labour turnover rate	
Absenteeism	
Days lost	Productivity
Sales per employee*	
Value added per employee*	
Degree of unionisation	

* These ratios are provided in the Bacchus Beer ratio model Bacrat.

Table 13   Assigning weights to the sections of the company

Section	Importance	Strength	Overall score (importance × strength)
Culture	4	+4	+16
Leadership	4	+1	+4
Structure	1	+2	+2
Corporate resources	4	−1	−4
Finance	5	−3	−15
Marketing	5	−4	−20
Production	2	−1	−2
Personnel	2	+3	+6

section. In contrast, a high positive score indicates that the section under consideration is likely to have as strong a positive influence on the company as possible. For example, when a company has a strong technical team and has a major technical lead in an industry where technical superiority is the crucial internal factor, then such a factor could be assigned a score of +5. Finally a score of 0 indicates that the section does not have any strength at all.

When the importance and strength of each section have been determined, these two numbers are multiplied and an ordinal score for each relevant section in the company is obtained. Each of these scores indicates the relative strength or weakness in each section. Finally the score for each section can be shown graphically on a company assessment diagram (Figure 24, p. 76). The advantage of the graphical exposition is that it tends to make the analysis more 'alive' and more easily understood.

A hypothetical example to illustrate how the stages of the company analysis are carried out

Stage 1: Division of the company. This company was divided into the following sections: culture, leadership, power, marketing, finance, production and personnel.

Stage 2: Analysis of the sections. A detailed analysis of the sections selected in Stage 1 was carried out.

Stage 3: Attributing weights to each section. After each section had been analysed, the weights shown in Table 13 were assigned.

Implications of the weighting in Table 13

Culture

In this analysis the culture of the company is considered to be extremely important and in this case it is an element of considerable strength – it has a score of +16. This implies that the prevailing culture must be well suited to the company and also appropriate to the industry in which it operates, and, additionally, its culture must be in some way significantly superior to its competitors.

Leadership

Leadership is considered to be extremely important to this company; however, the quality of leadership the company has is considered to be mild. This could indicate that there is room for the development of more aggressive leadership.

Structure

The structure of the company is not considered to be of great importance, and in this case it has a small positive effect: $+2$.

Corporate resources

The corporate resources – finance, personnel and image which corporate headquarters provides – are considered to be very important. In this case it is felt that the support of such resources is a mild weakness.

Finance

Unfortunately for this company finance is considered to be rather weak – it has a score of -15. Implicit in this score is the message that those weaknesses that have been revealed in the finance function must be dealt with.

Marketing

The ill-health of the marketing function is similar to that of the finance function: strength in marketing is considered to be vital and this company has an extremely low score (-20). Clearly steps must be taken to correct these faults.

Production

The analysis suggests that the production function is of lesser importance to the company than other functions, and it has some slight weaknesses in this area. However, these weaknesses are of lesser importance than the other functional weaknesses.

Personnel

The personnel function is considered to be of below average importance, and in this case the company is quite strong in this area.

CONCLUSION ON ANALYSING THE COMPANY

Analysing the company enables an assessment to be made of how well the company has adapted its internal profile to the environment in which it is operating. On completion of the analysis the manager should be made to make judgements about those sections in the company under analysis which display particular strengths and are likely to confer advantage and those sections in which it is relatively weak and which will leave the company vulnerable if no remedial action is taken. Figure 24 attempts to summarize the approach to analysing the internal strengths and weaknesses of the company.

References

1 Ackoff, R., *Concept of Corporate Planning*, Wiley, 1970.
2 Shapiro, B. P. and Levine, L. B., 'Hewlett-Packard: Manufacturing Productivity Division', Harvard Business School Case: 9–587–101.
3 Argenti, J., *Corporate Collapse: the Causes and Symptoms*, McGraw-Hill, 1971.
4 Selnick, P., *Leadership in Administration*, University of California Press, 1984.
5 Hensey, P. and Blanchard, K., *Management of Organizational Behaviour*, Prentice-Hall Inc., Englewood Cliffs, NJ, 1982.
6 Pfeffer, J., *Power in Organizations*, Pitman, 1981.
7 *Ibid.*
8 Ansoff, H. I., *Strategic Management*, Macmillan, 1979.
9 Crisp, J., 'Striving to Revitalise Its Core', *Financial Times*, 29 January 1986, p. 16.
10 Taylor, F. W., *The Principles of Scientific Management*, Harper Brothers, New York, 1911.
11 Mayo, E., *The Social Problems of an Industrial Civilization*, Harvard Business School, Boston, 1945.
12 Ghoshal, S. and Bartlett, C., *Matsushita Electric Industrial Co., Ltd (MEI)*, The Case Clearing House, Cranfield, 1987.
13 Mintzberg, H., *Power in and around Organizations*, Prentice-Hall Inc., Englewood Cliffs, NJ, 1983.
14 Ghoshal and Bartlett, *op. cit.*
15 Cromie, S., unpublished PhD thesis, University of Leeds, 1986.
16 Cyert, R. and March, J. G., *A Behavioural Theory of the Firm*, Prentice-Hall, Englewood Cliffs, NJ, 1963.
17 *Ibid.*
18 Porter, M., *Cases in Competitive Strategy*, Macmillan, The Free Press, 1983.
19 Ghoshal and Bartlett, *op. cit.*
20 *Ibid.*
21 Mikami, T., *Management and Productivity in Japan*, JMA Consultants, Tokyo 1982, p. 6.
22 Ansoff, H. I., *Corporate Strategy*, Penguin, 1965.
23 Carroll, C., *Building Ireland's Business Perspectives from PIMS*, IMI, Dublin, 1986.
24 See the PIMS studies for further information.

5 Modelling company goals

INTRODUCTION

In the accompanying suite of computer models Bacchus Beer's goals are modelled in the Bacchus Beer Goal Model: Bacgo. As Figure 25 implies, Bacgo is the starting point for the strategic planning and modelling process: it is in this model that the SBU goals are set, and it is against the benchmark of these goals that the effectiveness of the strategies will be judged. This

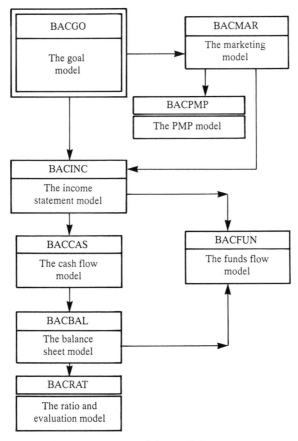

Figure 25 Bacgo is the starting point of the modelling process

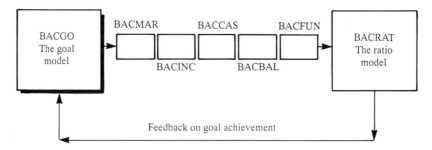

Figure 26 The modelling route to the evaluation of Bacchus's goals

judgement will take place in the final model: the Ratio and Evaluation Model, Bacrat. The modelling route to this evaluation is shown schematically in Figure 26.

THE OBJECTIVE OF BACGO

The objective of the model is to allow the planner to set the goals for Bacchus Beer for the years 1990 to 1994. These goals are set in the form of:

Table 14 The goals for Bacchus Beer

Year	1990	1991	1992	1993	1994
MARKETING					
Target sales (£)	6000	8000	14000	16000	20000
Return on sales (%)	10	10	10	10	10
FINANCIAL					
Return on investment (%)	12	12	13	13	14
Return on equity (%)	25	25	25	25	25
Dividend growth rate (%)	50	33	50	25	33
Dividend payable (£)	100	133	200	250	333
ASSETS AND LIABILITIES					
Additions (£)	1000	1000	1000	1000	500
Disposals (£)	0	0	0	0	0
Fixed assets (£)	3500	4500	5500	6500	7000
Share issues (£)	300	300	300	300	300
Share level (£)	900	1200	1500	1800	2100
Debenture issues (£)	500	500	500	500	500
Debentures (£)	1500	2000	2500	3000	3500
Long-term liabilities (£)	2400	3200	4000	4800	5600
PRODUCTION					
Premium Beer (Units)	150	200	250	320	400
Standard Beer (Units)	100	100	100	100	100
Super Beer (Units)	100	110	125	150	175
Total volume (Units)	350	410	475	570	675

- Marketing goals.
- Financial goals.
- Assets and liabilities goals.
- Production goals.

The actual goals that have been used are set out in Table 14.

It should be noted that although the goals of Bacgo are exclusively functional and quantitative, it is relatively easy to expand their scope and to include more qualitative goals, such as relative quality.

THE RATIONALE BEHIND BACGO AND ITS STRUCTURE

It is assumed that the starting point for the strategic planning process in Bacchus Beer is a review of the level of historic goal achievement and the setting of future goals. In passing, it should be noted that this is a rather simple model: it is merely setting targets at which the company will aim, and consequently there is very little computation. An implication of this is that it is rather easy to alter the goals should they be found to be unsatisfactory or inappropriate.

Each of the goals is now discussed.

Marketing goals

These goals are the target value of sales and the target return on sales that the company expects. Note it is relatively easy to add other marketing goals, e.g. promotion costs as a percentage of sales, or goals as set out in Chapter 4.

Financial goals

These are the principal goals of the model. Once again extra goals, such as liquidity ratios, can be added quite easily.

Assets and liabilities goals

These goals set the levels of assets and liabilities that the company wishes to have over the planning period. Once again these goals can be added to or amended very easily.

Production goals

Bacchus Beer has just three product lines – Premium, Standard and Super – and the target annual volumes for each product are set out above. Once again additional product lines can be introduced very easily.

THE STRUCTURE OF THE MODEL

Like all the other models in the suite, Bacgo has the following structure:

1 *An input worksheet.* This requests input data from the user. In this case the information is the company goals.
2 *An output worksheet.* This shows the output from the model after any calculations have been carried out. In this case, because there are so few calculations the output worksheet is very similar to the input worksheet.
3 *A graph menu.* This provides graphs of the data.
4 *A print menu.* This prints out aspects of the model – usually graphs or worksheets – requested by the user.
5 *A link to other models.* Each model is linked to other models so that data are automatically exported and imported. For example, the targets, or goals in the Bacgo model are automatically imported by the ratio model, Bacrat.

A NOTE ON RUNNING THE MODEL

You should now examine the Goal model Bacgo more closely. To do this, proceed as follows:

Place the disk in drive A and close the drive. Then
Type A:
Type Bacgo

After you have examined this model, you should leave it and proceed to the marketing model, Bacmar.

BUILDING YOUR OWN MODELS

After you have examined Bacgo, you should use it as an aid to build your own goal model. You should proceed as follows:

1 Run Bacgo.
2 Type Ctrl Break (this will break into the macro, which runs Bacgo automatically).
3 Save the model with a new name: for example, you could call this model Goal1.
4 Have two windows.
5 In the top window have a table view.
6 In the bottom window have a formula view.
7 Place the two windows in Sync.
8 Alter or develop the formulae in the bottom window and build your new model.
9 When complete, save and run.

6 Analysing the environment

INTRODUCTION

There is a growing body of evidence to show that those companies most committed to environmental assessment and strategic planning tend to achieve the best operating results.

Channon has shown[1] that one of the major strategic errors of British enterprises since World War II has been its failure, by and large, to recognize that the post-war business environment was fundamentally different from the one which prevailed pre-war. Thus from 1945 among the major changes were the rise of new global competition; the demise of the seller's market and the rise of the power of the buyers; the fall of the British Empire and, with that, the loss of secure markets for British goods; and the development of a freer system of world trade.

The first clear evidence of the benefits that can accrue from a systematic approach to strategic planning, and hence environmental assessment, was a study conducted in 1965 by S. S. Thune and R. J. House[2] in the United States. They found that those companies that engaged in formal long-range planning, when they were considered as a group historically, outperformed a comparable group of informal planners. Additionally, they found that the successful economic results associated with long-range planning tended to take place in the rapidly changing industries and among the companies of medium size.

THE GROWTH OF DISCONTINUITY AND TURBULENCE

Today it is more important than ever for planners to be aware of the increasingly turbulent and discontinuous nature of the environment faced by business. An implication of turbulence is that the past is not a good guide to the future. A consequence of this is that the traditional extrapolative methods of forecasting may today have very little currency. Indeed, research by Spivey and Wrobleski,[3] who examined past studies of econometric models used in the US government and for industry planning, found that non-econometric forecasts were at least as good, and that in the period 1970 to 1975 US econometric models were unreliable for three or more quarters into the future.

The difficulties in forecasting are well illustrated by the attempts of the leading UK forecasters to make accurate forecasts of the likely state of the UK economy just 1 year ahead. In June 1985 the *Financial Times* published an alphabetical list of the forecasts of selected indices of the UK economy that had been made approximately 1 year earlier by twenty-two leading forecasting institutions. The results are shown in Table 15. As can be seen, not only was there a wide level of variation in the forecasts, but all were incorrect. The major factor contributing to the general level of inaccuracy was the coalminers' strike in the UK, which occurred during this period: an example of turbulence.

The authors of the report, Wilkinson and Cassidy, commented, 'Like the unfortunate weathermen, forecasters of the UK economy are equipped with large computers, huge amounts of data and a punters' instinct and still they get it wrong'.[4]

This growth in environmental uncertainty has been documented well by Ansoff,[5] who asserts that, since the start of this century, there has been a general increase in the level of turbulence coupled with a decrease in the time available to make decisions. A consequence of these influences is that today firms must, in their assessment of their environments, rely less on traditional means of forecasting the future, and must develop their ability to be sensitive to weak signals of forthcoming change. One method of doing this is scenario planning through the medium of microcomputers. This issue is considered on p. 216.

A THREE-STAGE APPROACH TO ANALYSING THE ENVIRONMENT

Just as each individual's environment is unique, so the environment faced by every company is unique to it, and this makes the formulation of a general methodology for understanding and analysing the environment rather difficult. If each company's particular environment is unique, how can any generalized approach be of any value?

Research and the experience of company planners indicate that it is possible to make an effective judgement about the environmental prospects faced by a company by using a three-stage approach:

Stage 1: Segmenting the environment. The environment is divided into a number of discrete segments that generally are important for most companies.

Table 15 How forecasts for UK economy fared: percentage error from out-turn 1984

Forecaster	Date 1984	GDP	Consumer spending	Exports	Inflation	Unemployment	Average
Cambridge Econometrics	June	38	47	-17	13	-2	23
Capel-Cure Myers	June	25	80	-17	-9	0	26
CBI	March	17	100	-47	0	-3	33
City University	May	7			6	-3	5
Data Resources Incorporated	June	-11	-7	-6	13	-3	8
Grieveson Grant	June	90	17	-17	4	-6	49
Henley Centre	July	24	60	-20	4	-3	22
Hoare Govett	June	38	67	-11	52	0	34
Item Club	June	13	67	-9	0	-3	18
James Capel	July	4	27	-29	-4	-3	13
Laing and Cruickshank	June	50	27	-9	6	-6	19
Liverpool University	May	71			-27	-8	35
London Business School	June	-4	7	14	-2	0	5
National Institute	May	-30	7	2	25	-3	13
OECO	June	4	67	-20	3		24
Oxford Economic Forecasting	May	4	-7	-3	17	-3	7
Phillips and Drew	July	21	93	-2	2	-3	24
Rowe and Pitman	June	33	60	2	4		25
Simon and Coates	July	4	47	-18	8	0	14
Staniland Hall	June	8	27	-30	8	0	14
Treasury	March	29	127	-26	-6	0	47
Wood Mackenzie	June	21	67	-15	0	-6	22
Out-turn		2.4	1.5	6.6	4.8	3.1	

Note. Out-turn is real percentage increase year on year for GDP, consumer spending and exports. Inflation is a 12-month rise in RPI. Unemployment is fourth quarter adult total in millions. Error: figures are percentage overestimate, except negative figures, which are underestimate. Errors are calculated as closely as possible from variables actually forecast, e.g. consumer prices rather than RPI.

Stage 2: Analysis of the segments. Each segment is analysed in detail, and the threats and opportunities it poses are assessed.

Stage 3: Attributing weights to each segment. Weights are attributed to each segment to reflect the segment's anticipated impact – in terms of opportunities to exploit or threats to be countered.

In selecting the segments for analysis it is important to realize that not all industries will require all environmental segments to receive an equal depth of analysis. For example, if the company being considered is engaged in the manufacture and sale of vodka, then the environmental analysis for this company will be biased towards a rather detailed examination of segments such as the level of competition, the marketing environment, and the advertising environment, as these three elements are of crucial importance in the vodka business. However, if the analysis were concerned with a company engaged in the manufacture and sale of jet aircraft engines, then, in addition to analysing the competitive environment, considerable emphasis would probably be placed upon the technical environment, with particular reference to the technical developments of rival companies and the technical requirements of prospective customers.

STAGE 1: SEGMENTING THE ENVIRONMENT

Here it is assumed that the environment comprises the following segments:

- Competitive.
- Marketing.
- Economic.
- Legal/government.
- Social/cultural.
- Technological.
- Geographical.
- Other.

Although each of the segments is separated above, in practice they will be overlapping, and the distinction between each of them will not always be clear. For example, the segments 'Economic' and 'Legal/government' will frequently be closely intertwined. The segment 'Other' has been included as a catch-all or new category for environmental influences not captured by the other segments named in the list. Just what this segment contains, if it is used at all, will be determined by the particular circumstances the company under analysis is facing.

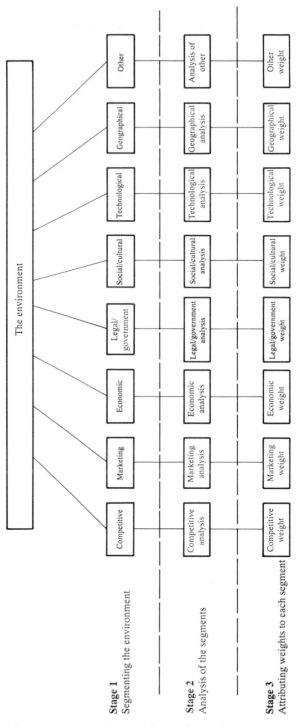

Figure 27   A three-stage approach to analysing the environment

STAGE 2: ANALYSIS OF THE SEGMENTS

The various segments into which the environment has been sub-divided are now analysed, using the methodology given below.

The competitive segment

In 1980 Professor Michael Porter of the Harvard Business School published his seminal work *Competitive Strategy: Techniques for Analyzing Industries and Competitors*.[6] This work was the first rigorous analysis and exposition of the fundamental competitive forces that prevail in all industries and that determine their levels of profitability. Some of the basic findings of Porter's work are summarized below.

Porter asserts that the competitive climate that prevails in an industry is not just a matter of luck or fortune. Rather, there are five fundamental competitive forces – 'Threat of Entry, Threat of Substitutes, Power of Buyers, Power of Suppliers and the Level of Rivalry Among Current Competitors' – and that the combined strength of these forces determines the profit potential of an industry. The power of these forces varies from industry to industry, and therefore to understand the strategic position and potential of any company, a strategist must understand these forces and then build a strategy that will enable the company to defend itself against them, or influence them in its favour.

The five competitive forces are shown in Figure 28, and each of them is now discussed in greater detail below.

The threat of entry

When new competitors enter an industry, by definition they make it more competitive – there are more 'players' competing in the market. More specifically, new entrants have the effect of increasing industrial capacity, and will employ strategies such as price competition and advertising to gain market share. Therefore, from the point of view of existing competitors, efforts should be made to counter this threat.

The strength of the threat of entry depends upon two major factors – the barriers to entry that existing competitors have erected plus the anticipated reaction from those existing competitors. In general the higher the entry barriers and the stronger the likelihood of adverse reaction by existing competitors, the smaller will be the threat of entry.

Porter lists seven main barriers to entry:

- Economies of scale.
- Product differentiation.
- Capital requirements.

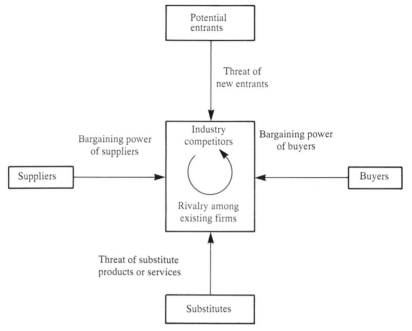

Figure 28   Forces driving industrial competition

- Switching costs.*
- Access to distribution channels.
- Cost disadvantages independent of scale.
- Government policy.

The height and nature of barriers to entry will vary from industry to industry and two contrasting examples are provided below.

Entry barriers in the motor industry

The major players in the world motor industry have now erected entry barriers that would seem to preclude the entry of any new independent competitors. Just two of the more important entry barriers are *capital investment* and *lead time*.

---

* These are the costs incurred by a consumer of a product or service who switches from one brand or product to another, and in certain industries these costs can be extremely high. For example, an accounting firm that has installed a certain brand of computer cannot easily switch to another brand even though the alternative may be in every respect a superior model. The switching costs are not just the costs of changing the hardware and the software but also of changing existing records and data bases to the new system, staff retraining and perhaps a change in the format of the information provided by and for clients. It is these latter costs that are the major impediments to switching.

It has been estimated that, in 1985, the average cost of designing and tooling for a new car was in the region of $800 million, and this acts as a major barrier to entry. In fact no country, except Japan, has been able to develop since World War II a world-scale domestic motor industry without the partnership of a multinational producer.

An additional problem for new entrants is that the minimum lead time for the development of a new car is around 5 years – a remarkably long lead time for a consumer product. It may be the case, however, that CADCAM will offer car manufacturers the opportunity to reduce the costs of introducing a new model and also speed up the process.

The height of these barriers to entry is well illustrated by the doubts surrounding Malaysia's efforts to develop an indigenous motor industry:

MALAYSIAN CAR TAKES TO THE ROAD

Malaysia's industrialisation efforts enter a new but uncertain phase today when the country's National Car, the Proton Saga, rolls off the production line for the first time. The M$560M (£177m) project is the brainchild of Dr Mahathir Mohamed, the Prime Minister...

Partnering the Government owned Heavy Industries Corporation of Malaysia (Hicom) are Mitsubishi Motors and Mitsubishi Corporation, both of Japan...

From the start the Proton project, the centre piece of a wider heavy industrialisation programme, has been shrouded in controversy because of doubts whether a small country like Malaysia (population 15m) can support an indigenous car industry without heavy protection and costly subsidies...

Dr Mahathir admitted earlier this year that the first 7,500 units being produced in 1985 will cost M$35,000 (£11,000) each. They are to retail at around the same elevated price as the Saga's nearest competitors, $20,000.

'We expect to lose money for the first three to four years', says Datuk Wan Nik Ismail, the project's executive director.[7]

Entry barriers to the philatelic industry

By way of contrast, an industry with minimal barriers to entry is the 'Retail Stamps' segment of the philatelic industry. This industry is concerned with selling postage stamps and covers (i.e. postage stamps on envelopes that have passed through the post) to collectors. It is characterized by very large numbers of dealers who operate on a part-time basis, have low overheads, and market their products at relatively low levels of expense, through the philatelic press.

The threat of substitutes

Although it could be argued that all the products produced by rival companies in a particular industry are substitutes for each other, this is too

narrow a view. Substitutes also include products from outside the industry
that are capable of performing a function previously carried out by products
of the industry. For example, the laser disk, although designed to provide an
alternative to the video recorder, has also evolved into a device for storing
information for computers. It therefore represents a substitute method of
data storage and is a rival to computer disks. In general the greater the
number of alternatives for a product or a service, the greater will be the threat
of substitutes.

Porter[8] suggests that those substitutes which should be monitored most
closely are:

- Those products that are providing a better performance/price standard
  than the industry standard.
- Products produced by industries earning high profits.

The power of buyers

The greater the power of buyers, the more they can adversely affect an
industry's profitability and its room for strategic manoeuvre. Porter has
found that power of a buyer group seems to be strongest when the following
conditions apply:

1 It is concentrated or purchases large volumes relative to seller sales.
2 The products it purchases represent a significant fraction of the buyer's
   costs or purchases.
3 The products it purchases from the industry are standard or
   undifferentiated.
4 It faces few switching costs.
5 It earns low profits.
6 Buyers pose a credible threat of backward integration.
7 The industry's product is unimportant to the quality of the buyers'
   products or services.
8 The buyer has full information.

The strength of the buyer group *vis-à-vis* the supplier group will vary from
industry to industry and again two contrasting examples are given.

Buyer power in the defence industry

In the defence industry it is normally the case that the government is the only
buyer. Even when defence industry products are purchased by foreign
governments, it usually requires approval by the government of the country
in which the product is manufactured. In the UK government defence

acquisitions are made by the Ministry of Defence Procurement Executive (MOD PE), and this committee has the power to set terms and conditions of contracts.

Buyer power of water consumers

In contrast to this extreme concentration of buyer power, companies purchasing water from a local water authority or utility have little power – they must accept the terms or conditions of the supplier or else go without.

Although it will frequently be the case that a company will be disadvantaged when faced by a powerful buyer, in practice, this will not always be so. For example, in the UK it is commonly asserted that those (relatively small) companies that supply the large retail multiples are severely disadvantaged because of the enormous disparity in their power *vis-à-vis* the buyer. In fact many of these smaller supplying companies have benefited substantially, both commercially and in terms of their strategic behaviour, from such associations, as the following quotation shows:

HOW TO DEAL WITH THE BIG FISH

Pinney's of Scotland, David Stapleton's company, is the only supplier of smoked salmon to Marks & Spencer. It has become twice the size of its nearest rival, and expects to see its turnover rise from 5m to more than 7m in the year (1985) to September.

Based in Dumfriesshire, Pinney's is an example of the way in which it is possible to turn a cottage industry into a leader in its field by applying techniques perfected by much larger businesses like production and cost control. It also shows that while a high exposure to one customer (M & S accounts for half of Pinney's sales) has its drawbacks, such dependence can actually help the supplier make its business more efficient and widely based...

The M & S link has been important both because of the technical help the store has offered in developing new products like smoked salmon pâté or salmon roulade and because of the flexible attitude it can afford to take over pricing.

If the price of any particular ingredient suddenly shoots through the roof, for instance, M & S can minimise the damage to sales of that product by spreading the increase across all five of Pinney's M & S lines. 'Much of what we have achieved would not have been possible without M & S', admits Stapleton.[9]

The power of suppliers

The power of suppliers tends to show the other side of the coin. Thus powerful suppliers can, through their supplying policies, determine the profitability and room for strategic manoeuvre of the companies they are supplying. Suppliers tend to be relatively powerful when the industry:

1 Is dominated by a few companies and is more concentrated than the industry to which it sells.
2 Is not obliged to contend with other substitute products for sale to the industry.
3 Is not an important customer of the supplier group.
4 Has products that are an important input to the buyer's business.
5 Has products that are differentiated or has built up switching costs.
6 Poses a credible threat of forward integration.

The level of rivalry among current competitors

Different industries generate different levels of rivalry among competitors. For example, the level of rivalry prevailing in professions such as law and accounting tends to be much less intense than the rivalry that prevails in the life insurance industry.

According to Porter, the intensity of rivalry is chiefly determined by the following factors:

* Numerous or equally balanced competitors.
* Slow industry growth.
* High fixed or storage costs.
* Lack of differentiation or switching costs.
* Capacity augmented in large increments.
* Diverse competitors.
* High strategic stakes.
* High exit barriers.

In the UK the big four clearing banks – Lloyds, National Westminster, Barclays and Midland – have for many years enjoyed a relationship with each other that has had a relatively low level of rivalry. The four banks offered almost identical services to customers at almost identical costs and had relatively stable market shares. However with the development of a greater degree of deregulation, the internationalization of banking, the convergence of the services offered by banks and other non-banking institutions, such as building societies, and the entry of new competitors, it seems that the intensity of rivalry will increase.

Conclusion on the competitive segment

Surveying and analysing the competitive map that all industries have is a crucial step in environmental assessment. After determination of the competitive forces that prevail in the industry, the second step is to determine just where the company under analysis is located and which competitive forces work in its favour or against it.

When the analysis of the competitive environment has been completed the threats and opportunities that prevail should then be weighted, as shown in Stage 3 below.

The marketing segment – overview

Overlapping with and complementing the competitive segment is the marketing segment. Analysis of this segment could be described as providing a measure of the potential demand for the goods and services that the company offers. Although throughout this section the goods or services will be couched in terms of consumer goods and services, the same general analytical approach can also be applied to industrial goods and services.

The fundamental determinants of demand

There are a number of environmental indicators which, it is usually agreed, are frequently the fundamental determinants of the demand for goods and services. These are the following.

The size and affluence of the market

A primary determinant of demand is the absolute size and affluence of the market for the product. This importance can be illustrated by reference to the world's most prosperous market – the United States. The size and affluence of this market has made it almost essential for global competitors to have a significant presence in it. Indeed Porter has commented: 'In many industries, globalisation has hinged critically on foreign firms having access to the US market because of its uniquely large size'. The factor of size has also been instrumental in the development of the concept and reality of a single Europe.

The trends in the market

Although the size and affluence of the total market are of great importance, within all markets there are other indicators and trends that are of great significance when considering the potential of a market. Among the more important trends are the following:

1 *Total population trends.* Is the total population growing, static or declining? Generally, but not always, (see p. 169) those markets that are growing will tend to offer the best prospects.
2 *Trends in segments of the population.* Products tend not to be targeted for 'the whole population' but rather for particular segments within the whole population. It is therefore important to know how the different target segments are changing. For example, there has been a steady increase in the UK of the proportion of the population over the age of

65 years, with the increase being particularly marked for women. This trend has obvious marketing and business implications for those companies in areas such as the provision of sheltered accommodation for older people, food products, health products, mobility products, communication products, holidays, etc.

3   *Income trends*. Is the level of income in the population increasing, static or declining, and how is the distribution of income among the various segments changing? Thus in Europe in general, with the advent of equal pay and sex discrimination legislation, there has been a steady decrease in the differential between male and female earnings. This is a significant change in the distribution of income. Other important changes in income distribution that have occurred and are occurring are the shift in income distribution towards the professional classes, the relative and increasing disparity in income distribution between the employed and the unemployed, etc.

Stage in the industry/product life cycle

The product life cycle has already been discussed in Chapter 2. From the perspective of environmental assessment it is important for managers to be informed about the stage in which their industry is at in its life cycle. For example, in the vending industry it is considered that the machine-vending of cigarettes is in the decline stage, while the machine-vending of drinks, food and other products is still in the growth stage.

Measuring the market potential

The potential for a market can be measured by market analysis as shown immediately below.

When the analysis of the marketing segment has been completed, it should then be weighted, as shown in Stage 3 below.

The marketing process

Introduction: distinction between marketing and selling

Although the terms *marketing* and *selling* are frequently used interchangeably, there is a clear distinction between them. A marketing orientation implies that the fundamental and ultimate determinant of the success of a company, in the market place, is the acceptance of its products or services by consumers. In other words, companies most effectively adapting their goods and or services to the needs and wishes of consumers will tend to be the most successful and *vice versa*. In contrast to this, a selling orientation implies that goods or services are already in existence, i.e. their characteristics are given,

Table 16   The contrast between a marketing and a selling orientation

Marketing orientation	Selling orientation
Products or services developed in response to consumers' needs and wishes	Consumers acquired in response to products or services

and the task is how to sell them to consumers. The contrast between the two orientations is shown in Table 16.

The importance of having such an orientation has, perhaps, been expressed most clearly by Leavitt:

> Every major industry was once a growth industry. But some that are now riding a wave of growth enthusiasm are very much in the shadow of decline. Others which are thought of as seasoned growth industries have actually stopped growing. In every case the reason growth is threatened, slowed, or stopped is not because the market is saturated. It is because there has been a failure of management.

FATEFUL PURPOSES

> The failure is at the top. The executives responsible for it, in the last analysis are those who deal with broad aims and policies . . .
> The difference between marketing and selling is more than semantic. Selling focuses on the needs of the buyer. Selling is preoccupied with the seller's need to convert his product into cash; marketing with the idea of satisfying the needs of the customer by means of the product and the whole cluster of things associated with creating, delivering, and finally consuming it.[10]

These quotations, which were first published in 1960 in the *Harvard Business Review*, were certainly true then and, as world economies and industries have been internationalized, are probably more important today. The commercial benefits that can accrue from having such a strong and applied marketing orientation is clearly seen in Japan's phenomenal industrial success.

The marketing process could be described in general terms as the process by which a company achieves its strategic goals through adapting its products and or services to the needs and wishes of its consumers. This general process can be sub-divided into a number of linked stages: market identification, market segmentation, product positioning, and marketing mix strategy. Each of these constituent elements is now discussed and illustrated hypothetically through reference to the Bacchus Company.

Stage 1: market identification

In this stage the company attempts to identify in its environment market opportunities that it may be able to exploit successfully. This is the stage at which marketing research is undertaken in order to ascertain the extent and nature of the opportunities, and to assess the company's internal ability to exploit them. At this stage there is a general lack of detail in the proposed actions: it is essentially exploratory and is really concerned with seeing if there is a possible match between the markets and the company's capabilities, including its existing (and potential) range of products and or services.

Market identification for Bacchus Beer

At this stage Bacchus could undertake the following activities:

- Market research to provide the following information:
  1 The types, sizes, growth rates, locations and values of the market segments for its three product lines. Forecasts of future demand in each of these markets.
  2 Information on competing product lines, including the number of competing products; the number and sizes of competing companies; and for each rival product line: sales values, sales volumes; prices; growth rates; special features; methods of promotion; and forecasts of future developments.
  3 Information on methods of distribution, including customer attitudes to distribution practices.
  4 Profiles of customers, including information on items such as customer attitudes to existing products and services; new features sought by customers; other customer needs not satisfied by existing products; preferred buying methods; price sensitivity; groupings of customers according to age, region, affluence, etc.; and forecasts of future customer demands and needs.
- An internal audit of its own capability to supply the market in a satisfactory manner.

Stage 2: market segmentation

In this stage the company attempts to refine the information gathered in the first stage of the process. Here, assuming that the company wishes to service the markets identified, and an appropriate match with the company's capabilities has been identified, the markets are sub-divided or segmented into various sub-markets. It could be said that market segmentation is in the eye of the beholder, and that unique and creative segmentation will often confer unique competitive advantage for companies. However, although there are no precise rules as to how markets ought to be segmented, the guidelines given in Chapter 2 for 'Defining the business' (p. 26), plus the suggestions set out below provide a range of issues that ought to be examined when markets are being segmented.

Frequently used bases of segmentation for consumer goods include:

1 *Demography*. Age, sex, family size, income, occupation, religion, race, etc.
2 *Geography*. Country, region, city, town, climate, etc.
3 *Social basis*. Class, education, occupation, etc.
4 *Product function*. Use sought, benefits sought, rate of usage, etc.
5 *Buyer behaviour*. Of actual and potential consumers.

It should be noted that market segmentation is often more straightforward for consumer goods than for industrial goods, mainly because of the greater range of uses to which many industrial goods can be put and also because there can be much greater customer heterogeneity. For example, a manufacturer of small electric motors may sell his products to such customers: automobile manufacturers, aircraft manufacturers, small general engineering companies, etc. Each of these customers has a very different set of uses and requirements.

The criteria for deciding which segments are most attractive will vary from industry to industry, but in general the following tend to be often considered as important influences:

- Current and future growth rate of the segment in terms of volume and value.
- The degree and nature of the existing competition: threat of new entrants, threat of substitutes, power of buyers, level of rivalry among existing competitors, levels of profitability.

Market segmentation for Bacchus Beer

Bacchus has segmented its markets on the following bases:

1 *Demographic*. Super Beer is bought by affluent males aged 25 to 35; Premium beer is bought by affluent males aged to 18/25, while Standard is bought by less affluent males aged 18/35.
2 *Geographical*. Location of customers: it is assumed that all customers will be drawn from the national market only.
3 *Distribution*. Super and Standard are sold principally through pubs and restaurants, while Premium, in addition to these outlets, has substantial sales through off-licence shops.

Stage 3: product positioning

Once a company has decided upon its target markets the next stage is to determine how it ought to position its products in these target markets in relation to competitors' offerings. This involves assessing how competitors' products meet customers' needs and then developing marketing strategies

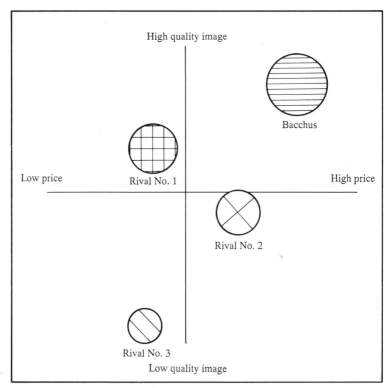

Figure 29   A product-positioning map for Bacchus Super Beer

(at the later Stage 4: marketing mix stage) to meet these needs in a superior fashion. Product positioning is a vital part of the process, because it is here that managers must 'see to the heart' of the reasons for competitors' success and, more importantly, decide upon how they will position their own products or services so that consumers are induced to buy them. It is suggested that this can be accomplished in three steps:

Step 1   Decide upon the criteria that distinguish the various products currently available in the target market. These criteria will be provided by the market research undertaken in Stage 1 of the marketing process. In the case of consumer goods typical criteria could include price, quality, service, image, etc.

Step 2   Draw up a series of product-positioning maps for competitors. A product-positioning map shows graphically how products compete, using two key customer criteria as axes. The products are represented by circles whose areas are proportional to their annual sales. Thus, for example, two fundamental criteria for beer could be price and image. A hypothetical product-positioning map for Bacchus Super Beer, using these criteria, is shown in Figure 29.

Step 3 Decide upon possible positions for Bacchus's products on the product-positioning maps. On the basis of the maps, it would appear that Bacchus's should position its Super Beer so that potential consumers perceive it to have the following attributes:

(a) Very strong.
(b) Very high quality.
(c) Expensive and exclusive.
(d) Associated with success.
(e) Associated with health.

Stage 4: marketing mix strategy

In order to position a product or service in a desired location in its target market segment, a company has at its disposal a great number of instruments. These include:

1 The quality of the product in terms of features such as style and image.
2 The distribution, i.e. by wholesaler, agent, etc.
3 The promotion of the product in terms of advertising, methods of selling.
4 The price of the product.

These various instruments, which are used to influence consumers, have been grouped together by McCarthy under the four headings product, place, promotion and price, and these four broader sets of strategy instruments have become known as the marketing mix. The most commonly used elements of the marketing mix are shown in Table 17.

In this stage the task is to blend various elements from the marketing mix into a combination that enables the company to position its products in its markets by an appropriate mix of the product, place, promotion and price variables, so that it achieves its goals. The detail of the marketing mix is now considered.

Table 17 The marketing mix[11]

Product	Place	Promotion	Price
Quality	Distribution channels	Advertising	Level
Features and options	Distribution coverage	Personal selling	Discounts and
Style	Outlet locations	Sales promotion	allowances
Brand name	Sales territories	Publicity	Payment terms
Packaging	Inventory levels and		
Product line	locations		
Warranty	Transportation carriers		
Service level			
Other services			

Product strategy

The 'product' activities are concerned with developing products (and their associated services) or services that satisfy customers' needs effectively. (The word 'effectively' rather than 'profitably' has been used because it is more general. Thus a non-profit-seeking leisure centre might seek to satisfy its users' needs with no reference to the profitability of doing so.) Among the more important features that distinguish products are the following:

1 *Quality*. What is the relative quality of the product, and its associated services, in relation to other competing products that are available?
2 *Features*. What particular features does the product have that distinguish it from competing products?
3 *Options*. Are there options that are not available on competing products?
4 *Style*. How well is the product styled in relation to immediate and other non-immediate competing products?
5 *Brand name*. Does the product have a brand name with connotations?
6 *Packaging*. What is the quality of the packaging of the product in relation to that offered by competitors?
7 *Product line*. Is the product just a single offering or is it part of a wider and more comprehensive product line?
8 *Warranty*. What is the warranty period and the quality of the warranty in comparison with the warranties offered on competing products?
9 *Service level*. Is the level of service that accompanies the product inferior or superior to that of comparable products?

Product strategies for Bacchus beer

The product strategies to be followed by Bacchus for just one of its brands – Super Beer – are as follows:

1 *Quality*. The relative product quality of Super beer to be regarded by consumers as higher than that provided by competing products.
2 *Feature*. Purity of brewing.
3 *Brand name*. Strong brand name associated with successful people.
4 *Packaging*. Expensive and exclusive.
5 *Product line*. Associated with Bacchus's other product lines.
6 *Service level*. Outlets assisted by Bacchus's staff to ensure quality of the product. Also emergency delivery service available.

Place strategy

The 'place' activities are concerned with deciding upon where the product will be sold, the method of distribution, and associated decisions such as inventory levels.

The distribution strategy and practices adopted by a company should flow from its corporate marketing strategies. It is important that the relationship has this direction, because decisions about distribution have such far-reaching strategic implications. The more important of these include:

- *Responsiveness to customers' needs and wishes.* The nature, quality and level of customer service will be influenced strongly by the chosen method of distribution.
- *Profitability.* The method of distribution chosen – in most cases there is a choice of method, usually calling for a trade-off between the costs and benefits of the alternatives.
- *Costs.* Distribution costs are significant in most industries. For example, Christopher[12] indicates that, on average, distribution costs are about 15 per cent of sales turnover for a typical company.
- *Product.* The characteristics of the product will be influenced by the method of distribution chosen. For example, a decision to distribute a product internationally may make it necessary to change some physical aspects of it so that it conforms to international standard specifications.
- *Pricing.* The pricing policy adopted will be influenced not just by manufacturing and actual distribution costs but also by the nature of the distribution adopted. Thus a decision by an organization to have broad, intensive, national distribution will tend to demand a lower price level than a decision to have limited distribution with a small number of exclusive, high quality outlets.
- *Promotion.* The promotional requirements for a product or service are also a function of the distribution methods employed. Thus the promotional requirements for intensive national distribution are very different from those required for smaller regional sales.
- *Relationships with other firms.* The degree to which an organization sub-contracts out its distribution will have major long-term implications for its relationships with other firms and its flexibility for strategic change. Thus an organization that contracts out its distribution may have to enter into long-term legal contracts that cannot be changed easily.
- *Control.* The greater use a company makes of intermediaries to carry out its distribution, the less control will it have over the marketing of its products.

Because of these and other strategically important aspects of distribution it is important that distribution policies reflect corporate policies rather than constrain or set them.

Distribution strategies of Bacchus Beer

Bacchus's distribution strategies are:

1 *Method.* Company's own trucks used to make deliveries on a schedule
   agreed with outlets.
2 *Outlets.* Pubs, restaurants and hotels, all in the higher social class sector.

Promotion strategy

The third element in the marketing mix is 'promotion'. This could be considered as the process through which a company communicates with and
influences its targeted market segments, with the goal of helping to position
its products or services in their desired locations and generating the desired
responses from these segments.

Although, from the perspective of the conventional firm making products
or offering services, the promotional goal often will be ultimately to generate
maximum sales at minimum cost, this is too narrow a view. Promotion will
not necessarily have sales generation as a direct or primary goal and it may
also have multiple goals. Among the more common generic promotion goals
are the following.

Awareness

Companies frequently wish to develop in their target audience just an awareness of their products, their brands, their services or even their existence. This
may be used to:

1 Develop potential customers' awareness of the existence of a new product
   or service. For example, when a new product is introduced, the aim may
   not be to cause the potential customer to buy the product, but to develop
   an awareness of the new product's existence and inculcate a predisposi-
   tion towards future purchase. The advertising and promotion, say, of
   management consultancy and accounting service generally does not have
   the goal that those influenced by the promotion will purchase the services
   immediately, but, rather, that they will be predisposed to do so in the
   future.
2 Refresh existing customers' memories of the existence of a company, a
   brand, a product, or service through reminding them of its existence. This
   is often the goal behind the promotion of products that are at the mature
   stage of their product life cycles. This is the type of motivation lying
   behind advertising of company names, products and services through
   diaries, calendars, etc.

Attitude

The generic goal 'attitude' is somewhat similar to the 'awareness' goal in that when a promotion has such a goal, its aim is to leave the targeted sector primarily with a desired attitude of mind towards a product, a service or indeed an issue, and the developed attitude may not result in action. For example, the promotion campaign waged in the UK in 1986 by the Department of Health and Social Services against the disease AIDS (the Acquired Immune Deficiency Syndrome) had largely the goal of developing attitudes: 'The aim of the campaign, says the Department of Health and Social Security, is twofold. To prevent the spread of AIDS and to allay people's fears and misconceptions about its transmission'.[13]

Action

When companies wish their promotion campaigns to lead directly to sales, then action, in the form of purchases by the target market segments, is the goal. Although immediate sales in response to promotion are the most frequently considered criterion for the success of a promotional campaign, there will often be lags in the process. For example, advertising campaigns designed to promote the purchase of ephemeral products such as popular records, films, plays, etc. are only successes if the required numbers of the targeted market segments buy almost immediately. In contrast, in the promotion of sales of products such as housing or industrial buildings, immediate sales are generally not expected.

Competitive signals

Companies may use promotion to signal to their competitors, and other interested parties, selected information about themselves. The information could include strategic intentions, future goals, or internal health. For example, many public companies, in order to act as a stabilizing influence in the degree of competition prevailing in their industry and also to maintain harmonious relationships with the financial community and society in general, often publish, in national newspapers, their annual operating results, their achievements and their plans for the future.

In general the primary goal of any promotion strategy should be to help the company achieve its marketing goals. More specifically it will often be the case that the promotion goals will be to ensure that blend of promotional devices which will achieve the maximum degree of influence in the targeted market segments at the minimum cost. Thus any promotion strategy should contribute to the marketing process through:

- Being appropriate to the product and the market segment that has been identified and is being targeted.

- Helping position the product in the desired location in the segment.
- Being appropriate to the means of distribution chosen.
- Being appropriate to the resources which the company has.

Promotion strategies for Bacchus Beer

The promotion strategy for just one of Bacchus's product lines – Super Beer – is now given. The goal of the promotion strategy is action, i.e. to lead as quickly as possible to increased sales of Super Beer. This is achieved through advertising in professional magazines, and promotion of relatively expensive sports, e.g. golf, show jumping etc.

Price strategy

Traditional economic theory claims that price is the primary basis of competition and the primary determinant of demand. Empirical evidence[14] and casual observation suggest that this is often untrue.

Although price may indeed strongly influence sales and may be an important influence upon the nature and the degree of competition in an industry, it is only one of many factors. Price is just one element of the marketing mix that may be employed to achieve its marketing objectives. Indeed there is now evidence to suggest that although most managers still consider price to be the most important influence on sales, in reality sales are also strongly influenced by a vector of other elements drawn from the marketing mix. Porter has argued that any competitive strategy based upon price competition alone is inherently dangerous:

> Some forms of competition, notably price competition, are highly unstable and quite likely to leave the entire industry worse off from the standpoint of profitability. Price cuts are quickly and easily matched by rivals, and once matched they lower revenues for all firms unless industry price elasticity of demand is high enough. Advertising battles, on the other hand, may well expand demand or enhance the level of product differentiation in the industry for the benefit of all firms.[15]

This quotation highlights a characteristic of price that makes it fundamentally different from each of the other elements in the marketing mix: the speed with which any company can unilaterally make a price change. This characteristic makes heavy reliance upon price alone as a method of gaining competitive advantage rather risky. A more satisfactory approach is to use price in conjunction with other complementary elements – product, place, and promotion – in the marketing mix.

A company's pricing strategy should:

1 Help the company achieve its corporate goals in such areas as profitability, market share, growth, range of products, etc.

2 Help the company achieve its more specific marketing goals, such as market share, market growth rate, etc.
3 Materially contribute to the marketing process through:

   (a) Being appropriate for the market segment that has been identified and is being targeted.
   (b) Helping position the product in the desired location in the segment.
   (c) Being appropriate to the means of distribution chosen.
   (d) Being consistent with the means of promotion chosen for the product.

In most companies pricing strategies and practices tend to be dominated by one or more of the following major sets of influences: demand influences, competitive influences, and cost influences.

Demand influences

The demand for a product is a fundamental influence on pricing strategies, and the price of a product is a fundamental influence on the demand for it. The two are mutually dependent. Generally the higher the price charged for a product, the less will be the volume of demand and *vice versa*. Consequently, when planning price strategies for products that have a high price elasticity of demand (such as international air travel), particular attention must be paid to the consequences of price changes. When such a view of pricing prevails, companies should endeavour to develop accurate sales forecasts or simulations of the demand consequences that different pricing strategies are likely to have.

Competition influences

Most products and services are not unique – they must compete with rivals or substitutes. Consequently pricing strategies will normally require a response to the nature of the competition. This type of pricing strategy is one where the price charged for a product or a service is strongly influenced by the prices charged by competitors rather than by internal costs. The levels at which a company sets its prices will be clear signals of their positions within their market segments. A relatively high price signals that the product is differentiated in some way, e.g. in all the market segments in which it competes, Mercedes Benz tends to charge higher prices than its competitors; while a relatively low price often signals inferior quality, e.g. Eastern European cars tend to sell at a relatively low price.

Cost influences

The cost of manufacturing a product or providing a service will be a fundamental influence in pricing strategies. A price below cost will ultimately lead to extinction while a price too high relative to cost will encourage new entrants and stimulate customers to use substitutes. The main types of cost-based pricing strategies are cost plus pricing, target pricing and marginal cost pricing, and are discussed below.

1   *Cost Plus Pricing.* A cost plus pricing strategy determines the total cost per unit produced and then arrives at a price by adding to that cost a fixed percentage for profit margin. The total cost per unit is normally composed of the variable costs of production and marketing, plus an allocation of overhead to cover fixed costs.

2   *Target pricing.* The kernel of this strategy is that the price to be charged for a product should be set by meeting a predetermined return on the capital employed to produce and market it. Thus if a company had a policy that its return on capital employed should be 20 per cent, then all its products should be priced so that they generate this rate of return.

  Target pricing has an underlying assumption that the company setting the target price has the power to see that it is indeed followed in the industry. Consequently this type of pricing strategy tends to be adopted successfully only by companies that have this degree of power. This type of pricing strategy is often adopted by national monopolies and public utilities, for monopoly power guarantees the organization's ability to implement its pricing decisions.

  Perhaps the best known example of public company following this type of pricing strategy is General Motors. Until the advent of the strong import penetration of its domestic market in the US by the Japanese in the 1970s, GM set its automobile prices by a target pricing strategy, and the rest of the US automobile industry tended to follow the GM pricing lead. However, with the relative diminution of GM's US market power because of the success of the Japanese manufacturers, GM has been obliged to abandon this approach and adopt pricing strategies more strongly influenced by competitive forces.

3   *Marginal cost pricing.* In marginal cost pricing all the variable costs of production and marketing are covered, but the fixed costs may be partly covered or not covered at all. There are a number of situations in which this type of pricing strategy may be particularly appropriate.

Although the influences of 'demand', 'competition', and 'cost' on price have been described above as separate, all three orientations are interrelated and interdependent, and the three perspectives should be employed when pricing strategies are being developed.

Pricing new products or services

The influences of 'demand', 'competition', and 'costs' are most easily discernible when considering products that are already in existence or new products related to existing products. However, when a new product is unique, then setting an appropriate price for it tends to be more difficult. A unique new product does not have the benchmarks of demand and competition; the only element known with certainty is the cost. In such a situation the following approach could be used:

1   Assume that the price of the product will at least cover marginal costs.
2   Through market research – say test marketing, analysis of substitute products and the estimation of the competitive reactions of the producers of substitutes – make estimates of the likely demand for the new product at different price levels, with different means of distribution and with alternative methods of promotion.
3   On the basis of the market research decide upon a pricing structure, methods of distribution and methods of promotion.

Conclusion on price strategy

Although for most products and services price is regarded by consumers to be the strongest and clearest signal of value – hence a fundamental lever for positioning a product within a targeted market segment – any marketing strategy relying exclusively upon price carries great dangers. Price is only one element in the marketing mix.

In general any pricing strategy should be integrated with all the elements in the marketing mix, and the price structure itself should be regarded as a variable that dynamically responds to its changing internal and external circumstances, particularly the following:

- *Internal.* The resources the organization has available to pursue its chosen price strategy; and the relationship between the pricing strategy and the costs of production and marketing.
- *External.* The product's stage in the product life cycle; the level and the nature of competition; and the price elasticity of demand for the product.

The economic segment

For most companies the economic segment of the environment is fundamental and will require detailed analysis. For the purposes of strategic analysis, it can be divided into two broad areas: the world economy, and the national economy. In the appraisal of the 'world economy', particular attention must be focused on the US economy, because this economy is so large and such a powerful influence on the performance of many other economies. Of course special attention should also be paid to the economies of other major trading partners.

The state of the 'world economy'

Because of the influence of global economic events, e.g. the world price of oil, it is usually inadequate to consider national economic policies without taking cognisance of this broader global economic context in which all national economies must exist. This broader economic context can include an assessment of such fundamental indices as:

- The performance of the major industrial countries in their:
  1 Rates of inflation.
  2 Real growth rates of GNP.
  3 Current account balances.
  4 Levels of employment.
  5 Interest rates.

  Such an appraisal should enable a judgement to be made about the general state of the world economy and its stage in the 'business cycle'.

- Information on and analysis of other global issues, such as:

  1 The economic development and performance of other nations.
  2 Global efforts at monetary reform.
  3 The behaviour of the currency markets.
  4 The international capital markets.
  5 Commodities.
  6 Trade talks.
  7 Activities of the International Monetary Fund.
  8 Activities of the World Bank.
  9 Third World indebtedness.

The state of the national economy

The analysis of the global economy can form the economic context within which the national economy can be appraised. This can be done on a hierarchical basis, as shown below:

- The top economic goals of the government are assessed. The information for this can be obtained from party manifestos, government statements, budget statements etc. For example, current economic issues that tend to receive most attention from governments include the following. Does the government place a higher priority on controlling inflation or increasing employment? Is the government expansionary in its stance or deflationary?
- The specific policies advocated and implemented to achieve these goals are studied. These policies fall under the following main headings:

1 *Fiscal policies.* What is the level of government spending and what are its policies on taxation? For example, is government, through public expenditure, attempting to raise the level of demand and hence reduce unemployment. Is the government's tax strategy designed to increase investment or increase public spending power?

2 *Monetary policies.* How tightly are monetary measures such as the money supply and the PSBR being constrained?

3 *Inflation policies.* What is the government's attitude towards inflation and what does it believe are its causes? What steps is it taking to influence the level of inflation?

4 *Foreign exchange and balance of payments policies.* What is the government's attitude towards stability in the value of the national currency? How do changes in the value of the national currency affect the economy in general and the organization under analysis in particular?

5 *Unemployment policies.* How committed is the government to full employment, and what policies does it use to achieve its employment goals?

6 *Privatization policies.* How strongly committed to the privatization of nationalized industries is the government? What is the objective of privatization – to increase competitiveness, to raise revenues for the government, to prove an ideological theory, etc.?

7 *Regional policy.* How committed is the government to strong regional policies to prevent the concentration of industry and commerce in favoured locations?

The operation of most of the above economic indicators can be quantitatively assessed, as there tend to be good statistical records for them publicly available. Once the impact of the economic segment has been assessed, it can be weighted, as shown in Stage 3 below.

Inflation

Irrespective of the underlying causes of inflation, the rate of inflation that prevails can be a significant environmental influence on a company's performance and expectations. High rates of inflation are generally portrayed as being 'bad' for business and therefore generally are regarded as an environmental threat, while low rates of inflation are generally portrayed as being 'good' and therefore are considered as an environmental opportunity. This view of the likely impact of inflation is, however, too narrow. Different companies and industries are affected in different ways by inflation, and it may be the case that some companies are actually advantaged by periods of high inflation. This is because inflation tends to act as a 'tax' on current assets and as a 'subsidy' on fixed assets, and consequently the effect of inflation on different organizations is influenced by the proportion of current to fixed assets. Thus, for example, banks, whose assets are skewed towards money and other similar products, must, in periods of inflation, earn a return on equity that is at least as great as the rate of inflation: otherwise their net worth is being eroded by inflation. By way of contrast, organizations that have a very high proportion of fixed assets – property companies, for example – may find that the value of these fixed assets is understated on their balance sheets during a period of inflation. Such companies may earn a return on equity that understates the full value of the assets, which will be realized when the asset is eventually sold.

Therefore, in a period of inflation, it is important for strategic planners not just to take cognisance of the actual level of the inflation rate, but also to understand the strategic and operating implications of inflation for their industry and their organisation. The Boston Consulting Group has clearly expressed the importance of understanding this aspect of inflation:

> One day we may return to a world of low or at least stable rates of inflation. Until then, managers must expand their planning activities to include continuing detailed evaluation of the impact of inflation on their businesses. This requires much more than inflating a revenue or cost stream according to simple pricing or cost increase assumptions. Business need not passively accept the invisible redistribution of wealth brought about by inflation. By actively seeking out the second and third order effects of inflation, managers can avoid its ravages and perhaps turn it to their advantage.[16]

The legal/government segment

Government at all levels – regional, national and international – has increasingly come to play a larger role in business and society. In the section above, 'The state of the national economy', the role of the national government in formulating and implementing economic policies was considered, but it is also important to take cognisance of the other pervasive roles that governments can play.

When an analysis is being carried out, it is important to consider the level of the government influence. Thus it can be, for example, regional (the role of a local development office in the provision of packages of assistance for local start-up businesses), national (the role of the central government in determining the level of taxation), or international (the role of the European Community in determining the levels of tariffs to be imposed upon foreign imports). For the purposes of this exposition, however, the national or central government will be the principal level of aggregation.

It is convenient for the purposes of environmental analysis to divide the role of government into two categories – government acting as an aid to business and government acting as an impediment to business, although it will probably be the case that government will simultaneously be performing both acts.

Government as an aid to business

Government can act either deliberately or unintentionally as an aid to business. Some of the main ways in which it does this include the following:

Government as a buyer

Government is frequently a major purchaser of goods and services, and is generally regarded by business as an excellent customer because it will not default on payment and also because government purchases, as well as being a mark of approval, also are frequently relatively large. For example, the construction industry in the UK, particularly in the areas of civil engineering such as road contracts and bridge contracts, relies heavily on government purchases. Accounting and consulting companies also tend to regard government contracts in a favourable light.

Government as a sustainer of R & D

In many industries today the costs of engaging in the R & D necessary for the successful development of new products is frequently beyond the financial capabilities of individual companies. In such circumstances it may be the case that government underwriting of the costs may be the only way in which it is feasible to undertake the research. This is especially true in the defence and aerospace industries.

Government as the provider of protection

Frequently government will protect an industry that is threatened by a foreign competitor. This is usually done through the provision of subsidies to the threatened industry, through the erection of tariff barriers against foreign products, through the erection of quotas against foreign goods and through the exercising of preferential procurement practices.

Government as an aid to controlling wage costs

Governments frequently introduce incomes policies that ease the difficulties of businesses in meeting wage demands they believe to be excessive.

Government assistance in training

There are many government schemes that help reduce the full cost of training through rebates, tax relief and grants.

Government assistance for start-up businesses

In regions of high unemployment especially governments frequently have generous schemes that can significantly reduce the cost of starting up and then running a business.

Government as a provider of new business opportunities

In many Western countries since the early 1980s there has been a general tide favouring the privatization of state industries and generally promoting a climate of deregulation. This new climate has provided many business opportunities that were previously unavailable.

Government as an impediment to business

The development of the 'web of regulation'

A complaint from business in general has been that as the intervention of government in society has increased, so has the amount of legislation and regulation, so that today business suffers large, and frequently hidden, costs in conforming with regulations which, from a business perspective, seem to be pointless. A good example of this costly exasperation is provided by the difficulties in meeting the regulations to transport goods from one state to another in the European Community. The charge is often made by intra-European transporters that as the Community has developed, so have the cross-border regulations, and that today it is actually more difficult to transport goods between European Community states than before the European Community was founded. The long queues of trucks often seen at the borders of member states are a testimony to the truth of this claim.

Government as a controller of prices

Incomes policies are also frequently complemented by prices policies, which are generally regarded by industry with some hostility. The argument tends to be that it is impossible for governments to have the knowledge and skills to legislate for all the pricing situations that obtain in industry, and that statutory price controls build in rigidities that go against market trends and may unfairly penalize companies.

Government as a protector of the environment

In the 1980s especially there developed in most Western nations a greater awareness of the long-term costs of industrial pollution. This has led to legislation to curb the activities of companies that it was believed were causing pollution. Many industries feel that they are unfairly penalized because they are made by government to bear the costs of avoiding pollution while their foreign competitors may not suffer such costs.

Government as the guarantor of health and safety at work

Government, through legislation, today takes a much more proactive role in ensuring the health and safety of people at work. This concern is manifested in legislation to ensure such issues as standards of mechanical and electrical safety, standards of hygiene, maximum working hours per day and per week, etc. All these elements are regarded by certain businesses on occasions as costs they should not have to bear, and also an intrusion by government into the privacy of the organization's workplace.

Government as the guarantor of equal opportunity

Conforming to equal opportunity legislation, i.e. equal rights to employment and promotion without regard to sex, age, race or religion, throughout Europe has been largely regarded by business as a cost.

Government as the defender of competition against monopoly

In most Western countries governments seek to ensure that industries do not become monopolized. Although this is regarded as desirable from a social point of view, and also from the point of view of the smaller firms in the industry, the operations of monopoly legislation is regarded somewhat negatively by larger firms in certain industries, and with the development of global markets and global competitors there is a body of opinion which says that for a company to be internationally competitive it may well need to be a national monopoly in order to have the necessary critical mass.

Government as the defender of the rights of the consumer

Most Western governments have enacted legislation to protect the consumer against unscrupulous business practices. This legislation ranges from laws on consumer credit to laws on advertising standards, the honest labelling of goods, and the safety and health standards of products. The more extensive these laws are, the more hostile business tends to be towards them.

Government as the decider of industry location

Frequently it will be the case that government may coerce an organization to locate in a region it does not favour. This can be achieved through differential levels of assistance or, more coercively, through withholding planning permission for construction in one region and granting it in another.

The social/cultural segment

Although it could be argued that the social and the cultural segments of the environment are separate, here it is considered that they are so overlapping that they are grouped together to form a single segment. The social/cultural segment is considered to be that undefined but nonetheless very real set of values, beliefs and attitudes that somehow expresses the general attitude that society has towards life and work.

Just because the social/cultural segment is not so clearly visible as such other segments as, say, the technological segment, it does not mean that its influence is any less important. For example, the profound changes that have taken place in retailing – out-of-town shopping centres, weekly visits for groceries to shops rather than daily visits, speed of purchase rather than price being a major buying influence – have occurred largely because of social/cultural influences that were difficult to see as they occurred yet whose material effects have been clear.

The social/cultural segment of the environment can be thought of in two broad areas – how it affects the products and services of business and how it affects employee attitudes towards their work.

How social/cultural factors affect products and services

The degree of attention planners need to give to the analysis of this factor is a function of the industry. For example, planners engaged in such fast changing and socially sensitive industries as fashion, television, records, and advertising need to be extremely sensitive to social changes, whereas planners in industries such as quarrying and heavy engineering do not need the same levels of sensitivity. The following are indicative of the types of element that should be considered.

Education

The level, availability and participation rate in education can have major implications for many products and services. Thus, for example, in Western Europe, as the general level of education has increased, so the sophistication of products and the promotion strategies of products have developed.

Health and fitness

In the 1980s there has been an increase in people's concern about health and fitness. This has been manifested in the increased participation rate in many sports, the development of restaurants and foods geared to this market, adverse publicity for products (such as alcohol and tobacco) that are considered injurious to health, and the development of sports people as ideal role models for young people. This social/cultural change has implications not just for sports-related businesses, but also for how other products and services are promoted, and how potentially 'unhealthy' products overcome their poor image. For example, the tobacco industry is a major sponsor of sporting events.

Family size

Family size has generally decreased since 1945, and today in most Western countries the average number of children per family is less than three. This has implications not just for the suppliers of children's goods – baby food, prams, clothes, etc. – but also for seemingly unrelated products such as houses and cars, where design and size is frequently a function of family need.

Family units

Family units have generally become less stable – there has been an increase in the levels of divorce and an increasing tendency for young people to leave home and live apart from their parents. This has implications for promotion, packaging, etc.

Religion

There has been a decrease in the power of churches and their appeal, especially to young people. This has had a major influence on such issues as how people spend their leisure, the types of moral attitudes that are socially acceptable, and retail opening hours.

Geographical mobility

The advent of cheap international travel has greatly increased the scope for international travel both for business and for pleasure. It has also greatly increased people's knowledge of foreign environments and tended to make goods and services more 'cosmopolitan', e.g. the growth of ethnic restaurants.

Domestic mobility

The development of mass motoring has meant a major social change not just in recreation but also in retailing. Thus many retailers have moved from downtown sites to out-of-town shopping centres with good car parking facilities. A further complementary social factor in retailing has been the rise of freezer ownership, which has led to the weekly shopping trip as opposed to the 'daily' necessity of shopping, which used to be prevalent.

The role of women in society

With the great increase in the proportion of women working outside the home and the development of equal opportunity legislation, there has also been a change in society's attitude towards the role of women and a change in the attitude of women towards their own role. Thus there has been a diminution of the domestic role of women and an increase in their broader role in society.

How social/cultural factors affect attitudes to work

There is a wide diversity in the attitudes, both managerial and shop-floor, to work and business. This diversity is most easily seen when international comparisons are made, although it has been claimed that regional comparisons within countries are also observable. Perhaps the clearest example of differing attitudes towards work can be seen when the Japanese work ethic and the Western European work ethic are compared. A report by the Japanese External Trade Organisation (JETRO) showed the width of the gap:

DIVISIONS OVER THE WORK ETHIC

The Japanese notion of overtime, for example, does not go down well in Europe. While about 75 per cent of the companies surveyed said they asked their employees to work overtime, getting them to agree to the request, they said, was much more difficult than in Japan.

Reasons for the difficulty in ordering overtime ranged from 'the employees give too much emphasis to their private lives' to local labour laws. Some 40 per cent of the companies said that employees had refused to obey orders when told to do overtime work . . .

The study is directed at Japanese businessmen contemplating their own moves into Europe, so it includes some touching descriptions of labour conditions in Europe. These go some way toward explaining why many Japanese management practices cannot be happily transplanted to European soil.

For example, the study notes: 'Western Europe is more advanced compared with Japan in social security systems. Local employees, unlike Japanese employees do not consider their work to be the centre of their lives. If push comes to shove, they consider work something they have to do to live. This is where the difficulty lies in expecting local employees to contribute as much to their companies as Japan'.[17]

At a national or regional level, with the development of a permanent class of long-term unemployed people, there is increasing government concern in many European countries that such people will, because of the effects of such enforced unemployment, become completely unemployable in any capacity.

Finally, as with the other segments of the environment, strategic planners should be aware of the important elements of social change for their industry and their business, and be able to assign a weight to the importance of this environmental influence.

The technological segment

As indicated on p. 89, the world is in an era of unprecedented technological change, and strategists must incorporate this dimension of the environment into their analyses. Although, at one level, technological change is all pervasive – for example, all industries are to some extent affected by the microcomputer/information technology revolution – at another level it is important to realize that some industries will be much more affected by technological change than others.

Not only will these changes in the environment have fundamental influences on manufacturing industry, they will cause major changes in the service sectors. For example, with the advent of relatively inexpensive and widely available electronic information data and information transmission those accounting and consultancy firms that fail to embrace this new technology may be disadvantaged.

It is important to realize that technological change affects not just final products but may also affect the production methods and indeed the raw materials. Thus Henry Ford's adoption of the production line to produce the Model T Ford was a technological change in the production process that temporarily gave the Ford company enormous competitive advantage over its rivals, and changed the 'rules of the game' for the manufacture of automobiles.

A more recent example of how technology, and other factors, have changed the 'rules of the game' is provided by the rise to pre-eminence of the Japanese automobile industry. Table 18 shows a comparison between US and Japanese manufacturing systems. The data shows clearly that Japan has won this technological battle.

Although it is difficult to measure, except with hindsight, the importance of technological change to an industry, two measures that may give a reasonable indication are suggested:

1 The amount the industry spends on R & D. This could be either an absolute amount or it could be a relative measure such as R & D expenditures as a proportion of sales.
2 The PIMS* measure of innovation. This measure defines the level of innovation as the proportion of revenues that accrue from products that have been introduced in the last 3 years. This measure does give a good indication of the relative importance to the industry of new products.

When the analysis of the technological environment has been completed, the threats and opportunities that prevail should then be weighted, as shown in Stage 3 below.

* See Reference 14.

Table 18 US–Japan comparison of auto manufacturing systems, 1982[18]

		US	Japan
1	Parts stamped per hour	325	550
2	Manpower per press line	7–13	1
3	Time needed to change dies	4–6 hours	5 minutes
4	Average production run	10 days	2 days
5	Time needed per small car	59.9 hours	30.8 hours
6	Average daily absentee rate	11.8%	3.5%
7	Ave. ann. employees turnover	15–20%	2%
8	No. of quality inspectors	1 per 7 workers	1 per 30 workers
9	Inventory/gross sales	16.6% (GM)	1.5% (Toyota)
10	No. of suppliers	Over 3,000 (GM)	300 (Toyota)

The geographical segment

The 'sea change' that the globalization of business has brought has altered the 'rules of the game' for business strategy, and this additional perspective must be integrated into environmental analysis. The trend towards the internationalization of business, with marketing, production, finance and personnel strategies planned on, or at least taking cognisance of, the global dimension, has been and will continue to be inexorable.

It is easy to use the importance of having international perspectives in those industries that are clearly perceived to be global, e.g. television set manufacture, vehicle manufacture and aircraft manufacture. Vehicle manufacturers' predominantly global view has led to the development of world cars, i.e. cars whose sourcing, manufacture and sales are planned and implemented on a global rather than on a national basis. For example, the General Motors (GM) world car the Corsa/Nova is assembled from parts sourced from many European countries:

> GM has put new component capacity into Cadiz (steering columns, steering gears, front-wheel-drive axles) as well as at Logrono (seat trim overs, headliners, instrument panels, consoles and bumper fascias in Spain.
>
> Other components are made in Northern Ireland (seat belts, exterior mouldings), England (steering columns, exhaust valves), France (batteries and heaters) and Portugal (rubber and plastic vehicle components).
>
> There is also major investment in Austria where new engine transmission plants are made side by side. They will supply not only the Corsa, but other Opel vehicles.[20]

The 'other' segment

This is really just a catch-all category meant to reflect any environmental segment not captured in the above categories. Depending upon the circumstances of an environmental analysis, this segment may or may not be included.

STAGE 3: ATTRIBUTING WEIGHTS TO EACH SEGMENT

In this stage of the environmental analysis the segments of the environment that have been selected in Stage 1 of the process and analysed in Stage 2 are given weights that summarize the impact each segment is expected to have on the company under analysis. The weights are calculated as follows.

The *importance* to the company under analysis of each segment of the environment that has been analysed is ranked on an ordinal scale running from 0 to 5. Thus if a segment is considered of crucial importance to the company, it merits a score of 5; if it is of average importance, it merits a score of 3; and if it is of no importance at all, it scores zero. For example, in the office automation industry the technological segment of the environment is of crucial importance and would probably score 5, while in the delivery of domestic coal industry the technological segment is of minimal importance, and would probably score zero, or perhaps 1.

Once the importance of each factor has been determined, the *strength* of each factor in the period under analysis is then ranked on an ordinal scale from −5 to +5, −5 indicating that this factor is likely to have as strong a negative influence on the company as possible. For example, it is likely that today most European shipbuilders would assign a score of −5 to the segment 'the competitive environment'. In contrast, a score of +5 indicates that the segment under consideration is likely to have as strong a positive influence on the company as possible. For example, when a company that has a profitable proprietary product is faced with excess demand and is obliged to ration its sales, then the market could be assigned a score of +5. Finally a score of 0 indicates that the factor does not have any strength at all.

When the importance and the strength of each factor have been determined, these two numbers are multiplied and an ordinal score for each relevant segment in the environment is obtained. Note that the values obtained may not be summed: all each value indicates is the likely relative impact that each segment is likely to have on the company. Finally, the score for each segment can be shown graphically on an environmental assessment diagram, as shown in Figure 30. The advantage of the graphical exposition is that it tends to make the analysis more 'alive' and more easily understood by a group.

A hypothetical example to illustrate how the stages of the environmental analysis are carried out

Stage 1: Segmenting the environment. For this company, it was decided that the relevant segments of the environment were economic, government/ legal, competitive, marketing and technological.

Stage 2: Analysis of the segments. A detailed analysis of the segments selected in Stage 1 was carried out for the period immediately preceding the date of

Table 19   Assigning weights to the environmental segments

Segment	Importance	Strength	Overall score (importance × strength)
Competitive	4	+1	+4
Marketing	1	+3	+3
Economic	5	−2	−10
Legal/government	2	−3	−6
Technological	3	−4	−12

the analysis, and also projections about the future trends in each of the segments for the next planning period or period of analysis of the company were made.

Stage 3: Attributing weights to each segment. After each segment had been analysed, the weights shown in Table 19 were assigned.

Implications of the above weighting

Competitive segment

The competitive segment of the environment is of very strong importance to this company. However, it is seen that this company appears to be in a strong

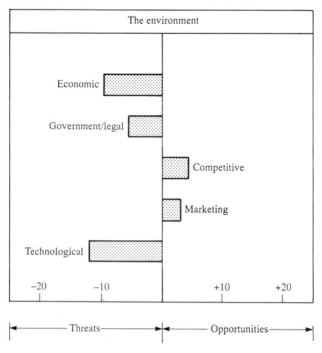

Figure 30   An environmental assessment diagram

position *vis-à-vis* its competitors in that it feels that over the next planning period the competitive environment will be slightly positive. The company should strive to maximize its competitive advantages.

Marketing segment

The marketing segment of the environment is not considered of great importance (competition must take some other form) and the company believes that its impact will be fairly positive over the next planning period. The company should strive to make the most of the opportunity the marketing segment of the environment is presenting.

Economic segment

It would appear that the economic climate is particularly important to this company and that in the next planning period it is not very conducive. It must regard the economic segment as a 'threat' and consider what actions it can take to minimize this threat.

Legal/government segment

Although the legal/government segment is generally a threat in the next planning period, its importance is not considered to be great, so that there will probably be fewer efforts to minimize this threat than for the other two threats.

Technological segment

Similarly, although the technological environment is considered not to be quite so important in the environment, in the next planning period it appears that the company will be confronted with major technological threats.

CONCLUSIONS ON THE IMPORTANCE OF ENVIRONMENTAL ASSESSMENT

Although most environmental change tends to lack the immediacy of, say, a cash flow crisis or a failure to meet a delivery schedule, this lack of immediacy should not cloud the strategists' views of its importance. As the above sample of evidence shows:

- It is a fundamental part of strategic management.
- Planners in companies must be sensitive to the environment and scan it for the signals of change that will affect their industry in general and their company in particular.
- Those companies most strongly committed to it tend to achieve better results than those that are not.

References

1 Channon, D., *The Strategy and Structure of British Enterprise*, Macmillan, 1973.
2 Thune, S. S. and House, R. J., 'Where Long Range Planning Pays Off: Findings of a Survey of Formal, Informal Planners', *Business Horizons*, vol. xiii, August 1970, pp. 81–87.
3 Spivey, A. W. and Wrobleski, W. J., *Surveying Recent Economic Performance*, Reprint 106, American Enterprise Institute, February 1980.
4 Wilkinson, M. and Cassidy J., 'Pit Strike Proves a Handicap for the Economic Forecasters, *Financial Times*, 3 July 1985.
5 Ansoff, H. I., *Strategic Management*, Macmillan, 1979.
6 Porter, M., *Competitive Strategy: Techniques for Analyzing Industries and Competitors*, Macmillan, The Free Press, New York, 1980.
7 Sherwell, C. and Sulong, W., 'Malaysian Car Takes to the Road', *Financial Times*, 9 July 1985.
8 Porter, *op. cit.*
9 Dawkins, W., 'How to Deal with the Big Fish', *Financial Times*, 5 July 1985.
10 Leavitt, T., 'Marketing Myopia', in Kotler, P. and Cox, K., *Marketing Management and Strategy*, Prentice-Hall, Englewood Cliffs, NJ. 1980, pp. 3–20.
11 McCarthy, E. J., *Basic Marketing: a Managerial Approach*, 4th ed., Richard D. Irwin Inc., 1971, p. 44.
12 Christopher, M., *The Strategy of Distribution Management*, Heinemann, 1986.
13 McEwan, J., 'Too Little and Too Late?' *Financial Times*, 14 August 1986. p. 18.
14 Schoeffler, S., 'The Nine Basic Findings of Business Strategy', *PIMSletter*, No. 1, 1980.
15 Porter, *op. cit.*, p. 17.
16 The Boston Consulting Group, Inflation's Invisible Hand, *Perspectives*, No. 1, 237, 1981.
17 Rappaport, C., 'Divisions Over the Work Ethic', *Financial Times*, 2 December 1985.
18 Tsurumi, Y. 'Japan's Challenge to the US: Industrial Politics and Corporate Strategies' in Sheth, J. and Eshaghi, G., *Global Strategic Management Perspectives*, South Western Publishing Co., 1989.
19 McNamee, P. B., *Tools and Techniques for Strategic Management*, Pergamon, 1985.
20 Case study by P. B. McNamee (unpublished).

7 Modelling a company's environment

INTRODUCTION

In the accompanying suite of computer models Bacchus Beer's environment is modelled in the Bacchus Beer marketing model: Bacmar. It is in this model that the alternative environmental scenarios for Bacchus are simulated, and it is these scenarios that 'feed' the later (mainly financial) models in the suite, as is shown schematically in Figure 31. In the model it is relatively easy to generate alternative scenarios by varying the values of the marketing levers, i.e. price, promotion expenditure, distribution expenditure and quality levels, for each of the three brands of beer, and also by varying the values that have been given to the various environmental influences, i.e. market growth rates and inflation rate.

It should be noted that in this model, because of disk space limitations, the environmental segments that have been deemed to influence sales have been confined mainly to marketing influences. It is relatively easy, however, to expand this set of influences to accommodate the influence of the other environmental segments discussed in Chapter 6.

PREAMBLE AND OBJECTIVES

The objective of this model is to simulate alternative *marketing scenarios* for the company and then to select a scenario that will best represent Bacchus's future circumstances. This scenario will forecast the future sales of the company, and these forecasted sales will be imported into later models in the suite and used to generate various reports: namely, income statements, cash flow statements, balance sheets, funds flow statements and ratio analysis statements. It is therefore of crucial importance that the data and the relationships that obtain in this marketing model are correct, as incorrect marketing information will corrupt all subsequent models.

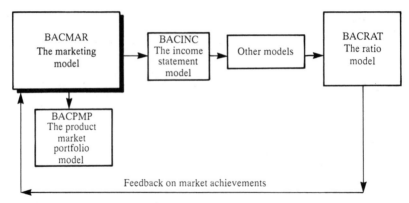

Figure 31   Bacmar feeds later models in the suite

PRODUCT LINES

Bacchus Beer has the following three product lines:

- *Super Beer*. This beer commands a very high price and is bought principally in bottle form mainly by affluent males aged 25 to 35 years.
- *Premium Beer*. This beer is strongly promoted and has a cachet of youth and quality. It is bought in bottle and can form mainly by relatively affluent males aged 18 to 25.
- *Standard Beer*. This beer is sold at average prices and is purchased principally in draught form but also in can form. Its main market is the less affluent male aged 18 to 35.

Bacchus's experience has shown that each of these market segments is sufficiently different to merit a unique marketing approach tailored to the segment. For example, in the Standard segment increased sales are largely price-dependent, whereas in the Super segment increased sales are influenced by advertising and other types of promotion rather than price.

The marketing department believes that there are two main influences on sales: the *marketing levers* and the *environmental factors*.

THE MARKETING LEVERS

The marketing levers are those instruments Bacchus can employ to influence sales. They are price, promotion, distribution and quality. The marketing department has developed a table that shows how the different marketing levers affect the sales of each segment (Table 20).

Table 20 How the various marketing levers affect different segments of the beer market

Marketing lever	Super		Premium		Standard	
	Rank	Elasticity	Rank	Elasticity	Rank	Elasticity
Price	4	0.99	4	0.9	1	0.95
Promotion	1	0.90	1	0.9	3	0.95
Distribution	3	0.85	2	0.9	2	0.85
Quality	2	1.10	3	0.95	4	0.95

The elasticities Bacchus uses have been developed through experience, and reflect the correlations believed to exist between the change in the use of a particular marketing lever and resultant sales. The elasticity is a decimal and is defined as: '*The percentage change in sales volume caused by a 1 per cent change in a marketing lever.*'

For example, if in 1991 and 1992 there was an increase in promotion expenditure for Super Beer of 1 per cent, then the resulting change in volume would be:

1%   *† 1.25   =   1.25%
Increase in expenditure   *   Elasticity =   Resulting increase in volume

When forecasting future sales, Bacchus incorporates all the marketing levers in a multiplicative forecasting model for each product line. For example, a major part of the Bacchus forecasting model for the future sales of Super is the following relationship:

Sales of Super Beer = Price factor Super * Promotion factor Super
                          * Distribution factor Super * Quality factor Super

The environmental factors

Bacchus considers that the other major influences on sales are environmental factors beyond its control. The principal factors it believes influence its sales are recent segment growth rate, volume size of segment's largest competitor and the inflation rate. These factors may be further elaborated:

1   Each product line is sold in a different and distinct market segment; therefore the growth rates of the three segments, rather than the simple growth rate for the 'beer market' are required. See Chapter 6 for the issue of market segmentation.

† *Note:* In all the formulae below   * = multiplied by.

2   The volume size of the largest competitor is needed for calculations in the product market portfolio model (see Chapters 10 and 11).
3   As well as being used as an influence on sales the inflation rate is also used to determine the rate of interest in the income statement model. The rate of interest is defined in that model as: Interest Rate = Inflation Rate * 1.2, i.e. it is set at 20 per cent above inflation.

A more complete version of the Bacchus forecasting model for each product line combines the marketing levers factors and the environmental influences in a multiplicative model, as shown below. Thus for Super Beer future sales are assumed to be a function of the following relationship:

Sales of Super Beer = Beer price factor Super * Beer promotion factor Super * Beer distribution factor Super * Beer quality factor Super * Beer segment growth rate factor Super * Inflation rate factor Super

THE COMPLETE BACCHUS MARKETING MODEL

The complete Bacchus Marketing model is now set out below.

The total value of Bacchus Beer sales are:

Sales value = Sales value Super + Sales value Premium + Sales value Standard

where the forecast sales for each product line is computed as follows:

Sales value Super = Sales volume Super * Price Super, and
Sales volume Super = Sales volume Super last year

Marketing levers
: * Price factor Super
: * Promotion factor Super
: * Distribution factor Super
: * Quality factor Super

Environmental factors
: * Market growth rate factor Super
: * Inflation factor Super

Sales value Premium = Sales volume Premium × Price Premium, and
Sales volume Premium = Sales volume Premium last year

Marketing levers
: * Price factor Premium
: * Promotion factor Premium
: * Distribution factor Premium
: * Quality factor Premium

Environmental factors
{
* Market growth rate factor Premium
* Inflation factor Premium

Sales value Standard = Sales volume Standard × price Standard, and
Sales volume Standard = Sales volume Standard last year

Marketing levers
{
* Price factor Standard
* Promotion factor Standard
* Distribution factor Standard
* Quality factor Standard

Environmental factors
{
* Market growth rate factor Standard
* Inflation factor Standard

The input data that has been used to drive the Bacmar model is given in Table 21.

THE STRUCTURE OF THE MODEL

Like all the other models in the suite, Bacmar has the following structure:

1 *An input worksheet.* This requests input data from the user. In this case the information is the marketing and environmental data.
2 *An output worksheet.* This shows the output from the model after any calculations have been carried out. In this case, because there are so few calculations, the output worksheet is very similar to the input worksheet.
3 *A graph menu.* This provides graphs of the data.
4 *A print menu.* This prints out aspects of the model – usually graphs or worksheets – requested by the user.
5 *A link to other models.* Each model is linked to other models, so that data is automatically exported and imported. For example, the sales values are imported into the income statement model, Bacinic.

A NOTE ON RUNNING THE MODEL

You should now examine the Marketing model Bacmar more closely. To do this proceed as follows:

Place the disk in drive A and close the drive. Then
   Type A:
   Type Bacmar

After you have examined this model, you should leave it and proceed to the income statement model, Bacinc.

Table 21   The data used to drive the Bacmar model

	1990	1991	1992	1993	1994
STRATEGY DECISIONS					
Price (£)					
Super	15	15	16	16	18
Premium	11	12	12	12	12
Standard	9	9	9	10	10
Price elasticity					
Super	0.99	0.99	0.99	0.99	0.99
Premium	0.9	0.9	0.9	0.9	0.9
Standard	0.95	0.95	0.95	0.95	0.95
Promotion expenditure (£)					
Super	250	300	320	350	400
Premium	80	100	110	115	130
Standard	55	70	80	85	120
Promotion elasticity					
Super	0.9	0.9	0.9	0.9	0.9
Premium	0.9	0.9	0.9	0.9	0.9
Standard	0.95	0.95	0.95	0.95	0.95
Distribution expenditure (£)					
Super	10	11	12	13	14
Premium	12	13	14	15	16
Standard	4	5	6	7	8
Distribution elasticity					
Super	0.85	0.85	0.85	0.85	0.85
Premium	0.9	0.9	0.9	0.9	0.9
Standard	0.85	0.85	0.85	0.85	0.85
Quality expenditure (£)					
Super	10	11	12	13	14
Premium	9	12	20	20	20
Standard	4	4	5	5	5
Quality elasticity					
Super	1.1	1.1	1.1	1.1	1.1
Premium	0.95	0.95	0.95	0.95	0.95
Standard	0.95	0.95	0.95	0.95	0.95
ENVIRONMENTAL FACTORS					
Market growth rate (%)					
Super	10	10	10	10	10
Premium	12	15	16	16	16
Standard	10	10	10	10	10
Market elasticity					
Super	1.01	1.01	1.01	1.01	1.01
Premium	1	1	1	1	1
Standard	1	1	1	1	1
Inflation rate (%)	9	10	10	10	10
Inflation elasticity					
Super	0.95	0.95	0.95	0.95	0.95
Premium	1	1	1	1	1
Standard	1	1	1	1	1
Sales volume largest competitor					
Super	150	160	165	180	185
Premium	300	400	600	700	1000
Standard	2500	3500	5000	5600	10000

BUILDING YOUR OWN MARKETING MODELS

After you have examined Bacmar you should use it as an aid to build your own marketing or forecasting model. You should proceed as follows:

1 Run Bacmar.
2 Type Ctrl Break (this will break into the macro, which runs Bacmar automatically).
3 Save the model with a new name: for example you could call this model Mkt1.
4 Have two windows.
5 In the top window have a table view.
6 In the bottom window have a formula view.
7 Place the two windows in Sync.
8 Alter or develop the formulae in the bottom window and build your new model.
9 When complete, save and run.

8 The current strategic position

INTRODUCTION

The primary aim of this chapter is to show how an SBU's current strategic position can be displayed clearly. Once this is known, then it is rational to use it as a base upon which to build future strategies. It should be noted that this approach is concerned mainly with SBU rather than corporate-wide issues.

The current strategic position of an SBU can be inferred from the following perspectives:

1 An assessment of the current strategic position.
2 A financial analysis of the current strategic position.
3 Key financial and strategic ratios.
4 An assessment of the SBU's position in the corporate portfolio.

Many elements in 2, 3 and 4 above are modelled for Bacchus Beer. Some ratios have, however, been omitted because of disk space limitations.

ASSESSMENT OF THE CURRENT STRATEGIC POSITION

The information concerning the company and its environment that was gathered in Chapters 4 and 6 is now brought together and integrated so that a total view – internal and external – of the company's strategic position is obtained. Thus the environmental assessment diagram and the company assessment diagram are joined, as shown in Figure 32, to provide a summary of the current strategic position.

This method of display enables managers to focus on areas of strength and opportunity, and also on areas of vulnerability and threat, and then formulate appropriate responses or strategies. Thus in the case of Figure 32 it would appear that the following issues should receive primary consideration.

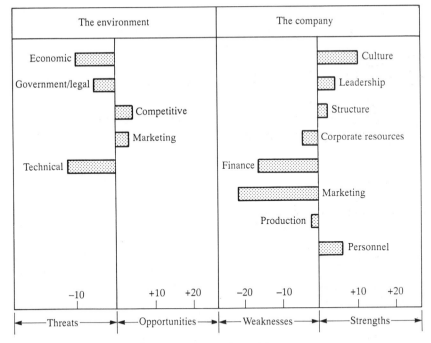

Figure 32 Summarizing the current strategic position

Company appraisal issues

The company appears to enjoy considerable strength in its behavioural dimensions. Therefore, from the quality of the management and personnel, it is relatively strong. Consequently, for the forthcoming planning period, the following question should be asked: 'In what way can these important strengths be used to confer advantage or at least overcome other weaknesses?'

The company appears to be relatively weak in its marketing and its finance functions (note that the detail of these weaknesses is revealed in the Functional Analysis stage, as set out on pp. 71–82), and these weaknesses must receive priority attention and action must be taken to redress them.

Environmental appraisal issues

Figure 32 shows that the necessity of improving the company's marketing capability is even more important than the company analysis revealed. The Marketing and Competitive segments of the environment appear to be relatively benign and lack of marketing capability may, in these circumstances, lead to the loss of great opportunities.

Thus, from this very simple example, a total view of the current strategic position of the company is provided, and also some fundamental strategic options are suggested. How these fundamental strategy developments are translated into precise company-wide strategies and operations is considered in Chapter 12.

A FINANCIAL ANALYSIS OF THE COMPANY'S STRATEGIC POSITION

As money is the universal numeraire of all businesses, it is appropriate for any strategic analysis to contain a financial analysis. Although a very large number of possible financial analyses could be carried out, the following historic and projected financial statements are the main ones suggested:

1 *Income statement.* This will show the SBU's sales performance and its profitability.
2 *Cash flow statement.* This will show the SBU's liquidity and vulnerability.
3 *Balance sheet.* This will show how well the SBU is using its assets and also the composition of its liabilities.
4 *Funds flow statement.* This will show how the SBU is acquiring its funds and how it is using them.

KEY FINANCIAL AND STRATEGIC RATIOS

These ratios could comprise the following:

1 *Financial ratios*
    (a) Profitability ratios: gross profit (£); net profit before interest and tax (£); gross profit margin (%); net profit margin (%); return on investment (%); return on equity (%); and earnings per share (£).
    (b) Liquidity ratios: current ratio; quick ratio; average collection period: debtors; turnover ratio; and creditors' ratio.
    (c) Gearing ratios: debt to equity and debt coverage.
    (d) Activity ratios: total asset turnover; fixed asset turnover; and stock turnover.
2 *Strategic ratios*
    (a) Measures to show growth
        (i)   Sales (£).
        (ii)   Profit before interest and tax (£).
        (iii) Return on sales (%).
        (iv)   Investment (£).
        (v)   Return on investment (%).
    (b) Measures to summarize strategic direction[1]

3   *Strategic effort*
    (a) Marketing/sales (%).
    (b) R & D/sales (%).
4   *Competitive position*
    (a) Market share (%).
    (b) Relative market share.
    (c) Relative market dominance.
    (d) Relative quality.
5   *Market characteristics*
    (a) Growth rate (%).
    (b) Concentration.
6   *Capital/production structure*
    (a) Investment/value added (%).
    (b) Investment/sales (%).
    (c) Value added/sales (%).
    (d) Fixed assets/sales (%).
7   *Productivity*
    (a) Value added (£).
    (b) No. of employees.
    (c) Productivity (£ current).
    (d) Investment per employee (£ current).
    (e) Investment productivity ratio.
    (f) Real productivity (£ constant 1991).
    (g) Real productivity (1991 = 100).

AN ASSESSMENT OF THE SBU'S POSITION IN THE CORPORATE PORTFOLIO

In addition to the above means of assessing an SBU's current strategic position, it is also important to recognize its relative strategic position within the corporation's portfolio of businesses. An SBU can be assessed in terms of whether it is growing, static or declining in strategic importance through use of the ratios in Table 22.

In addition to this type of portfolio analysis, a product market portfolio analysis should be carried out. This is considered in detail in Chapter 10.

CONCLUSION ON ASSESSING THE CURRENT STRATEGIC POSITION

Assessing the current strategic position is carried out by distilling much of the data obtained in the strategic analysis into vital and significant indicators. Usually the financial and strategic ratios set out above achieve this.

Table 22   The strategic relationship between an SBU and corporate headquarters

	Year 1	Year 2	Year 3	Year 4
Overall company				
Sales (£)				
Value added (£)				
Net profit before interest and tax (£)				
Investment (£)				
For each SBU				
% of corporate sales				
% of corporate value added				
% of net income				
% of investment				

Reference

1 Buzzell, R. D. and Gale, B. T., *The PIMS Principles: Linking Strategy in Perform-ance*, The Free Press, NY, 1987.

9 Modelling the current strategic position

INTRODUCTION

The current strategic position is modelled, as shown in Figure 33, using the following models: Bacchus income statement, Bacinc; Bacchus cash flow, Baccas; Bacchus balance sheet, Bacbal; Bacchus funds flow, Bacfun; and

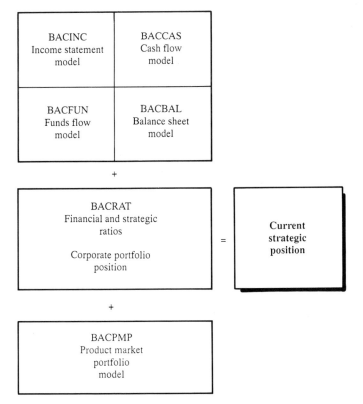

Figure 33   How Bacchus's current strategic position is assessed

Table 23　Income statement for Bacchus for 1990 to 1994 (£)*

	1990	1991	1992	1993	1994
Sales	5824	8584	13189	14104	17083
Cost of sales	4139	6035	9096	9812	
Gross profit	1685	2550	4093	4292	

LESS					
Mkting, selling and distn	385	470	510	550	650
Admin. expenses	736	1013	1442	1555	1821
Net profit before interest and tax	564	1066	2142	2188	
Interest payable	(162)	(240)	(300)	(360)	(420)

Net profit before tax	402	826	1842	1828	
Tax	(141)	(289)	(645)	(640)	
Net profit after tax	261	537	1197	1188	
Dividend payable	131	269	599	594	
Unappropriated profit	131	269	599	594	
Retained earnings	239	507	1016	1700	

* 1994 figures are not complete because of the nature of some of the formulae used to calculate future cost of sales.

Table 24　Cash flow statement for Bacchus for 1990 to 1994 (£)

	1990	1991	1992	1993	1994
SHORT-TERM CASH INFLOWS					
Sales receipts	5576	8032	12268	13921	16487
SHORT-TERM CASH OUTFLOWS					
Direct labour	458	664	980	1075	1350
Payments to creditors	4872	7142	9923	11607	3590
Mkting, selling and distn	385	470	510	550	650
Admin. expenses	736	1013	1442	1555	1821
Interest paid	162	240	300	360	420
Dividends paid	110	200	434	596	279
Tax paid	96	141	289	645	640
Net short-term cash flows	(1244)	(1838)	(1609)	(2466)	7720
OTHER ITEMS					
Share issues	300	300	300	300	300
Debenture issues	500	500	500	500	500
Additions	(1000)	(1000)	(1000)	(1000)	(500)
Net cash flow	(1444)	(2038)	(1809)	(2666)	8020

Table 25   Balance sheet statements for Bacchus for 1990 to 1994 (£)*

	1990	1991	1992	1993	1994
Fixed assets	3500	4500	5500	6500	7000
Accumulated depreciation	800	1250	1800	2450	3150
Total fixed assets	2700	3250	3700	4050	3850
Closing stock	4269	7293	10498	14375	
Debtors	1165	1717	2638	2821	3417
Bank	0	0	0	0	0
Total current assets	5434	9010	13127	17196	
Creditors	1581	2383	3231	3590	
Overdraft	3708	5746	7555	10220	2201
Tax payable	141	289	645	640	
Dividend payable	65	134	299	297	
Total current liabilities	5495	8553	11730	17423	
Net current assets	(61)	457	1397	(227)	
Total net assets	2639	3707	5097	3823	
Share capital	900	1200	1500	1800	2100
Retained earnings	239	507	1106	1700	
Long-term liabilities	1500	2000	2500	3000	3500
Capital employed	2639	3707	5106	6500	
Difference	0	0	0	0	

* Some values are missing from 1994 because of the nature of the calculations.
Note: Some values do not add up exactly due to rounding.

Bacchus ratio model: Bacrat. It should be noted that the product market portfolio model also contributes to the assessment, but because this is such a major strategy topic, it is considered separately in Chapters 10 and 11.

THE OBJECTIVE OF THE MODELS

The objective of all the models, when taken together, is to show the current strategic position of Bacchus Beer, both at the SBU level and at the corporate level. These models allow the manager to see the effects of strategies that have been set in the marketing and goal models upon Bacchus.

Table 26 Funds flow statements for Bacchus for 1990 to 1994 (£)*

	1990	1991	1992	1993	1994
Income from operations	564	1066	2142	2188	
Share issues	300	300	300	300	300
Debenture issues	500	500	500	500	500
Disposals	0	0	0	0	0
Annual depreciation	350	450	550	650	700
Total sources	1714	2316	3492	3638	
Additions	1000	1000	1000	1000	500
Interest paid	162	240	300	360	420
Tax paid	110	200	434	596	297
Dividend paid	110	200	434	596	297
Total applications	1368	1580	2023	2601	1857
Surplus or deficit	346	736	1469	1037	63
CAUSED BY					
Inc. or dec. debtors	248	552	921	183	596
Inc. or dec. creditors	(397)	(803)	(848)	(359)	
Inc. or dec. in stock	1939	3024	3204	3878	
Change in working capital	346	736	1469	1037	
Difference	0	0	0	0	0

* Some values are missing from 1994 because of the nature of the calculations.
Note: Some values do not add up exactly due to rounding.

THE STRUCTURE OF THE MODELS

Although these models are similar in structure to the marketing and goal models, there is a significant difference in that they do not have an input worksheet. This is because the data for these models are imported from the goal and marketing models. Consequently, if new goals or strategies are being set, they must be set in the goal and marketing models, and these models must be run first so that the changes will be imported. Indeed when examining the structure of the models, particular attention should be paid to the import building blocks and the variables they import. The import building block is a key distinguishing feature of the Javelin approach to modelling. Further information on modelling the effects of new strategies is provided in Chapter 13.

The actual results for each model are set out in Tables 23 to 29.

Table 27 Key sales and financial ratios for Bacchus for 1990 to 1994 (£)*

	1990	*1991*	*1992*	*1993*	*1994*
MARKETING GOALS					
Sales (£)	5824	8584	13189	14104	17083
Target sales (£)	6000	8000	14000	16000	20000
Return on sales (%)	7	10	14	13	
Target return on sales (%)	10	10	10	10	10
FINANCIAL GOALS					
Return on investment (%)	10	14	23	18	
Target return on investment (%)	12	12	13	13	14
Return on equity (%)	35	48	71	52	
Target return on equity (%)	25	25	25	25	25
Dividend growth rate (%)	46	105	123	(1)	
Target dividend growth rate (%)	50	33	50	25	33
Dividend payable (£)	65	134	299	297	
Target dividend payable (£)	100	133	200	250	333
ASSETS AND LIABILITIES					
Additions (£)	1000	1000	1000	1000	500
Target additions (£)	1000	1000	1000	1000	500
Fixed assets (£)	3500	4500	5500	6500	7000
Target fixed assets (£)	3500	4500	5500	6500	7000
Share issues (£)	300	300	300	300	300
Target share issues (£)	300	300	300	300	300
Debenture issues (£)	500	500	500	500	500
Target debenture issues (£)	500	500	500	500	500
Long-term liabilities (£)	1500	3200	4000	4800	5600
Target long-term liabilities (£)	1500	3200	4000	4800	5600

* 1994 figures are not complete because of the nature of some of the formulae used in calculations.

Table 28   Key strategic ratios for Bacchus for 1990 to 1994 (£)*

	1990	1991	1992	1993	1994
STRATEGIC RATIOS					
Sales (£)	5824	8584	13189	14104	17083
Net profit before tax (£)	402	826	1842	1828	
Return on sales (%)	7	10	13	14	
Investment (£)	2639	3707	5106	6500	
Return on investment (%)	10	14	23	18	
STRATEGIC EFFORT					
Marketing to sales (%)	7	5	4	4	4
R & D to sales (%)	1.1	0.8	0.5	0.5	0.4
Market share (%)					
Premium	20	28	42	36	33
Standard	1	2	2	2	3
Super	10	13	14	16	16
1990 RMS for					
Premium	0.75				
Standard	0.07				
Super	0.76				
1991 RMS for					
Premium		0.81			
Standard		0.07			
Super		1.00			
1992 RMS for					
Premium			0.94		
Premium			0.08		
Super			1.11		
1993 RMS for					
Premium				0.80	
Standard				0.07	
Super				1.26	
1994 RMS for					
Premium					0.60
Standard					0.05
Super					1.38

Table 28   Continued

	1990	1991	1992	1993	1994
MARKET CHARACTERISTICS					
Market growth rate (%)					
Premium	12	15	16	16	16
Standard	10	10	10	10	10
Super	10	10	10	10	10
Concentration (%)					
Premium	47	61	85	79	87
Standard	19	25	32	37	59
Super	23	25	27	29	32
CAPITAL AND PRODUCTION STRUCTURE					
Investment to value added (%)	0.64	0.69	0.81	0.66	
Investment to sales (%)	0.45	0.43	0.39	0.46	
Value added to sales (%)	0.29	0.30	0.31	0.30	
Fixed assets to sales (%)	0.60	0.52	0.42	0.46	0.41
Productivity in current terms (£)	7.95	11.59	12.79	12.26	
Productivity in real terms (£)	7.95	10.54	11.63	11.15	

* Some values are missing from 1994 because of the nature of the calculations.

Table 29   Bacchus's position in the corporate portfolio, 1990–4

	1990	1991	1992	1993	1994*
CORPORATE POSITION (£)					
Sales	149994	236783	142250	318381	
Value added	52532	83510	43005	108452	
Net profit before interest and tax	50858	80950	41387	105028	
Investment	37086	64847	78424	113580	
BACCHUS'S POSITION **Per cent**					
Corporate sales (%)	3.9	3.6	9.3	4.4	
Corporate value added	3.2	3.1	9.5	4.0	
Corporate net profit before interest and tax	0.8	1.0	4.4	1.7	
Corporate investment	7.0	5.7	6.5	5.7	

* Some values are missing from 1994 because of the nature of the calculations.

A NOTE ON RUNNING THE MODELS

You should now examine each of the models in turn more closely. To do this proceed as follows:

Place the disk in drive A and close the drive. Then
Type A:
Type in Bacinc

After you have examined this model, you should leave it and proceed to Bacbal, then Bacfun and finally Bacrat.

BUILDING YOUR OWN MODELS

After you have examined each model, you should use them as aids to build your own models. You should proceed as follows:

1 Run the model.
2 Type Ctrl Break (this will break into the macro which runs the model automatically).
3 Save each model with a new name; for example, you could call them Income1, Cash1, Bal1 and Rat1.
4 Have two windows.
5 In the top window have a table view.
6 In the bottom window have a formula view.
7 Place the two windows in Sync.
8 Alter or develop the formulae in the bottom window and build your new model.
9 When complete, save and run.

10 The product market portfolio

INTRODUCTION

One of the major problems facing strategic planners, particularly in large, diversified corporations, is that of information overload. Generally in such companies the volume of data concerning both the environments in which the company operates and the company's internal functioning is so massive that it makes a succinct, quantitative view of the company's strategic position difficult to obtain. The challenge for strategic planners is to distil such data into a few crisp indicators of corporate, SBU, and product line strategic position.

In the 1970s the Boston Consulting Group (BCG) devised an approach known as the product market portfolio, which has become accepted by many as having effectively met this challenge.

THE PRODUCT MARKET PORTFOLIO: AN OVERVIEW OF ITS PHILOSOPHICAL BASIS

The BCG approach starts, as did Chapter 1, with the assumption that strategic position can be inferred from how well a company relates to its environment. However, the technique is more precise than this. It claims that there is just one overwhelmingly important determinant of a company's competitive position – its *relative market share* – and that, symmetrically, there is just one overwhelming important determinant of environmental conditions – *market growth rate*. These two co-ordinates are the key determinants of competitive position. In other words, the stronger a company is relative to its competitors measured by these co-ordinates alone, then the stronger will be its strategic position. Additionally BCG asserts that the best measure of performance and position is *cash*.

In summary therefore this approach claims that strategic position is 'driven' by one major influence, 'the market' and that performance can be measured by means of one numeraire, 'cash'. Table 30 summarizes the approach. The model is now examined in greater detail.

Table 30   A summary of the drivers of the product market portfolio

Determinants of strategic position The Market		Measure of performance
External	*Internal*	
Market growth rate	Relative market share	Cash

A note on the level of aggregation

The expostion of the product market portfolio below is conducted at the product level. This is to facilitate readers' comprehension, as it is the simplest way in which to use the model. However, it is important to realize that the matrix can be used at two levels of aggregation, which are, in ascending order:

1   *The SBU level.* Here the portfolio is composed of products or product lines and the task is to infer the strategic position of an SBU's *portfolio of products.*
2   *The corporate level.* Here the portfolio is composed of SBUs and the task is to infer the strategic position of a corporation's *portfolio of SBUs.*

RELATIVE MARKET SHARE AS A DETERMINANT OF COMPETITIVE POSITION

There is considerable evidence[1] to show that the financial benefits accruing from a product are directly correlated with its *market share*, i.e. those products which have the highest market shares will tend to make the greatest financial contributions. However, market share does not adequately indicate what a product's expected financial contribution ought to be. As BCG has shown, it is not market share that is important in determining the strategic position of a product but rather its market power, where this is determined by a product's market share relative to the market share enjoyed by rivals. BCG has called this competitive strength 'relative market share' and it is considered to be 'its share of its served market' divided by the market share of its largest competitor.

The importance of using relative market share (RMS) rather than market share is illustrated by a hypothetical example. If it is known that two products A and Z in different industries have market shares of 20 per cent and 40 per cent respectively, then this information alone does not reveal the true competitive position of each product. On the basis of this information alone Z would appear to have a superior competitive position: it has a 40 per cent market share as opposed to A's 20 per cent market share. However, when the

Table 31 Actual and relative market shares for 'A' and competing products

	A	B	C	D	E	F	G	H	I
Actual market share (%)	20	15	15	10	10	10	10	5	5
Relative market share		1.33	0.75	0.5	0.5	0.5	0.5	0.5	0.25	0.25

Table 32 Actual and relative market shares for 'Z' and competing products

	Z	Y	X	W
Actual market share (%)	40	50	5	5
Relative market share	0.8	1.25	0.1	0.1

market shares of all of the significant rival products in each industry are revealed, as shown in Tables 31 and 32, it can be seen that this is not the case.

Indeed it is product A rather than Z that enjoys the superior competitive position, as it is stronger relative to its rivals. Thus A has a relative market share of 1.33, i.e. it is *1.33 times* as large in its served market as its largest competitor, while Z has a relative market share of 0.8, i.e. it is only *0.8* the size of its largest competitor. From this it should be apparent that if a product is a clear market leader, it must, by the above definition, have a relative market share of greater than 1.0, and similarly, if a product is not a market leader, it must, by the above definition, have a relative market share of less than 1.0.

A special case: the issue of a relative market share of exactly 1.0

When a product has a relative market share of exactly 1.0, this is an intriguing strategic situation, as it indicates that the product is a *joint market leader*, i.e. there is at least one other product in the market that has an equal volume of sales. In this type of situation it is likely that there will be intense competitive pressure – often manifested in severe price erosion, quality enhancement and or promotion battles – as joint leaders vie with each other in their attempt to win outright leadership. The competition will normally be extremely fierce, as each joint leader will believe that with some additional effort and resources it could become the outright leader, with all the benefits that this position will normally bring.

Plotting relative market share

In the product market portfolio matrix the relative market share of each product is plotted, as shown in Figure 34 on the horizontal axis using a log scale. This will normally range from 0.1 to 10, with a score of 1.0 being at the centre of the axis. This means that outright leaders are shown on the left-hand side of the matrix, followers on the right-hand side, and joint leaders on the centre line of the matrix.

The scoring on the horizontal axis will be tailored to the particular circumstances which occur in any analysis. For example, the scoring could range from an RMS of 0.01 to an RMS of 100.

MARKET GROWTH RATE AS A DETERMINANT OF COMPETITIVE POSITION

Generally markets that have high growth rates will tend to be more attractive than those that have lower growth rates. The logic behind this is inescapable – in high growth markets a product can increase its market share without necessarily harming competing products, whereas in a low growth market it will often be the case that a product can only increase its market share at the expense of rivals. In the latter situation rivals are likely to resist attempts to 'steal' their market share; this resistance will usually comprise strategies such as price reduction, promotion battles or quality enhancement – strategies that often depress the profitability levels for all.

Plotting the market growth rate

In the matrix the growth rate of the market is plotted, as shown in Figure 34, on the vertical axis, using a simple percentage scale. The range on the axis will depend upon the analysis being undertaken. Generally it should be drawn so that the average market growth rate is near the centre of the axis. This enables markets to be divided into two types: high growth markets will be in the top half of the matrix and low growth markets will be in the lower half.

The market growth rate and the relative market share are thus the co-ordinates that determine the strategic location of products in the matrix.

THE VALUE OF ANNUAL SALES

The final element in the construction of the matrix is the portrayal of the annual sales of each product in the SBU. This is effected by plotting, for each product, circles whose areas are proportional to each product's annual sales. These circles are located at the co-ordinates provided by the intersection of each product's relative market share and market growth rate.

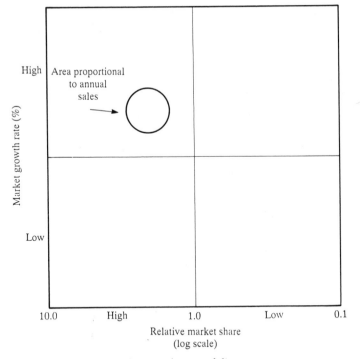

Figure 34 Constructing a product market portfolio

CASH: THE NUMERAIRE OF PERFORMANCE

Complementing the marketing dimension of the product market portfolio is its finance dimension. The numeraire of performance employed by the matrix is cash, and generally a product's location in the matrix should lead to it having certain cash characteristics, as shown in Figure 35. The anticipated cash characteristics of the matrix can be revealed most easily by dividing it, as shown in Figure 35, into four quadrants.

Cash characteristics of quadrant 1 products: 'dilemmas'

Products occupying quadrant 1 tend to have large negative cash flows. They have low relative market shares in high growth markets, and so, although their competitive positions are weak, the market characteristics are very attractive. These types of product are usually at the initial stages of their life cycles, and so it would be expected, from this perspective alone, that they would be net absorbers of cash. However, the matrix reveals that such products are in an even worse position than the product life cycle model reveals: they are in the growth stage and they also face competition from at

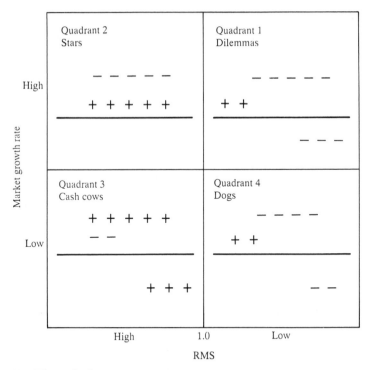

Figure 35   The cash characteristics of the product market portfolio

least one rival that has a relatively strong position in the market, i.e., a relative market share of greater than 1.0. Consequently such products present strategic planners with a dilemma. On the one hand, for these products to gain market share, considerable resources (cash) must be invested and there is no guarantee that this investment will produce an acceptable return. Indeed it is likely that the leading rival product, i.e. the one with a relative market share of more than 1.0 and which should enjoy a superior cost position, will react in a resolute fashion to any move made by low market share competitors. On the other hand, however, these products, as stated above, are at the initial stages of their life cycles and consequently are likely to be the products upon which the future of the company will be built, so that failure to invest in them now may leave the company without a balanced product line in the future. Because of the difficulties and great risks of this strategic position they are often known as 'dilemmas'.

Cash characteristics of quadrant 2 products: 'stars'

The products that occupy quadrant 2 tend to have neutral cash flows. They have high relative market shares, i.e. RMS > 1.0, in high growth markets:

they are enjoying strong competitive positions. However, in spite of this they may be cash neutral, or indeed even absorb cash. They have high relative market shares because they are in high growth markets, and so, in order to *sustain* their positions, will normally require substantial investments (cash) to protect those positions (through perhaps price-cutting, promotion or quality enhancements) against the competitive onslaughts in which relatively weaker rivals will engage in their efforts to strengthen their positions in this attractive market. Products in this quadrant are known as 'stars'.

Cash characteristics of quadrant 3 products: cash cows

Products occupying quadrant 3 tend to have large positive cash flows. They have high relative market shares, i.e. RMS > 1.0, in low growth markets. The positive cash flows are determined both by the product's stage in its life cycle and its market position relative to rivals. Thus such a product is in the mature or decline stage of its life cycle, and so the market is less attractive to new entrants and existing competitors. Compounding this lack of attractiveness of the market is the extremely strong position of the leader: because it enjoys the highest relative market share, the leader should, all other things being equal, have the lowest unit costs. Consequently it ought to be able to deal relatively easily with competitive warfare from weaker rivals. Products in this quadrant therefore tend to generate cash in excess of their needs. This excess cash can be used to pay dividends, overheads and, perhaps most importantly, to fund investments in other cash-absorbing parts of the portfolio, namely 'dilemmas' and 'stars'. Products in quadrant 3 are known as 'cash cows'.

Cash characteristics of quadrant 4 products: 'dogs'

Products occupying quadrant 4 tend to have negative, or perhaps neutral, cash flows. They have low relative market shares in low growth markets, and thus they tend to have the worst of all worlds: poor market growth rates, poor relative competitive positions, and passing through the final stages of their life cycles. There is really only one way in which such a product can improve its strategic position, and that is by wresting market share from other competitors. However, it is unlikely that such an action will be successful. The other competitors, who will have the advantage of having larger market shares, will be likely to have lower unit costs and consequently will be in a strong position to resist this move. Indeed BCG calls products in this quadrant 'dogs', and has described them as essentially worthless. Furthermore it has asserted that the maintenance of dog products is fraught with danger in that they may absorb increasing amounts of cash and ultimately develop into 'cash traps' – products causing cash to haemorrhage from the company.

Thus in summary the 'cash aspect' of the product market portfolio makes a dual contribution. First, it enables planners to see how well the actual cash contributions from products accord with cash contributions predicted by their positions in the product market portfolio. If there is a significant discrepancy between the actual and the expected, it ought to be a cause for deeper investigations of the reasons. Second, it enables planners to perform an important central treasury function: namely, to examine the cash balance of the SBU, i.e. ensuring that the cash flow is in balance, where the balance is such that the cash generated by cash cow products, plus perhaps star products, is sufficient to ensure funding for 'dilemma' products and 'dog' products, and to meet overheads and dividend payments.

The product market portfolio is thus a beguilingly simple device, which integrates the market function and the finance function into a unified strategic tool that can be used to:

- Describe the strategic position of each individual product of a company and also its portfolio of products.
- Diagnose the strategic position of each individual product of a company and also its portfolio of products,
- Prescribe strategies for each individual product of a company and also its portfolio of products,

An example of how a product market portfolio is constructed manually: a product market portfolio for Bacchus Beer

Table 33 shows the sales and market data necessary for the construction of a product market portfolio for Bacchus Beer. It should be noted that this type of data can easily be obtained from most companies' management information systems.

Table 34 shows the calculations that were necessary in order to construct the product market portfolio. It should be noted that all the circles, which reflect the value of annual sales, are scaled to the smallest value: Premium Beer in 1990 (circled). Finally, Figure 36 shows the completed matrix for two years – 1990 and 1994.

STRATEGIES AND LOCATIONS IN THE PRODUCT MARKET PORTFOLIO

Introduction

The product market portfolio is not just a financial description of a company's products. It also shows their strategic locations, and their particular locations will often suggest particular strategies. Below are set out the suggested strategies for various locations. It does not follow that these

Table 33 Data for the Bacchus Beer product market portfolio

	1990	1991	1992	1993	1994
Bacchus Beer sales value (£)					
Premium	2479	3889	6785	6717	7156
Super	1706	2397	2929	3637	4589
Standard	1638	2298	3474	3750	5336
Bacchus Beer sales volume					
Premium	225	324	565	560	596
Super	114	160	183	227	255
Standard	182	255	386	375	534
Market growth rate (%)					
Premium	12	15	16	16	16
Super	10	10	10	10	10
Standard	10	10	10	10	10
Sales volume largest competitor					
Premium	300	400	600	700	1000
Super	150	160	165	180	185
Standard	2500	3500	5000	5600	10000

suggested strategies should be followed blindly; at the heart of successful strategic management is creativity, and the blind application of these suggested strategies is a denial of this. Indeed one of the major contributions that the product market portfolio can make to strategic thinking is to help planners focus on the fundamentals that will determine the success or otherwise of a strategy. For example, a company with an ill-defined concept of the

Table 34 Data for a product market portfolio for Bacchus Beer

	1990	1991	1992	1993	1994
Bacchus Beer circle radius for					
Premium	1.23	1.54	2.04	2.02	2.09
Super	1.02	1.21	1.34	1.49	1.67
Standard	1.00	1.18	1.46	1.51	1.80
Bacchus Beer RMS for					
Premium	0.75	0.81	0.94	0.80	0.60
Super	0.76	1.00	1.11	1.26	1.38
Standard	0.07	0.07	0.08	0.07	0.05

market segments that it serves may quantify its products as having rather low relative market shares, and consequently view all of them either as 'dilemmas' or as 'dogs'. However, a more creative approach to market segmentation may reveal that its products, when measured against competitors in carefully segmented served markets, are actually high relative market share products.

Such a redefinition has major strategic implications. For example, the UK freezer manufacturer Norfrost could be considered, if a broad view of the freezer market is taken, to have a rather low relative market share when its production is compared with rivals such as Electrolux, Phillips, Westinghouse or Whirlpool. However, when a narrower, or more segmented, view of the market is taken, then Norfrost becomes a high relative market share

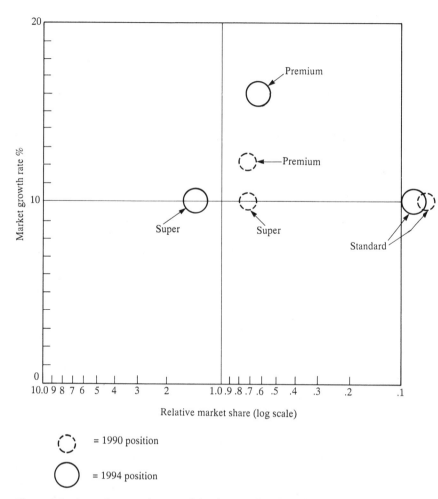

Figure 36 A product market portfolio for Bacchus Beer for 1990 and 1994

producer. This company produces just one single standard product – a small, 4 cubic feet chest freezer – and when its relative market share of this particular market segment is considered, the company is revealed to be the world leader, producing, at a lower cost than any rival. The message is that strategic insights will be yielded only by a careful segmentation of markets and an appropriate recognition of genuine competitors.

Building market share: a natural strategy for 'dilemmas'

This strategy tends to take a long-run view of the contribution that a product can make to a business in that it implicitly asserts that the most enduringly profitable, or cash-generating, products are those that have the strongest strategic position, and that the strongest strategic position is determined by relative size in the market. Therefore this strategy places a higher premium on developing a strong market position in the future than in having cash throw-offs today, i.e. profits today are foregone for more substantial profits tomorrow. It is assumed that a strong market position can be developed by means of:

1 Price reduction.
2 Quality or value-for-money enhancement.
3 Product innovation.
4 Improvements in distribution.
5 Increase in promotion.
6 Market segmentation.

A textbook example of this strategy is provided by Matsushita's introduction of the video cassette recorder (VCR). This product was introduced to the market in 1966, but it was not until the 1980s that it became a commercial success:

> The company quickly built production volumes to ensure it could accommodate the fast growing world wide demand. Capacity which was only 205,000 units in 1977, was increased 33-fold to 6.8 million units by 1984 ... Distribution channels that had been opened with TV products were now loaded up with the new product lines and brand names and images that had been established to introduce the earlier consumer electronic products were used to sell the VCRs ... By the mid-1980s, VCRs were contributing almost 30% of the company's total sales and an estimated 45% of its profits.[2]

However, it should be noted that although the strategy of building market share appears rather logical, simple and attractive, it is fraught with risks. Indeed even the assumption that those markets that have the highest growth rates are the most attractive may not always be correct. For example, although many extremely fast growing markets, such as those for personal computers, have appeared to be rather attractive, they have in reality experienced such high levels of competition and technical change that the majority of competitors have not in the long run (over say 10 years) been profitable. Indeed the attrition rate for PC companies has been so high that most competitive victories have often been pyrrhic and, with the benefit of hindsight, were merely flickers before extinction.

In contrast to the mirage of glamour that may be associated with such fast growing markets, there are many examples of mature industries that have had a much more pedestrian growth rate and image but which have provided the firms concerned with higher and more enduring levels of profitability. For example, Table 35 shows the average return on sales and the average return on assets by industry for the world's largest companies for 1989.

Additionally, seeking after larger and larger market shares may be inappropriate in certain industries. Thus Fruhan[3] has shown empirically that for the US computer industry, the US retail grocery industry and the US domestic trunk airline industry the major efforts of competitors to gain large market shares were unsuccessful, costly and inappropriate. He suggests that any company striving for large market share should first of all ask the following questions:

1 Are you operating in an industry where extremely heavy financial resources are required?
2 Are you in an industry where an expansion strategy might be cut off abruptly by a regulatory agency?
3 Are you in an industry where some agency is even now planning new regulatory hurdles?

Table 35 The average return on sales and the average return on assets by industrial sector for the world's largest companies[4]

Industrial sector	Return on sales (%)	Return on assets (%)
Aerospace	3	3
Beverages	6	6
Building materials	6	5
Chemicals	6	5
Computers	3	3
Electronics	4	3
Food	3	5
Forest products	5	5
Metal products	5	5
Minerals and crude oil	9	5
Pharmaceuticals	10	9
Publishing	7	7
Rubber and plantations	2	2
Transportation equip.	2	1

4 If the answer to any of these questions is YES, and if yours is the kind of company that fights for market share, then reassess your battle plan.

Furthermore, although the phenomenon of a high relative market share being strongly correlated with profitability has been robustly verified[5], there are many examples in many countries of low relative market share companies that for many years have enjoyed superior levels of profitability to their larger rivals. These companies have a competitive advantage that is based on a strategy other than size or unit costs. For example, in the oil tanker industry many of the most successful companies have fleets that are substantially smaller than the majors. Their success is built upon flexibility and intimate knowledge of their markets and customers.

Indeed the example of the oil tanker industry points out a danger inherent in the BCG approach. This is the assumption that there are just two strategic options available to 'dilemma' products, namely gain market share or withdraw from the market. Many companies may be prepared to do neither – they simply wish to remain as a relatively small player that does not upset the competitive status quo of the market and have a source of competitive advantage other than cost.

Finally it should be noted that a strategy of building market share will, as stated above, usually be a cash-absorbing experience, and that companies will normally only have sufficient cash to support a limited number of such products in their portfolio. Once again such products can be seen to be 'dilemmas' – if they are not supported, the future of the company may be being sacrificed, while if they are supported, they may drain cash with no ultimate pay-off. Indeed the latter was one of the strategic causes of Rolls-Royce's collapse in 1971. Table 36 shows Rolls-Royce'a aero-engine products in 1979.

If low, average and high growth rates are assumed for the mature, production and development stages of the life cycle, then Figure 37 represents a possible product market portfolio for Rolls-Royce. Clearly this matrix was overloaded with 'dilemmas' – there were not sufficient mature products to fund the development products.

Table 36 Rolls-Royce aero engine products, 1970[6]

Life cycle stages	Commercial	Military	VSTOL
Mature	Dart Avon (Turbo Prop) Tyne		
Production	Spey Conway	Spey (TF41)	Gnome H-1400
Development	Olympus 593 RB 211 M 45 11 Viper 600	RB190 Adour	Pegasus BS360

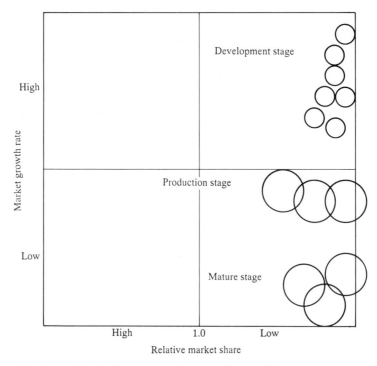

Figure 37   A possible Rolls-Royce product market portfolio in 1971

Holding market share: a natural strategy for 'stars'

Holding market share is usually an appropriate strategy when the product and its market have become more mature and it is considered desirable to maintain the status quo. Consequently it is often an appropriate strategy for products that are in the 'star' or 'cash cow' quadrants. Many advantages lie with products that occupy either of these positions: they have developed strong strategic positions in the market, they have the leading relative market shares, and their unit costs should be the lowest in the industry.

Usually holding this (optimal) market share is not easy. There will be a variety of lower market share competitors who will be striving continuously to snatch some share of the market from the leader. These efforts will often comprise strategies such as:

- Market segmentation.
- Product innovation.
- Cross-subsidization.
- Increased promotion.

An example of this is provided by the activities of the Miller Brewing Company in the 1970s in the U.S. At this time Miller beers gained market share on Anheuser-Busch through clearly segmenting the beer market into Premium, Light and Super Premium categories, and then engaging in very strong television promotion of selected segments. It has been claimed that Miller was able to do this because it was part of the relatively cash rich Philip Morris group, which cross-subsidized its beer division with cash from other divisions.

Support for 'star' products is essential for the long-run strategic security of a company. These are the cash-generating products of the future, and failure to support them will enable rival 'dilemma' products to gain market share. Eventually the incumbent 'star', F, as shown in Figure 39, will drift downwards (as the rate of market growth declines) and eastwards (as it loses relative market share), and ultimately become a cash-absorbing 'dog' product, G.

Harvesting may be a natural strategy for 'dogs', 'dilemmas' and 'cash cows'

With this strategy as much cash as possible is taken from the product and as little new investment as possible is undertaken. Under such a strategy, although the cash flow from the product is maximized, because of expenditure controls, its market share is likely to contract and the plant and equipment used to manufacture the product is likely to become obsolete. Although this strategy may appear to take a rather short-term view, there are a number of circumstances in which it is necessary for the strategic health of the company. For example:

1   When the product has a poor market share in a declining market, and the future prospects are rather dismal, i.e. it is a 'dog'.
2   When the product has a low relative market share in a growing market but the company does not have the resources necessary to support it. Thus it will normally be the case that a company only has the resources for a limited number of 'dilemmas'. In this situation not fully supported 'dilemmas' could be harvested. Indeed such products could even be the cash-generators of the company.
3   When the product is a 'cash cow', and the company believes that it is approaching the end of its commercial life and that additional investment will not yield an acceptable return, then it may be harvested.
4   When the company is in financial difficulties, and must maximize its cash flow as soon as possible.

Consequently harvesting is concerned with maximizing short-term earnings and cash flow, both from operations and the working capital released.

The cash so obtained could be used for many purposes, including the promotion of other products in the company's portfolio with better prospects.

Withdrawal or divestment

This strategy is employed when a company decides to withdraw from a particular product market configuration. The decision to withdraw could be based on a large number of reasons, including:

1 Insufficient critical mass: the product's strategic position, measured by relative market share, is insufficient to enable it to compete with larger rivals.
2 Poor financial performance: the product's financial contribution does not meet company benchmarks, and it believes that the proceeds from the disposal of the product line would be superior to continuation.
3 Portfolio incompatibility: the product no longer fits harmoniously with the rest of the portfolio of products.
4 Poor management: the product is poorly managed and there is no prospect of any improvement.

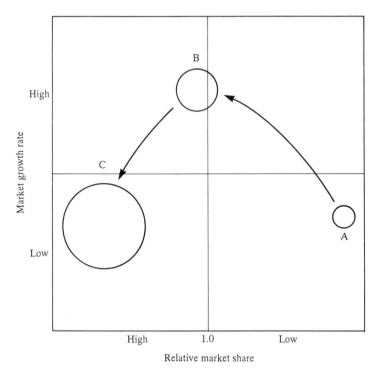

Figure 38   Ideal movements of products in the matrix

MOVEMENTS IN THE PRODUCT MARKET PORTFOLIO

There are two main types of movement that take place in the matrix: movements of products and movements of cash.

Movements of products

As well as taking cognisance of the locations of products in the product market portfolio, it is instructive to note how they are moving in the matrix over time. The product market portfolio is a dynamic strategic tool, and it is possible to gain significant strategic insights by plotting the movements of products over time.

Figure 38 shows the ideal movement of products – from A to B to C – over time. These movements reflect a well-managed portfolio in which the products are moving in an 'ideal sequence'. As the figure shows, the product's movements can be related to its life cycle.

In contrast to this sequence, there are also 'disaster sequences', as shown by F to G, H to I and J to K in Figure 39. In these sequences the products are

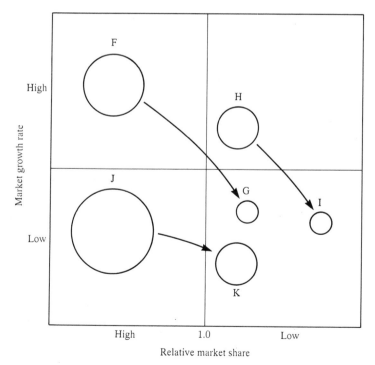

Figure 39   Disastrous movements of products in the matrix

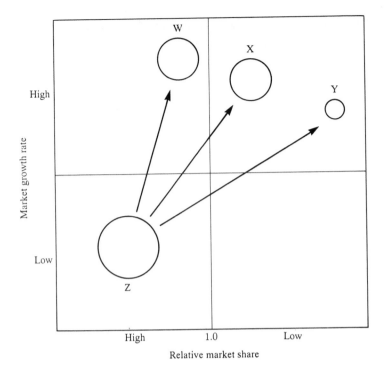

Figure 40   Ideal movements of cash in the matrix

failing to receive sufficient corporate support, and are falling in the matrix to 'dog' positions.

Movements of cash

Complementing the movements of products, there are movements of cash, and once again there are 'ideal movements' and 'disaster movements'. Figure 40 shows the ideal movement of cash from Z to Y, X and W. Z is generating cash in excess to its needs and this cash is being used to fund the products of the future.

In contrast to this, Figure 41 shows the 'disaster movements' of cash: cash from U being returned to U, cash from U going to T and cash from U going to S. In the case of cash from U being returned to U, this is a most difficult situation.

From the perspective of the personnel associated with U it seems entirely logical that its cash surpluses should be returned to it: after all, this product has had a record of earning cash surpluses and it would seem from the points of view of rationality and natural justice that these benefits should be returned to those who earned them. In fact it could be argued by personnel associated with U that no cash should be given to 'dilemmas' or any other such products: after all, the 'dilemmas' have never shown a profit, unlike U. The 'dilemma' category is likely to be a heavy absorber of cash, while products in the 'star' category are likely to be cash neutral or perhaps absorbers. However, the 'cash cow' products are net generators of cash, and this cash should be used, first, to enable the 'cash cow' products to maintain their positions, and, second, to sustain and build the relative market shares of 'stars' and 'dilemmas'. The 'dilemmas' will with this support become 'stars', and these 'stars' will fall vertically in the matrix as the growth rate of the market declines, so that eventually they will become 'cash cows'. This occurs when the products of one SBU are subsidized by the profits of another.

LIMITATIONS OF THE PRODUCT MARKET PORTFOLIO

Although the product market portfolio approach to strategic management has been widely accepted as making a significant contribution, there are a

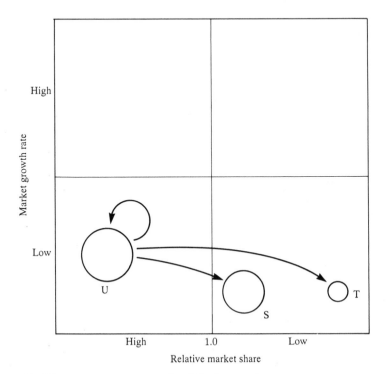

Figure 41 Disastrous movements of cash in the matrix

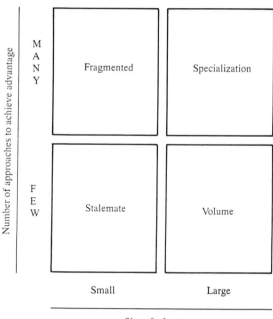

Figure 42   BCG strategic planning tool, 1981

considerable number of criticisms of the approach. The principal ones are set out below.

Two factors determine strategic position

The matrix relies on just two factors – relative market share and market growth rate – to determine strategic position. Although these are important determinants, they do not exclusively determine strategic location, and in most companies strategic decisions are made on the basis of more comprehensive information. Indeed BCG recognized this shortcoming, and in the 1980s introduced a new matrix that had, as shown in Figure 42, as its axes 'Size of advantage' and 'Number of approaches to achieve advantage'. This matrix takes a broader view of the determinants of strategic position, and as well as expanding the number of factors, it is also less quantitative and more geard to qualitative factors.

Only have top relative market share products

The matrix seems to infer that unless one's products are in the top three or four in terms of relative market share, then one should leave the market. There are, however, many examples of firms that have for many years had low relative market shares and also thrived. For example, the US can manufacturer Crown Cork and Seal has for many years been a market share follower, and yet has consistently proved to be the most profitable competitor in the industry. Its success is based on strategies other than market share, e.g. innovation.

Relative market share and profitability

The link between relative market share and profitability may not be as strong as BCG suggests. This may be so for a number of reasons, including:

1 Low relative market share competitors that have entered the market last may be on the steepest cost curves.
2 Some low relative market share competitors may have an inbuilt advantage: for example, low cost suppliers, or government subsidy.
3 Not all products have experience-related* costs.
4 Large share competitors may be subject to government control and regulation.

High growth markets are best

The matrix implies that high growth markets are the most fruitful ones in which to operate. This may not always be so, because:

1 The entry barriers may be so high that the returns, even with high growth rates, are not deemed to be satisfactory.
2 The level of competition is so severe that it nullifies any advantage that the high market growth rate brings.

'Dog' products are worthless

The matrix suggests that 'dog' products are really worthless and should be sold. However, there are many examples of companies having dog products that, far from draining cash from the business, have made substantial cash contributions over many years. Indeed in many smaller countries if the relative market shares of their largest companies were to be compared with their US or Japanese rivals, they would by the BCG definition be described as 'dogs'.

The definition of relative market share

The BCG definition of relative market share has been considered by many strategists to be too narrow a view of power in the market. A more

---

* Experience-related costs are unit costs which are inversely proportional to the accumulated volume of production.

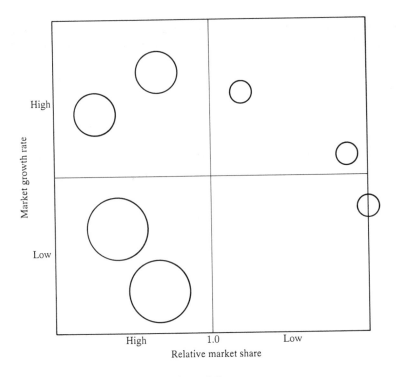

Figure 43   An example of a balanced portfolio

comprehensive definition is provided by the Strategic Planning Institute (SPI), which defines it as: 'Your market share divided by the sum of the market shares of your three largest competitors'. It is argued that this definition is a truer reflection of the competitive position of a product than the BCG one.

The served market

A crucial consideration in the construction of matrices is defining the served market. As the example of Norfrost showed, failure to do this properly will lead to matrices that do not reflect the strategic positions of products.

CONCLUSIONS ON THE PRODUCT MARKET PORTFOLIO

The development of the product market portfolio was a landmark in strategic management. Although it has received extensive criticism, it is still an excellent device for obtaining strategic insights into a company, as, when employed properly, it forces planners to raise issues such as the following.

At the product level

1 What is the served market for each product and are these markets correctly defined/segmented?
2 What is the position of each product in its market in relation to competing products?
3 Given the locations of each product in the matrix, what are their cash expectations and the cash realities of each product?
4 How has each product moved in the matrix?

At the portfolio level

What is the balance of the portfolio. Specifically are there:

1 'Cash cows' to fund 'dilemmas'?
2 'Stars' that will over time become 'cash cows'?

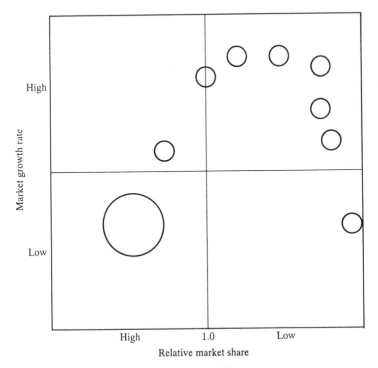

Figure 44 An example of an unbalanced portfolio

3 'Dilemmas' that will over time become 'stars'?
4 'Dogs', and are they being controlled?

The matrix's power to generate strategic insights is shown in the appendix to this chapter, in which a number of portfolios are drawn up for the Anheuser-Busch case. Finally, Figures 43 and 44 show examples of a balanced and an unbalanced portfolio.

References

1 Schoeffler, S., 'The Nine Basic Findings on Business Strategy', The PIMSLetter, no. 1, The Strategic Planning Institute, Cambridge, Mass, 1980.
2 Ghoshal, S. and Bartlett, C., *Matsushita Electrical Industrial Co. Ltd* (MEI), The Case Clearing House, Cranfield, 1987.
3 Fruhan, W. E., 'Pyrrhic Victories in Fights for Market Share', *Harvard Business Review*, vol. 50, no. 5, Sept/Oct 1972, pp. 58–67.
4 *Business Week*, February 1990.
5 Anderson, M. J. Jr and Harris, J. E., 'Strategies for Low Market Share Businesses', *Harvard Business Review*, vol. 56, no. 3, May/June 1978, pp. 95–102.
6 Wrigley L., *Rolls-Royce*, Case Clearing House, Cranfield, 1973.
7 Boston Consulting Group, *Annual Perspective*, 1981.

APPENDIX

THE CONSTRUCTION OF PRODUCT MARKET PORTFOLIOS FROM INCOMPLETE DATA

A well-known case study in strategic management concerns Anheuser-Busch Companies Inc. by Workman, D. J., Snyder, N. H., Bonaventura R., Cary, J., McMasters, S. and Cook, K. This case examines the strategy of the Anheuser-Busch company in the 1970s in the US and contains data that enable various type of product market portfolios to be constructed. The data are typical of published data on companies in that they are not set out in a way that enables product market portfolios to be constructed, but with amendment and appropriate assumptions this can be effected. The following are set out below:

1   A generic method of construction for product market portfolios that should work in most situations.
2   Examples of specific product market portfolios based on the Anheuser-Busch case.

A generic method for the construction of product market portfolios from the Anheuser-Busch case

In the construction of the portfolios the following is assumed:

Table 37   Data for an industry product market portfolio

Company	Barrels		RMS		Circle radius unscaled		Circle radius scaled	
	1974	1978	1974	1978	1974	1978	1974	1978
Anheuser	34.1	41.6	1.50	1.30	3.3	3.6	1.9	2.1
Miller	9.1	31.3	0.27	0.75	1.7	3.1	1.0	1.9
Schlitz	22.7	19.6	0.67	0.47	2.7	2.5	1.6	1.5
Pabst	14.3	15.4	0.42	0.37	2.1	2.2	1.2	1.3
Coors	12.8	12.6	0.37	0.30	2.0	2.0	1.2	1.2

Total barrels 1974: 146.9
Total barrels 1978: 165.6

Annual percentage change = 3.1%

Source: Exhibit 12.

1 The average growth rate of the market is plotted on the vertical axis and it is
   computed as follows:

Average growth rate
$$= \frac{\text{Barrel shipments for 1978} - \text{Barrel shipments for 1974}}{4}$$

Thus for Table 37 this average growth rate is computed as follows:

$$\text{Average growth rate for industry} = \frac{165.6 - 146.9}{4}$$
$$= 3.1\%$$

2 Relative market share (BCG definition) or relative market dominance is
   computed as follows:

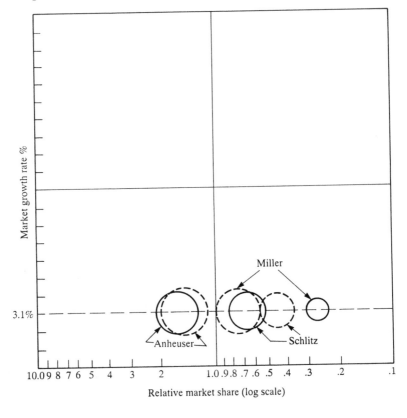

Figure 45   An industry product market portfolio

Your market share/largest competitor's share
Thus for Table 37 it can be seen that for 1978 Anheuser's and Schlitz's
relative market shares are computed as follows:

Anheuser 1978 RMS = 41.6/31.3 = 1.30
Schlitz 1978 RMS = 19.6/41.6 = 0.47

This is plotted on the horizontal axis, using a log scale (Figure 45).

3   The circles used in the product market portfolio are constructed so that
their areas are proportional to annual sales. However, in this case the
value of annual sales is not available for the different segments, so barrel
shipments (mil.) are used as a surrogate.

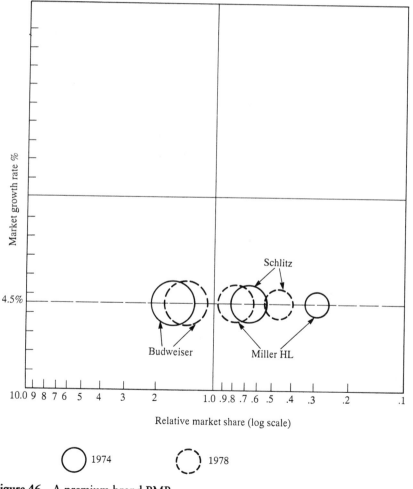

Figure 46   A premium brand PMP

The circles are constructed in two stages, as follows:

The area of a circle is $A = \pi R^2$

Therefore $R^2 = \dfrac{A}{\pi} = \dfrac{A * 7}{22}$

It is known that the area is meant to equal annual sales, i.e. in this case millions of barrels. Therefore the radius of the circle to represent annual sales can be computed from this formula:

$$R = \sqrt{\dfrac{A * 7}{22}}$$

In the case of Anheuser in Table 37 its circle radius for 1974 is computed as follows:

$$= \dfrac{34.1 * 7}{22}$$
$$= 3.3$$

All the radii can be computed in this fashion.

In the second stage, when we wish to draw the circles, it is useful to scale all the radii in relation to the smallest circle. This is effected by dividing each of the computed radii by the smallest one. In the case of Table 37, the smallest radius is that for Miller in 1974 – 1.7 – and each of the other unscaled radii are divided by 1.7 to yield the scaled radii.

Table 38 Data for a premium brand product market portfolio

Company	Barrels		RMS		Circle radius unscaled		Circle radius scaled	
	1974	1978	1974	1978	1974	1978	1974	1978
Budweiser	26.4	27.5	1.47	1.29	2.9	2.0	1.8	1.9
Mill. H. L.	7.8	21.3	0.29	0.77	1.6	2.6	1.0	1.6
Schlitz	17.9	12.7	0.68	0.46	2.4	2.0	1.5	1.3

Total barrels 1974: 52.1
Total barrels 1978: 61.5

Annual percentage change = 4.5%

Source: Exhibits 7, 9, 10, 11.

Table 39 Data for a light category product market portfolio

Company	Barrels		RMS		Circle radius unscaled		Circle radius scaled	
	1974	1978	1974	1978	1974	1978	1974	1978
Mich. L.	0	0.9	–	0.10	–	0.5	–	1.0
Natural	0	2.3	–	0.26	–	0.9	–	1.8
Lite	0.4	8.8	+	3.8	+	1.7	+	3.4
Schl. L.	0	0.7	–	0.08	–	0.5	–	1.0

Total barrels 1974: 0.4
Total barrels 1978: 12.7

Source: Exhibits 7, 9, 10, 11

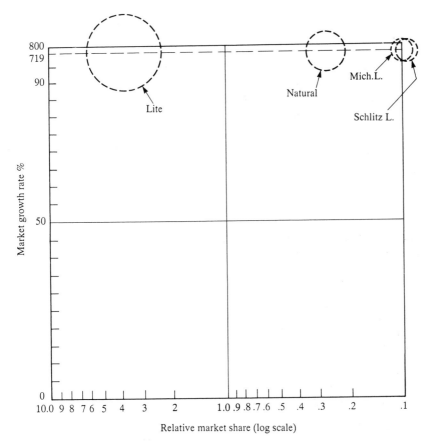

Figure 47 A light category PMP

Examples of specific product market portfolios based on the Anheuser-Busch case

Table 37 and Figure 45 show industry level product market portfolios, illustrating Anheuser-Busch's competitive situation in relation to the major competitors in the industry. Note that the market growth rate has been computed on the basis of *all the beer sold.*

Table 38 and Figure 46 show a brand level product market portfolio for premium brand beers, how the premium brand beers are competing with each other, i.e. illustrating Budweiser, Miller High Life and Schlitz.

Note that the various brands occupying the premium segment are given in Exhibit 7 and their market data is contained in Exhibits 9, 10 and 11. In addition the total sales of the segment are assumed to be the sum of the three brands listed in Table 38.

Table 39 and Figure 47 show a light category product market portfolio, i.e. for Michelob Light, Natural and Schlitz Light. Note that the various brands occupying the light segment are given in Exhibit 7 and their market data is contained in Exhibits 9, 10 and 11. The total sales of the segment are assumed to be the sum of the three brands listed in Table 39.

Table 40 and Figure 48 show a super premium category product market portfolio, illustrating how the super premium brand beers are competing with each other, i.e. Michelob and Lowenbrau. Note that the various brands occupying the super segment are given in Exhibit 7 and their market data are contained in Exhibits 9, 10 and 11. In addition the total sales of the segment are assumed to be the sum of the two brands listed in Table 40.

Table 41 and Figure 49 show an Anheuser-Busch product market portfolio, illustrating products in relation to each other, i.e. Budweiser, Michelob, Michelob Light and Natural. Note that in constructing this portfolio the performance of the various beers that Busch makes must be related to their segment peers. Thus Budweiser must be compared with premium segment peers, Michelob must be compared with super premium segment peers and

Table 40 Data for a super premium category product market portfolio

Company	Barrels		RMS		Circle radius unscaled		Circle radius scaled	
	1974	1978	1974	1978	1974	1978	1974	1978
Michelob	3.1	7.4	+	6.17	+	1.5	−	2.5
Lowenbrau	0	1.2	−	0.16	−	0.6	−	1.0

Total barrels 1974: 3.1
Total barrels 1978: 8.6

Annual percentage change = 44%

Source: Exhibits 7, 9, 10, 11.

Michelob Light and Natural must also be compared with light segment peers. These different segments also have, as the table shows, different segment growth rates. Finally, the brand Busch has been excluded from the portfolio because Exhibit 7 does not indicate into which segment it fits.

Table 42 and Figure 50 show a Miller product market portfolio, illustrating Miller products in relation, i.e. Miller High Life, Lite, Lowenbrau and other. Note that in constructing this portfolio the performance of the various beers that Miller makes must be related to their segment peers. Thus Miller High Life must be compared with premium segment peers, Lowenbrau must be compared with super premium Segment peers and Lite must be compared with light segment peers. These different segments also have, as the table shows, different segment growth rates.

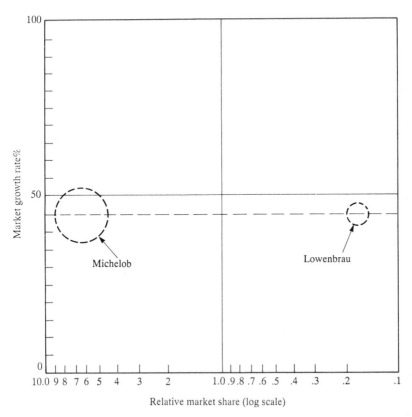

Figure 48 A super premium category PMP

Table 41   Data for an Anheuser-Busch product market portfolio

Company Growth rate	Barrels		RMS		Circle radius unscaled		Circle radius scaled		Growth of seg
	1974	1978	1974	1978	1974	1978	1974	1978	%
Budweiser	26.4	27.5	1.47	1.28	2.9	3.0	5.8	5.9	4.5
Michelob	3.1	7.4	+	6.17	1.0	1.5	2.0	2.3	44
Mich. L.	0	0.9	–	0.10	–	0.5	–	1.0	769
Natural	0	2.3	–	0.16	–	0.9	–	1.8	769
Total	35.2	41.6							

Source: Exhibit 9.

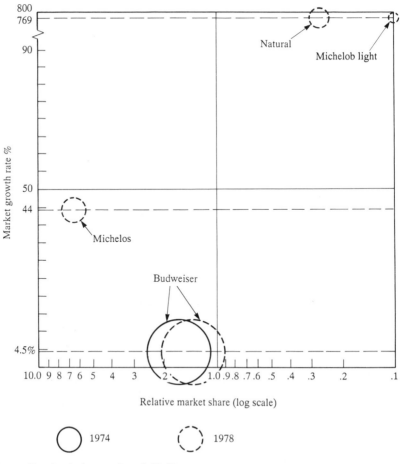

Figure 49   An Anheuser-Busch PMP

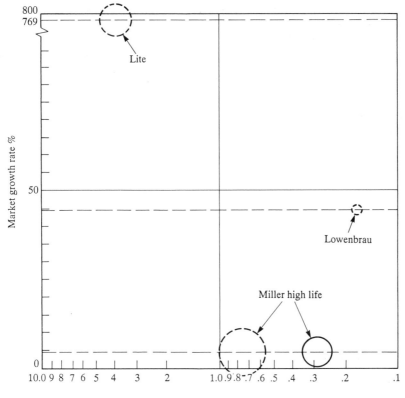

Figure 50   A Miller PMP

Table 42   Data for a Miller product market portfolio

Company Rate	Barrels		RMS		Circle radius unscaled		Circle radius scaled		Growth of seg
	1974	*1978*	*1974*	*1978*	*1974*	*1978*	*1974*	*1978*	*%*
Mill. H.L.	7.8	21.3	0.29	0.77	1.6	2.6	2.7	4.3	4.5
Lite	0.4	8.8	+	3.8	+	1.7	+	2.8	769
Lowenbrau	0	1.2	–	0.16	–	0.6	–	1.0	44
Other	0.9	0	–	–	–	–	–	–	
Total	9.1	31.3							

Source: Exhibit 12.

11 Modelling a company's product market portfolio

INTRODUCTION

In the accompanying suite of computer models Bacchus Beer's product market portfolio is modelled in the Bacchus Beer product market portfolio model, Bacpmp. As Figure 51 shows, Bacpmp is an optional model – the rest of the suite of models may be run without it. The figure also shows that Bacpmp does not require any input from the user – all its data is imported from the marketing model.

THE OBJECTIVE OF BACPMP

The objective of this model is to convert conventional marketing data, contained in the marketing model, into product market portfolios for the years 1990 to 1994. The computed figures for these portfolios are shown in Table 43, while the portfolios for 1990 and 1994 are shown in Figure 52.

THE RATIONALE BEHIND BACPMP AND ITS STRUCTURE

Javelin Plus cannot draw product market portfolios, but it can compute the key elements necessary to draw portfolios. Thus Bacpmp sets out, for each year, the following computations necessary for the construction of product market portfolios:

- The radii of the circles for Premium, Super and Standard brands. (These enable circles proportional to annual sales value to be drawn. Note that all the circles are automatically scaled to the smallest annual sales, in this case the sales of Premium Beer in 1990.)

- The market growth rates for Premium, Super and Standard brands, expressed as a percentage.
- The relative market shares for the Premium, Super and Standard brands, based on annual volumes.

THE STRUCTURE OF THE MODEL

Bacmar has the following structure:

1 *An output worksheet.* This shows for each brand, and for the years 1990 to 1994, the radii of the circles, the annual growth rates and the relative market shares.
2 *A graph menu.* This provides graphs of the data.
3 *A print menu.* This prints out aspects of the model – usually graphs or worksheets – requested by the user.

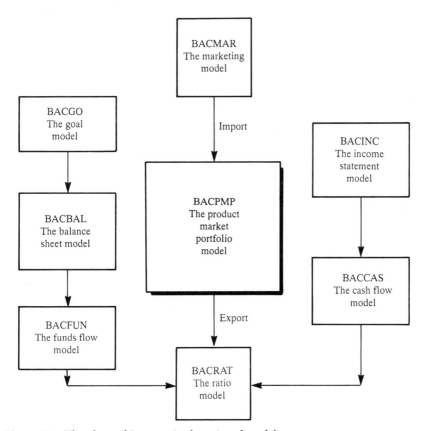

Figure 51 The place of Bacpmp in the suite of models

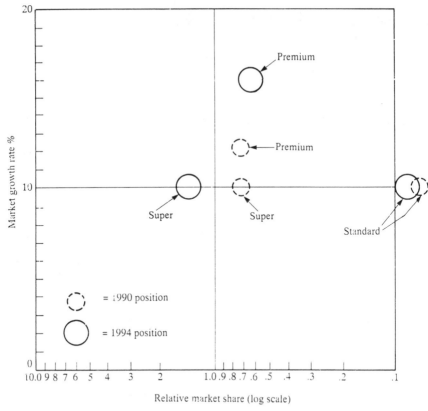

Figure 52   The Bacchus Beer product market portfolio for 1990 and 1994

4   *A link to other models.* Each model is linked to other models, so that data
    are automatically exported and imported. For example, all the data in this
    model are imported from the Bacmar.

A NOTE ON RUNNING THE MODEL

You should now examine the product market portfolio model Bacpmp more
closely. To do this proceed as follows:

Place the disk in drive A and close the drive. Then
    Type A:
    Type Bacpmp

After you have examined this model, you should leave it and proceed to the
income statement model, Bacinc.

BUILDING YOUR OWN MODELS

After you have examined Bacmar, you should use it as an aid to build your own portfolio model. You should proceed as follows:

1 Run Bacpmp.
2 Type Ctrl Break (this will break into the macro, which runs Bacpmp automatically).
3 Save the model with a new name: for example, you could call this model Pmp1.
4 Have two windows.
5 In the top window have a table view.

Table 43   The figures upon which Bacchus Beer's product market portfolios are based

	1990	1991	1992	1993	1994
Circle radius for					
Premium	1.23	1.54	2.04	2.02	2.09
Super	1.02	1.21	1.34	1.49	1.67
Standard	1.0	1.18	1.46	1.51	1.80
Market growth rate (%)					
Premium	12.00	15.00	16.00	16.00	16.00
Super	10.00	15.00	10.00	10.00	10.00
Standard	10.00	15.00	10.00	10.00	10.00
1990 RMS for					
Premium	0.75				
Super	0.76				
Standard	0.01				
1991 RMS for					
Premium		0.81			
Super		1.0			
Standard		0.07			
1992 RMS for					
Premium			0.94		
Super			1.11		
Standard			0.08		
1993 RMS for					
Premium				0.80	
Super				1.26	
Standard				0.07	
1994 RMS for					
Premium					0.60
Super					1.38
Standard					0.05

6   In the bottom window have a formula view.
7   Place the two windows in Sync.
8   Alter or develop the formulae in the bottom window and build your new
    model.
9   When complete save and run.

12 Developing strategies

INTRODUCTION

This chapter is concerned with the most exciting, risky and creative aspect of strategic management: the generation of strategies that will determine the future of the company. There is inherent uncertainty in making strategic choices about the future. On the one hand, the decision to embark upon a bold new strategy that is a major break with the past will have the excitement and appeal of novelty and perhaps the prospect of great rewards. However, it will usually also carry with it a higher level of risk and the possibility of total failure. On the other hand, the decision to continue following the strategies that have always worked in the past provides the comfort of knowing that the proposed future strategies have already been tried, tested and found to have been successful and are therefore likely to be low risk. However, if the company's environment is changing, then this approach may also, through ultra-conservatism, plunge it into total failure. Two examples illustrate how this polarity of vision can be disastrous.

Slatter[1] has given numerous examples to illustrate this, with one of the best known being Burmah Oil. In 1973 Burmah Oil was the twenty-fifth largest company in Britain, with sales of £496 million and profits of £49 million. Yet within 1 year the company was totally insolvent. Slatter points out that among the major causes of its demise were:

1   Financing the Signal Oil acquisition, a major project which developed financing difficulties.
2   A sharp drop in tanker rates, due to the OPEC oil crisis.

Burmah had engaged in massive expansion of its tanker fleet and developed terminal financial difficulties when tanker rates collapsed.

In contrast to the boldness of the Burmah strategy, there are many examples of companies and industries which, because of their failure to develop imaginative strategies to cope with their changing environments, have failed. A clear example is provided by the specialist steel industry of Sheffield in the UK, an industry which has almost disappeared.

In 1958 there were 105 special steel producers in Britain and by 1984 there were fewer than 10 makers of tool and high speed steel with none of them enjoying a significant market share. Additionally employment in the industry fell from 18,000 in 1970 to under 2,000 in 1984. Over the period 1970 to 1982 import penetration had increased from approximately 9 per cent to 64 per cent.[2]

THE NECESSITY OF DEVELOPING NEW STRATEGIES

It could be argued that if a company is meeting its goals, there should be no necessity to develop new strategies. After all, if success is being achieved, then why expend valuable managerial effort on generating new strategies? The fundamental reason for the development of new strategies is that the environment faced by all companies is constantly changing – for example, new competitors are arising, new markets are developing, new products are evolving and simultaneously existing competitors, markets and products are decaying – and continued success can only be ensured by successfully tracking the environment and adjusting strategies and structures in response to these changes.

Because of the enormous variation in the rates at which different industries change, there is great variety in the amounts of adjustment that successful companies in different industries need to make. The required adjustment will vary from the dramatic and fundamental change of strategy to the fine-tuning of existing strategies. For example, an industry that was subject to extremely rapid change was the US civil airline industry in the 1980s after deregulation. At that time there was an influx of new, innovative and aggressive competitors, an unprecedented rash of price-cutting and ruthless pursuit of passengers, and ultimately a series of failures and mergers as competitors jockeyed for survival. The importance of having an appropriate environmental alignment is illustrated by the contrasting fates of two US airline companies. In March 1986 Eastern Airlines, the long-established and third largest airline company in the US, was taken over by Texas Air Corporation – a relatively recent arrival in the airlines business and just half the size of Eastern. It was widely agreed by industry observers[3] that, in contrast to Texas, Eastern had failed to generate and implement the dramatic new strategies essential for survival in this new deregulated era.

A contrast to the volatility of the airline industry in the US is the relative stability of the environment faced by the legal profession in the United Kingdom and most other countries. In this 'industry', through strong official regulation, the environment faced by barristers and solicitors has been relatively stable, with new strategies requiring relatively little effort and innovation largely eschewed.

In addition to this universal necessity for tracking the environment, there are other more specific triggers that cause companies to develop new strategies. Perhaps the most frequent trigger occurs when a company fails to meet a key goal, such as 'dividend payment':

The year 1984 was strategically critical for ITT. We took actions that were necessary for the future success of the company. ITT is different today, more competitive.

Sales and revenues for the Corporation increased during 1984 but net income declined. Net income for the year totalled $448 million, at $2.97 per share, down from $675 million, or $4.50 per share, in 1983. Sales and revenues totalled $19.6 billion, up from $18.6 billion the year before.

In 1984, we accelerated our ongoing asset redeployment program; continued to reduce staff at headquarters in New York and Brussels and at key units; continued to lower debt, and reevaluated and revised our dividend policy. Our dividend is in line with our current earnings and allows us to continue our substantial research and development and meet our capital needs.[4]

RESISTANCE TO NEW STRATEGIES AND CHANGE

Although the development of new strategies is often presented as a logical managerial development, which will arise, almost naturally, as a result of assessing recent performance, in practice this may not be so. There are usually cultural impediments to change. Frequently managers will prefer to follow historical behaviour and strategies rather than embrace the new. The past strategies have become familiar and they feel more secure and comfortable with them, so that any strategy which is a break with the past may appear threatening.

Consequently when a new strategy is being considered, particularly a radical change, it is important to foresee how acceptable it will be. Too great a divergence from the past may generate such hostility and non-co-operation as to render its introduction impossible. The importance of the behavioural dimensions of strategy development and implementation was well expressed by Seymour Tilles of the Boston Consulting Group:

It is an inescapable fact that the shared values, beliefs, and behaviours of a company – its culture – changed only slowly. Yet rapid change is frequently required to meet an environmental or competitive challenge. How does one actually change behaviour in a corporation when all the unwritten rules may work to keep it the same?

The most dramatic way to change the corporate culture, and one frequently invoked, is to change the chief executive. Indeed, many experienced people believe that having the right person in the top job will resolve any difficulty.

While changing the chief executive can be effective, it is always a major risk and cannot be done very often in any one company. In any case, the new CEO will face an organisation that retains many of the same barriers to change that were there before, although he may deal with them differently.

While a committed CEO is necessary to achieve a change, any effort to accelerate change must address fundamental cultural variables: the status system, rituals and taboos, and the reward system. The challenge is to ensure that these cultural variables are consistent with the emerging needs of the company rather than past requirements ... it is important to remember that a culture that is inconsistent with a strategy dooms the strategy to failure. Changing the culture is part of changing the strategy.[5]

Therefore the successful generation and implementation of strategies must be at least acceptable and preferably attractive to the company's key managers.

DEVELOPING NEW STRATEGIES

New strategies are developed from the current strategic position, which was considered in Chapter 8. It is suggested that new strategies should be developed by means of a two-stage methodology, which is shown schematically in Figure 53.

The first stage is to decide upon a *fundamental* strategy for the company. It is assumed that there are just five fundamental strategies:

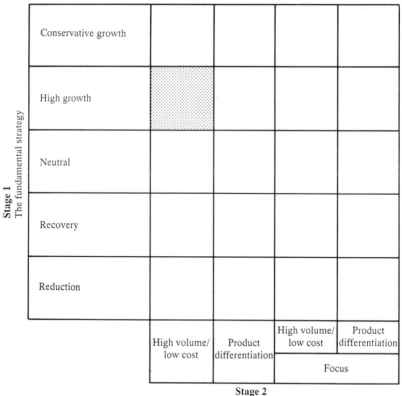

Figure 53   A two-stage methodology for developing strategies

1 Conservative growth.
2 High growth.
3 Neutral.
4 Recovery.
5 Reduction.

The second stage is to develop, following Porter,[6] an appropriate *generic* strategy. It is assumed that there are three possible generic strategies:

1 High volume / low cost.
2 Differentiate.
3 Focus.

Each stage is now considered in greater detail.

Stage 1: The fundamental strategies

Because of the distinction made between conservative growth and high growth, some benchmarks for distinguishing between each case are necessary. In this distinction 'Growth' is assumed to have three fundamental dimensions:

- Actual growth rates of the performance measures (for example, sales, profits, earnings per share, etc.) quantitatively expressed.
- The growth in the range of products a company provides.
- Growth in the range of markets served.

Conservative growth strategy

Generally, a company could be described as following a conservative growth strategy when:

1 Its growth rate is similar to the industry average.
2 Its growth rate is similar to its own historical performance.
3 It continues to serve the same or related markets with similar or related products.

Within the context of a conservative growth strategy various sub-strategies may be employed.

Greater internal efficiency

Growth in performance can be achieved without altering the product–market scope of the company but by improving its performance through stretching

Table 44   Objectives of scientific and technological research (%)[7]

Year	Labour saving	Resource saving	Energy saving
1950	9	5	2
1960	10	5	3
1970	11	8	5
1980	8	18	18

the gap between revenues and costs. The types of activity that would promote this could include the following:

(a) Reduction of costs.
(b) Improvement of quality.
(c) Price increases.
(d) Better human relations.
(e) Rationalization of production methods, products and markets.
(f) More efficient organizational structure.

The successful pursuit of increased internal efficiency has been a feature of the strategies employed by Japanese companies in general. In the 1970s, after the two oil shocks, when the price of oil increased in real terms by a factor of approximately four, Japanese industry and society faced a serious threat to its continued growth – the cost of oil. Because of its extremely heavy dependence on imported oil (in 1981 Japan imported 99.8 per cent of its oil),[8] the increase in energy costs threatened to destroy Japanese industry's growth aspirations. However, it successfully responded to this challenge by improving its internal efficiency through increasingly focusing its fundamental research efforts on areas such as 'energy saving', 'labour saving', and 'resource saving'. Thus the Japanese Management Association (JMA) has shown how the objectives of research changed between 1970 and 1980 to reflect this concern with increasing internal efficiency. Selected statistics from the JMA findings are given in Table 44. The fruits of this research were ultimately reflected in productivity rates and production costs, which now bestow a strong competitive advantage on many sectors of Japanese industry.

Deeper penetration of existing markets with existing products

Here the emphasis is on improving the effectiveness of the marketing of the existing products in the existing markets. It is therefore rather similar to internal efficiency strategy, except that the focus lies outside the company. This type of strategy is concerned with more effective use of the marketing mix, and could include activities such as advertising campaigns, warranty improvements, price reductions, etc., which attempt to cause existing purchasers to purchase in greater quantities, to attract customers from rival products or to persuade customers who previously were not consumers of the product to buy it.

Conservative growth was the strategy adopted by British Leyland in the UK in the early 1980s, when it attempted to increase its market share of the UK automobile market. 'Armed' with a somewhat out-dated range of models, the company attempted to retain existing customers and attract new ones, through marketing campaigns that featured special warranties and reduced prices.

Existing products in new markets

Here the emphasis is placed upon developing new markets for the company's existing products. These new markets can be divided into two main groups:

(a) Additional segments within existing markets and new geographical markets.
(b) Usually international or overseas.

The additional segments will arise when new uses can be found for existing products or when new segments can be persuaded to purchase the products.

An example of this strategy is provided by the Nissan company. In 1991, because of the slump of its UK sales, Nissan, the Japanese motor company, switched its sales effort for its UK-produced vehicles to foreign markets. 'Around 120,000 Nissans will be built in Britain this year, with 85 per cent of them bound for export to 29 countries. This compares with 61,000 exported to the European mainland last year...'[9]

New related products in existing markets

An alternative to market development is product development, where the growth is achieved by developing the product in some fashion so that its market appeal is extended. This type of strategy is a feature of the strategies of the manufacturers of DIY electric drills, such as Black and Decker and Bosch. Once an electric drill is introduced to the market, there frequently follows a series of related products – attachments for polishing, sanding, sawing, etc. This is a strategy of new related products in the same markets.

New related products in new markets

This is really a combination of the two strategies considered immediately above. In this case there is both market development (which can be domestic or international or both) and product development. Again Black and Decker provides an example of this type of strategy. Not only has the company introduced new related DIY products, but it has sought to extend its market segments by expanding into other domestic activities by developing ranges of gardening and household appliance products.

Circumstances appropriate to a conservative growth strategy

Like all the fundamental strategies there are no absolute guidelines for determining when each is correct. There are, however, general considerations that ought to sway decisions. These include:

1   *The environment.* Conservative growth tends to be appropriate when the current and future environments are considered to be relatively stable and there is modest growth in the economy.
2   *The competition.* Competitive stability makes this type of strategy appropriate. Stability implies that the major competitors, in the main, are satisfied with the status quo, i.e. they are earning returns they consider to be satisfactory, there is a low level of rivalry, there are no strong threats of substitutes or new entrants, and the power of buyers and suppliers is not regarded as excessive. In such situations modest aspirations may be the most appropriate, as attempts at aggressive growth may upset the relatively comfortable status quo through provoking fierce competitive reaction, with consequent depressed returns for all competitors.
3   *Resources.* Any strategy must be related to the company's resources. For companies that have somewhat limited resources there may be no alternative to Conservative Growth. Resource constraints limited British Leyland's strategic options in the 1980s.
4   *The company goals.* Of crucial importance to the fundamental strategy adopted are the goals of its top decision-makers. If these decision-makers have had modest goals in the past and have been largely satisfied with modest growth, then such strategies are likely to persist in the future.
5   *The company culture.* In choosing a strategy care must be taken to ensure that it either fits with, or can be fitted to, the company culture. The company culture is frequently a major impediment to strategic change. Thus the decision-makers who have been accustomed to rapid growth in the past will find it difficult to adjust their behaviour and actions to a strategy of conservative growth, and *vice versa*.

    In summary those new strategies that represent the smallest break with the cultural past will probably have the best prospects of subsequent successful implementation.

High growth strategies

From a quantitative perspective high growth strategy is occurring when one or more of the following conditions obtain:

1 Growth rate is significantly greater than the industry average.
2 Growth rate is significantly in excess of historical performance.
3 Previously accepted levels of historical measures of performance need to
   be adjusted.

In addition to these quantitative measures high growth could also be said to
be occurring when the company is adding to its portfolio of products and/or
markets and/or businesses.

There are two main methods of achieving high growth, namely through
internal, or *organic* means, and *external* means. Each of these approaches
may be pursued sequentially, or simultaneously.

Strategies to achieve internal high growth can be sub-divided into two main
categories:

- Increased sales of existing or related products.
- Sales of unrelated products.

Each of these is now discussed.

Internal high growth through increased sales of existing or related products

The strategies that may be employed to achieve this are really the same as the
various sub-strategies suggested when conservative growth was the fundamental strategy, namely:

1 Greater internal efficiency.
2 Deeper penetration – same markets, same products.
3 Same products in new markets.
4 New related products in same markets.
5 New related products in new markets.

Indeed the only real change for the designation of 'high growth' is that the
expected *level* of growth should be higher.

When new related products are added to the existing range of products the
company offers, this strategy is frequently described as growth through
Internal concentric diversification, because the growth is:

(a) *Internal*, as it is generated from within the company.
(b) *Concentric*, as the new products are in some way related to the existing
    product range – they will probably be in similar industrial classifications.
(c) *Diversified*, as the products are extensions to the existing range.

An example of the pursuit of high internal growth through the increased sales
of existing and related products is provided by the recent history of the

Table 45 Earnings of Minolta Camera Co. Ltd 1981–5

	1985 Mn.¥	(%)	1984 Mn.¥	(%)	1983 Mn.¥	(%)	1982 Mn.¥	(%)	1981 Mn.¥	(%)
Cameras and related equipment	106,843	44	98,535	46	93,751	49	94,553	49	95,473	55
Copying machines, microfilm equipment and others	138,010	46	115,356	44	98,843	51	99,817	51	78,562	45
Total sales	244,853	100	213,891	100	192,594	100	194,370	100	174,035	100

Minolta Camera Company Ltd of Japan. Table 45 shows the total revenues and the contributions made by the products 'cameras and related equipment' and 'copying machines and other equipment' for this company over the period 1981 to 1985.

As can be seen, the company, which traditionally has been regarded as a camera manufacturer, now derives more than half of its revenue from non-camera products. Minolta, since the camera market is relatively flat and extremely competitive, has concentrically diversified from cameras into other technologically related products whose growth prospects are superior. Judging from the 1985 annual report, this successful strategy of internal concentric diversification is likely to continue:

> Having built extensive businesses in cameras and business machines, we are eager to expand the scope of our operations. The high-quality imaging on which we have established our reputation encompasses optics, microelectronics, precision machining and other technologies. Combinations of these technologies have yielded successful products in many areas, including photomicry, medical equipment, and planetariums, and we will continue to apply our technological strengths to diversify our business activities.[10]

Internal high growth through increased sales of unrelated products

This strategy occurs when a company introduces products unrelated to its existing range. Because of the unrelated nature of the products, normally the markets will also be new.

An example of the successful adoption of this strategy is provided by the Lockheed Aircraft Company, whose main business was in the manufacture of aircraft and related products. It developed electronic data bases to help in its manufacturing processes, and these data bases were so comprehensive that outside organizations started to make use of them, and ultimately the Lockheed Aircraft Company diversified into the unrelated business of the commercial provision of electronic data base services on a world basis.

When unrelated products are added to the existing range, this strategy could be described as growth through *Internal conglomerate diversification* because the growth is:

(a) *Internal*, as it is generated from within the company.
(b) *Conglomerate*, as the new products are not related to the existing product range.
(c) *Diversification*, as the new products are extensions to the existing range.

Neutral strategy

A neutral strategy is defined as one where there is no significant deviation from the past strategy, i.e. the goals achieved, the company's activities and its

Table 46 Business failures in England and Wales, 1980–90

	Liquidations	Bankruptcies	Total failures
1980	6814	3814	10651
1981	8227	4976	13203
1982	11131	5436	16567
1983	12466	6821	19287
1984	13647	8035	21682
1985	14363	6580	20943
1986	13689	6991	20680
1987	10644	6761	17405
1988	9276	7286	16652
1989	10197	7966	18163
1990	13611	10831	24442

Source: Dun and Bradstreet

current competitive position have been historically satisfactory and similar achievements in the future would also be considered satisfactory. Therefore in this type of strategy no change is proposed.

Apart from the general circumstances outlined above, the following situations may help a company decide upon a neutral strategy.

Environmental reasons

If little environmental change is anticipated and if past achievements have been satisfactory, then there would appear to be little incentive to change.

Because of the competition

If the company has achieved a satisfactory competitive position, then, rather than upset this by introducing a change of strategy, which might provoke hostile competitive retaliation, it may be better to have no change.

Lack of resources

If the company only has the resources to continue the same strategy as it followed in the past, then it has no choice.

Goals already satisfied

If company goals have been satisfied by the achievements of the past strategy, then it is likely therefore that the goals will be satisfied by a similar strategy in the future.

Cultural reasons

From a cultural point of view, this is the easiest strategy to implement. People are familiar with it, it tends to be of little threat, and it requires little additional effort.

Conclusion

Although the neutral strategy is, for the reasons given under 'Cultural reasons', often very attractive to management, the simple re-application of the 'formula that brought access in the past' has great dangers. As many companies have found out to their cost, the assumption that the environment is static is indeed a large one, and one that many companies have found out to be incorrect.

Recovery strategies

In spite of the evidence of Table 46 and the painful business experiences many companies had in the late 1970s and 1980s, there are many who still consider business crisis or failure to be a unique and unexpected occurrence. It is not. It is as normal an occurrence in business as illness is in human beings. In all industries there is a dynamic of change and adjustment, and there will always be a certain proportion of businesses that are experiencing crises or failing. Although the levels and impact of business failure tend to be most severe in the types of recessionary times the UK has recently experienced, it should not be thought of as a phenomenon that is determined exclusively by recession. Thus, in the case of Japan, Mikami[11] has shown that over the period 1970 to 1979, because of the severity of competition, the rate of bankruptcies in Japan was two to three times greater than in the US.

These comments are not meant to detract from the seriousness of business crises or failures, but rather to put such events in the context of a 'normal' business occurrence and so increase the weight given to the importance of considering strategies that will prevent failure, i.e. strategies of recovery.

There is a continuum in the severity of the crisis that may require the instigation of a recovery strategy. At one end is the immediate prospect of insolvency and bankruptcy, naturally the strongest trigger, and at the other is a more general feeling of dissatisfaction. For the purposes of this section it will be assumed that a recovery strategy is appropriate when the company is not performing satisfactorily but there is not a prospect of immediate collapse. In other words, it is in a crisis that is not going to cause immediate failure, but will certainly cause failure to occur if remedial action is not taken fairly quickly.

The aim of any recovery strategy ought to be at the least to minimize the losses that are occurring and, if possible, to change a declining company into one achieving satisfactory returns and developing a long-term sustainable competitive position.

Although it is axiomatic that any successful recovery strategy must be tailored to the causes of the crisis, there are a number of fundamental general activities that appear to be appropriate in most recovery situations. Therefore the exposition of recovery strategy given below will be as follows:

- General activities for recovery.
- Causes of failure and how to recover.

Early action for recovery

The earlier in the developing crisis that action is taken, the more time and scope there is for manoeuvre and the greater is the likelihood of a successful recovery. Ensuring early action means having the managerial motivation to act upon adverse signals.

Reducing costs

Companies in crisis often are there because of a failure to control, or even know about, their costs. Therefore any recovery strategy should, as a starting point, consider existing costs and then, if appropriate, how they can be reduced or at least controlled.

Reducing the assets

Frequently in a crisis a company may have too large an asset base for the sales and profits it is generating. Simple arithmetic shows that a reduction in the value of the assets automatically increases the return on assets, and, additionally, the proceeds of the sales of such assets may be used to reduce the level of debt or increase the proportion of equity.

Increasing the revenue

A more positive solution may be to increase revenue. This may be achieved through a variety of means – quality enhancements, price changes, better marketing, new markets, etc.

Changing the top management

Perhaps the most crucial element in the development of a successful recovery strategy is having appropriate top management, particularly the chief executive officer or managing director. Frequently a successful recovery can only be effected if the top management is replaced. As the incumbent top management is normally aware of this threat, it is not unusual for them to attempt to mask a forthcoming crisis in order to help them preserve their positions as long as possible.

  A good example of the typical types of strategy taken to effect recovery are the actions that have been taken to try to turn round the UK electronics and computer company STC. In 1985 STC developed severe financial difficulties and then embarked upon a series of actions, outlined below, that was designed to return the company to profitability:

Twelve months ago when Sir Kenneth Corfield, the then chairman of STC, the telecommunications and computer group, addressed the annual meeting he said 1985 would be a year of consolidation and the longer-term outlook was highly encouraging.

Three months later STC was in the throes of a grave financial crisis and he was ousted in a boardroom coup.[12]

There has been a considerable amount of empirical investigation into the causes of decline and failure, and this research has resulted in a number of methods of predicting corporate failure. Most of the research tends to agree that the following are normally the main issues that must be dealt with to achieve recovery.

Management failure

Managerial failure is one of the most frequently cited causes of corporate decline. This type of failure can be manifested at one or more of the following levels:

1 *Dominant and powerful chief executive or small caucus.* When control is in the hands of just one person, or a small caucus, this concentration of autocratic power can lead to idiosyncratic decision-making, which may not be in the best interests of the company. Argenti[13] suggests that when the chairman of a company is also its managing director it tends to concentrate an excessive amount of power in the hands of one person, and such power structures often contribute to failure.

   In passing, it is rather paradoxical to observe that the chief executive who autocratically leads his company into decline is often the same person who built the company into its successful state. Often the strengths that were so essential for building the company become weaknesses when different strategic problems are encountered. Autocrats may help cause decline and failure because they themselves fail to change in line with changed circumstances.

   The answer to management failure is to replace top management. Normally, however, this will be feasible only when all other strategies have failed and the crisis is so severe that the prospect of bankruptcy of the company is imminent.

2 Poor board of directors. When the board of directors fails to discharge its duties properly, this is often a contributing factor to future failure. Poor performance by a board of directors can be expressed in a number of dimensions, including:

   (a) Lack of skills and knowledge, i.e. the board does not have balanced functional expertise or is ignorant of the competitive realities of the business and its industry.

(b) Lack of communication, i.e. there is little effective communication among the members.

(c) Lack of assertiveness, i.e. rather than acting as a forum for the informed debate of fundamental strategic issues concerning the company, the board may act as a rubber-stamping agency for a dominant chief executive.

The answers to the problem are the removal of those members of the board who have failed to make worthwhile contributions and their replacement with personnel who do have the necessary skills and knowledge, or augmenting the board with additional talent.

3 *Diffusion of managerial effort.* It is not unusual to find, particularly for companies that have engaged in diversificatrion, that strategic managerial effort may be absorbed by new and unrelated projects, with the consequently costly neglect of the core of the business. In passing, it is instructive to note that one of the major criticisms of those companies that have been recipients of hostile takeover bids by predatory financiers is that a disproportionate amount of top management's time is absorbed in defending the company against such bids rather than creative strategic planning and implementation.

A restriction on the range of the activities in which top management is engaged will help recovery. This may include the disposal of parts of the business and 'getting back to basics'.

Although all the functional areas can contribute to decline, researchers of the causes have found that the following are the most frequently occurring causes.

Financial inefficiency

1 *Poor financial control.* This is a most frequent contributing factor to decline and is often exhibited when companies have poor or nonexistent:

(a) Cash flow forecasting systems.
(b) Budgetary control systems.
(c) Cost control systems.

2 *Poor financial structure.* The financial structure may, especially when there is a period of stagnant or reduced growth, impose strains. This frequently occurs when the amount of debt the company has is too large relative to its equity.

Recovery should follow from the introduction of effective financial information and control systems, i.e. the following:

1   An accurate cash flow forecasting system.
2   An effective budgetary control system.
3   An effective cost control system.

The financial structure may be improved through:

1   Reducing the amount of debt. This could be achieved through the sale of assets and using the proceeds of such sales, or by leasing rather than purchasing assets.
2   Increasing the amount of equity. This could be achieved through asking existing investors for additional funds, attracting new investors, or being taken over.

Overtrading

When the rate of the company's growth is high and its consequent level of sales relative to its assets is very great, then these circumstances, often called overtrading, can occur, with consequent disastrous consequences.

Reducing the rate of growth of sales and consolidating sales to relate them more closely to the size of assets will aid recovery.

Marketing failure

When the efforts made by those concerned with marketing are poor, as measured by the various marketing indices referred to on pp. 73–74, then failure is likely.

There are a great number of possible strategies for recovery (see pp. 199–201). It is instructive to note that a 'reformation' of marketing strategies was one of the key ingredients of the UK computer company ICL's recovery strategy in 1985. An important element in its recovery was a realization of its inadequacy in the areas of market segmentation, product positioning and other basic marketing techniques.

Production failure

When the costs of production become high relative to competitors, this frequently is an indicator of failure. The Japanese concentration on production efficiency has been so effective that the production costs of many Western companies are now no longer competitive.

The answer is to reduce the costs of production, if possible. Methods could include improving the quality of the production equipment; acquiring additional production staff and expertise; shifting the location of production to a lower cost area; product redesign, with the objective of lowering production costs; improving the quality of the product; and reducing production costs.

Although not in danger of failure the West German power tool division of the West German automative and communications company Robert Bosch was, in the late 1970s and early 1980s, concerned about its inability to compete against Japanese competitors' prices. It embarked upon a campaign of cost engineering with the objective of reducing price without sacrificing quality. The results were impressive:

> The concept of cost engineering proved difficult for many to accept. Practising engineers, for example, tended at the start to state 'it can't be done' and to ask management which components they wanted taken out.
> Management insisted. Helped by the campaign, the price of the company's 2 kg hammer has been brought down from DM 800 to DM 300 with no loss of quality. Annual sales have increased 20-fold in the past few years, Lungerhausen (the managing director of the division) boasts. It is now the division's main line and sets a price and quality standard for the rest of the world to match.[14]

Two types of major strategic error seem to be the most frequent cause of failure.

Failure of the big project

Argenti has documented well how a single large project that goes wrong can have the most disastrous consequences for a company, with perhaps the best example being the decision of Rolls-Royce to develop the RB 211 jet engine. The problems associated with this huge project helped contribute to the company's collapse in 1971. A consequence of this finding is that a project that is large in relation to the total size of the organization should be embarked upon only with the greatest degree of caution.

In this type of situation, depending upon the scale of the crisis, there are a number of possible recovery strategies:

1 Abandon the project altogether. In spite of the money that has been sunk in the project, if it shows no signs of becoming viable, it may be better just to abandon it and stop the haemorrhage of resources it is absorbing.
2 Seek additional funding / resources to enable the project to continue. If it appears that the project will be ultimately commercially successful and that the crisis it is causing can be weathered if sufficient additional resources are made available, then this may be a viable option.

Acquisition failure

Although acquisition is frequently seen by top management as the most attractive and frequently a relatively low risk method of growth, it has also been for many companies a cause of failure. This failure can be due to:

1 Absorption of top management time in developing the acquired company.
2 Paying too much for the acquired company and simply acquiring companies that are poor performers and whose poor performance only becomes apparent after the acquisition.

Reducing the rate of acquisition, and / or divesting the company of some of the more troublesome acquisitions, may be the way to recovery.

Competitive pressure as cause of failure

When the competitive pressures become particularly severe, then failure can be expected. For example, in the Western European textile industry there have been many cases of textile companies failing because of the severe competitive pressures caused by the advent of new low cost entrants from the Far East.

The prospects of recovery are linked to the severity of the competition – the level of competition may be so severe that recovery is impossible. Assuming that if the competition is not as severe as that, the company should, following p. 208, attempt to structure itself so that it can profitably differentiate itself from its competitors.

Market or economic recession

A decline in the total market demand for a product could be due to either a change in demand for the product because of its stage in its life cycle – for example, the demand in Western Europe for electro-mechanical cash registers is now relatively small, as this product has been superseded by electronic cash registers – or because of a general decrease in the level of demand for all products caused by economic decline. In the UK in the late 1970s and 1980s, for instance, there was a severe increase in the number of bankruptcies in the construction industry. This was due in a large part simply to a fall-off in demand, which reflected the general economic recession in the country.

If the products manufactured by the company are in the last stages of their life cycles, then they should either be abandoned, or else, if it is feasible and economically sensible, be restructured so that their life cycles are extended.

Reduction strategy

If the causes of the decline in demand are due to economic recession, then the appropriate recovery strategy would be to reduce the scale of operations of the company, which could include reduction in the range of activities, range of products, range of markets, assets and personnel to match the reduced economic circumstances. Alternatively, and more positively, if the recession applied just to the company domestic market, then new sales could be sought in foreign markets.

The most common causes of business decline

Finally, Table 47 shows the causal factors of decline that Slatter has found in his empirical investigations into this topic.

Circumstances appropriate to recovery strategies

As the tenor of this section on recovery indicated, when certain conditions prevail, a company will frequently have a stark choice – liquidation or a recovery strategy. Therefore the circumstances determining when a recovery strategy is appropriate are somewhat different – it may be more true to assert that recovery strategies are triggered by the prospect of crisis rather than any managerial aspiration towards any particular style of strategy.

Stage 2: the generic strategies

Once a fundamental strategy has been selected, then the company should decide upon which of Porter's generic strategies it should follow. Thus the

Table 47 Frequency (in %) of causal factors of decline in forty UK recovery situations[15]

Causal factor	Total sample	Successfully recovered	Failed to recover
(Sample size)	(40)	(30)	(10)
Lack of financial control	75	73	80
Inadequate management			
Chief executive	73	67	90
Other	12	7	30
Competition			
Price competition	40	20	100
Product competition	18	17	20
High cost structure			
Operating inefficiency	35	36	40
High overheads	30	20	50
Scale effects	28	17	70
Changes in market demand			
Cyclical	33	40	30
Secular	18	17	20
Pattern of demand	7	6	10
Adverse movements in commodity market	30	30	30
Lack of marketing effort	22	17	40
Financial policy	20	20b	20
Big projects			
Capital	17	20	10
Revenue	15	20	10
Acquisitions	15	13	20
Overtrading	—	—	—

two strategy types – the fundamental and the Porter generic – should complement each other and together should enable the company to achieve its goals.

Porter[16] suggests that there are three broad generic strategies for creating such a position in the long run. These are overall cost leadership, differentiation, and focus. Each is now discussed.

Overall cost leadership

This strategy became increasingly popular in the 1970s, largely as a result of the prominence of the experience curve. A company that has a cost position lower than its competitors should earn average returns for its industry, and also enjoy a strong and defensible competitive position.

Although expensive to achieve, this position provides high margins that can be reinvested in new equipment and modern facilities in order to maintain leadership. Companies that have successfully followed this generic strategy include such well-known examples as Black and Decker power tools and Casio calculators.

Although overall cost leadership has conferred major advantages on those companies that have successfully followed it, it is risky and there are many examples of failure. Such a strategy requires very heavy capital investment, with no guarantee of a static environment that will yield fruits from such investment. Among the major changes that add to the risk of adopting this strategy are:

- Technological change that nullifies past investments or experience. For example, past investments in electro-mechanical cash register manufacturing equipment is now of relatively little value because of the development of electronic cash registers.
- Low cost learning by followers. Although the leader or pioneer in the industry will have to bear the heavy development costs of a low cost strategy (R & D, building production facilities, setting up channels of distribution and mounting effective marketing campaigns), following companies may be able to achieve similar positions much more cheaply. For example, the technology needed to manufacture electronic watches and calculators is now widely available and is no longer considered to be expensive.
- There may be too strong a focus on cost reduction, with a consequent lack of weight given to responding to changes in the environment and the market. This was one of the reasons for the demise of the Model T Ford.[17]
- The difference in cost between the leaders and the followers may be narrowed because of inflation, and changes in the costs of the factors of production. For example, Japanese shipyards now find it extremely difficult to compete against South Korean shipyards.

Differentiation

The objective of differentiation is that the company's products should come to be perceived, industry-wide and by their consumers, as being unique. Usually such products are of higher quality than rival products, and this cachet of quality enables them to command a premium price, i.e. the consumer is prepared to pay more than the 'normal' or average price because he wants high quality.

Differentiation can be achieved in a number of ways – quality, value for money, reliability, chic, customer service, etc. Some well-known examples of products that sell at a premium price because they have successfully differentiated themselves from others in the market include Lynx golf clubs, Nike running shoes and Volvo cars.

If differentiation is achieved, it provides a strategy for earning above-average returns in an industry (a higher price is usually charged). This helps provide a defensible competitive position.

It should be noted that achieving differentiation may sometimes preclude gaining high market share, as differentiation often requires a perception of exclusivity that is incompatible with high market share. Thus mass-produced, large volume fashion clothes, no matter how well they are made, cannot normally be sold on a differentiated strategy, as their numbers negate such a connotation. They may of course be sold as a differentiated product with a higher price if they can be differentiated by such a feature as 'up-to-dateness', unavailable elsewhere. In passing, it is instructive to note that Japanese automobile manufacturers such as Honda appear to be moving to a strategy where they will combine low cost plus differentiation (on the basis of quality).

Just as low cost strategy has its attendant risks, so also does a strategy of differentiation. Thus:

- The cost differential between the low cost and the differentiated competitor may become too great, and consumers may not be prepared to pay the differential. Leica cameras, although almost universally admired by photographers and certainly strongly differentiated from their Japanese competitors, are now so expensive, relative to Japanese cameras, that only the most dedicated and wealthy photographers can afford them.
- The consumers of the product may no longer feel that differentiation is so important. Many businesses buy IBM 'look-alike' personal computers because, presumably, they believe that the difference between the machines is not important.
- Imitators may erode the perceived difference between the differentiated and the low cost product. This is a major problem for IBM's personal computers. There are now so many IBM compatibles and 'look-alikes', which frequently claim to be better than the genuine IBM, that the perceived difference has been to some extent eroded.

Focus

This strategy focuses on a particular buyer group, segment of the product line, or geographic market. A focused strategy can take many forms. Its basic thrust is that a company can succeed best by serving a narrow strategic target very well. A company using this strategy will achieve differentiation through better meeting the needs of the particular target, lower costs or both, and it does this only from the perspective of its narrow market target. Once again, when such a strategy is successfully followed, then higher than industry average returns may be earned. An example of a focused low cost strategy is the strategy that the parts suppliers to many large Japanese companies followed; while an example of a focused differentiated strategy could be specialist health food shops, and specialist record shops focusing on one particular type of music.

As with the other generic strategies, there are certain risks attendant upon focusing, the main risks being:

- Cost difference between the low cost producer competitor and the focused company becomes more than consumers are willing to pay. Leica cameras may be in this category.
- The differences between the focused product and the low cost product become eroded. Japanese efforts at design and quality improvement have narrowed the differences between expensive focused Western cars and Japanese mass-produced products significantly.
- Non-focused large competitors may decide to focus on small market segments and use their resources to cater for these segments in a 'focused' way. It could be argued that large multiple retailers that open specialist shops within a large shop are adopting this strategy.

Stuck in the middle

Porter[18] claims that when a company fails to develop one of the three generic strategies satisfactorily, it will become 'stuck in the middle'. Such a company is too small to achieve a low cost position; it may lack market share and capital investment, i.e. it does not have the critical mass necessary to compete against the major competitors. In addition, it cannot achieve the degree of differentiation necessary to charge premium prices, as it may not have superior quality, superior reliability, chic, or whatever attribute is necessary for differentiation. Porter asserts that a company in such a position is almost certain to have low profitability. It will also probably suffer from a blurred corporate culture and a conflicting set of organizational arrangements and motivation system. Among companies that appear to have suffered this fate are British Leyland, which neither achieved volumes of production comparable with major rivals, such as Volkswagen, nor of the product differentiation companies such as BMW.

Porter suggests that a company stuck in the middle must make one of two fundamental decisions:

(a) It must take the steps necessary to achieve either cost leadership or at least parity, or,
(b) It must focus or achieve some differentiation.

Which strategy ought to be selected should be determined by the environmental prospects, the nature of the competition, and the company's resources, goals and culture.

CONCLUSION ON DEVELOPING STRATEGIES

Developing strategies is the most creative and perhaps most important part of the strategic planning process. It is at this stage of the process that the long-run future operations and hence destiny of the organization are decided. The next stage of the planning process is to refine the strategic guidelines into specific operations targets that will permit successful implementation.

GAP ANALYSIS

One approach that can be of considerable help to companies in developing an awareness of the need for strategic change and in providing guidance in the selection of appropriate strategies is gap analysis, which was devised by Argenti.[19] The approach proceeds by providing information on the changes in strategies or policies a company *must* effect if it is to achieve its specified goals or targets. Thus, for example, if the goal is to generate profits of £1 m in the forthcoming planning period and pursuing current strategies will yield profits of just £700,000, then gap analysis could be used to reveal the strategic actions necessary to achieve the goal.

The objective of the analysis is to show the gap or discrepancy that would develop between the goals or targets that had been set for the company and the performance that would actually be achieved if the company continued to follow its existing strategies. If no gap is forecast to develop, then existing strategies are satisfactory and no strategic change is necessary. However, if a gap is forecast, then this indicates that targets will not be achieved, and strategies should be sought and developed to close the projected gap.

The process of gap analysis can be carried out in the following linked steps:

Step 1   *Goals or targets are set.* These are the performance levels that are desired by the end of the planning period.

Step 2 *Current performance is extrapolated.* From environmental and internal data, the company's performance over the planning period is forecast. These forecasts are based upon the existing strategy continuing with no substantial change. For example, if a company had been pursuing a strategy of steady organic growth of 10 per cent per year in volume terms then, in a Gap Analysis, this rate of growth would be assumed to continue, with minor adjustments for changes in variables such as rate of economic growth in the markets for the product, changes in the costs associated with manufacturing and marketing the product, etc.

Step 3 *The forecast gap is measured.* Once the forecast has been made, then the difference between it and the goal or target can be measured. The difference is an indication of the size of the strategic adjustment that will be necessary to achieve goals or targets. Generally the greater the gap, the greater will be the required change in strategic direction necessary to close it.

Step 4 *Strategies to close the gap are developed.*

The generic nature of gap analysis

Gap analysis can be considered to be a generic approach to strategy development in that it can be tailored to any level in the company. The units by which the gap is measured can be determined by the objectives of the analysis and needs of the user.

At the corporate level, where goals are usually set in financial and marketing units such as sales values, return on investment, etc., strategies will tend to be set in similar terms. Consequently any projected gaps will tend to be measured in such units.

At the SBU level, where the goals tend to be more specific, gaps will be measured in units reflecting this orientation. These units could include annual sales volumes and sales values.

At the functional level targets are set as specific functional numbers: for example, quarterly sales of at least £500,000 for Product 1 and £300,000 for Product 2; 60 per cent of sales to be through Distribution Channel 1 and the remainder through Distribution Channel 2; the total number of employees not to exceed 125 people, etc. Gaps can therefore be measured in these units. Thus the generic nature of gap analysis is reflected not just in the process but also in the units of measurement: the choice of unit should be determined by the objectives of the analysis.

A case example to illustrate gap analysis

A simple case is set out below to illustrate how Gap Analysis may be employed to help see and then bridge the gap between a company's target annual sales and its sales forecast. In the analysis it is assumed that past conditions, internal and environmental, will continue to prevail and that future sales growth will continue to follow the historical pattern.

Bacchus Beer has carried out a Gap Analysis to compare its target sales over the period 1991 to 1994 with a simple forecast of its future performance. A gap analysis was carried out as follows.

Step 1   Goals or targets are set

The senior managers in Bacchus have set sales targets for 1992, 1993 and 1994, at £14,000, £16,000 and £20,000 respectively.

Step 2   Current performance is extrapolated

Current performance is extrapolated through analysing past trends and then building the forecast upon these trends. The forecasts are made on the assumption that future sales will continue to increase in line with past performance. The forecast of future sales may be made in two main ways: graphical extrapolation or using scenarios generated in the Bacchus marketing model, Bacmar. The computer scenario approach is given in Chapter 13, and the graphical approach is set out below. The graphical approach used here is the simplest possible: it uses free-hand straight line extrapolation. Other more complex forecasting approach may of course be employed.

Figure 54 shows Bacchus Beer's sales over the period 1988 to 1991 and the straight line is the free-hand drawn line of best fit. As can be seen, this approach suggests that sales in 1991, 1992 and 1993 will be £9,500, £12,500 and £13,500 respectively.

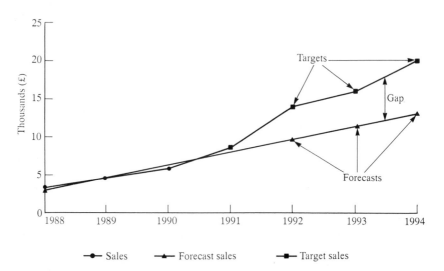

Figure 54   A gap analysis diagram for Bacchus Beer.

Step 3   The forecast gap is measured

The gaps between the target sales and the graphically forecast sales can be seen to be £3,500 for 1992, £3,500 for 1993, and £6,500 for 1994.

Step 4   Strategies to close the gap are developed

The analysis indicates that Bacchus is going to fail to meet its sales targets. If the company still wishes to pursue the targets, i.e. close the gap, it must change from its current fundamental strategy of conservative organic growth to a fundamental strategy of high growth. The latter fundamental strategy could be achieved by one or more of the following sub-strategies:

1   *Internal high growth.* This could be achieved through one or more of the following: increased sales of existing products, internal concentric diversification, or internal conglomerate diversification.
2   *External high growth.* This could be achieved through one or more of the following: external concentric diversification, external conglomerate diversification, or merger.

Conclusion

Gap analysis can be particularly useful as a neutral device for showing the extent of strategic change necessary to achieve corporate goals or targets, and can thus act as a stimulant to effecting change. Of fundamental importance to the quality of the analysis is the quality of the forecasts upon which it is based, and in today's turbulent environment long-run accurate forecasts are the exception rather than the rule. However, Chapter 13 shows how to build reactive forecasting models that can be changed very quickly in response to environmental change.

References

1   Slatter, S., *Corporate Recovery*, Penguin, 1984.
2   McNamee, P. B., *Management Accounting: Strategic Planning and Marketing*, Heinemann, 1988.
3   Hall, W. and Taylor, P., 'Falling prey to rigours of deregulation', *Financial Times*, 5 March 1986, p. 22.
4   ITT Annual Report for 1984, p. 40.
5   Tilles, S., 'Culture: Barrier to Change', *Perspectives*, No. 253, Boston Consulting Group, 1983.
6   Porter, M. E., *Competitive Strategy: Techniques for Analysing Industries and Competitors*, Collier Macmillan, 1980.

7 Mikami, T., *Management and Productivity Improvement in Japan*, JMA, Tokyo, 1982, p. 35.

8 *Ibid.*, p. 2.

9 'Nissan UK: Back on the Road?', *Observer*, 4 August 1991, p. 23.

10 Minolta Camera Company Ltd, Annual Report 1985.

11 Mikami, *op. cit.*

12 Lorenz, C, 'A painful process of change', *Financial Times*, 14 May 1986, p. 22.

13 Argenti, J., *Corporate Collapse: the Causes and the Symptoms*, McGraw-Hill, 1976.

14 Lorenz, C., 'How Bosch strengthened its defences', *Financial Times*, 2 May 1986, p. 20.

15 Slatter, *op. cit.*, p. 53.

16 Porter, *op. cit.*

17 See McNamee, P. B., *Tools and Techniques for Strategic Management*, Pergamon Press, Oxford, 1985.

18 Porter, *op. cit.*

19 Argenti, J., *Corporate Planning: a Practical Guide*, George Allen & Unwin, 1968.

13 Computer modelling of new strategies

INTRODUCTION

New Strategies for Bacchus Beer are developed, as shown in Figure 55, using the goal model, Bacgo; the marketing model, Bacmar; the product market portfolio model, Bacpmp; the financial models, Bacinc, Baccas, Bacfun and Bacbal; and finally the ratio model, Bacrat.

THE OBJECTIVE OF THE MODELS

The objective of the models is, when taken together, to allow a manager to set up new strategies, simulate their effects and then choose one that appears to provide optimal results. This is effected as follows:

- A *strategy* is selected. This will be a fundamental strategy aligned with a generic strategy. In Figure 55 the strategy of high growth and high volume/low cost has been selected for Bacchus. (A new strategy may, of course, be simply a continuation of a previously successful strategy.)
- The new strategy is *simulated*, i.e. the goal model, Bacgo, and the marketing model, Bacmar, are adjusted to reflect the new strategy, and then the models are run.
- The *results* of the new strategy are captured in the product market portfolio model, the financial models, and the ratio model, and then appraised.

Depending upon the appraisal, the new strategy is amended and the complete sequence run again. This sequence of runs then continues until the results obtained are acceptable and feasible. (Feasible results are, first, results capable of being achieved by the company's resources and, second, feasible in the environment in which the company operates.) The results, in other words,

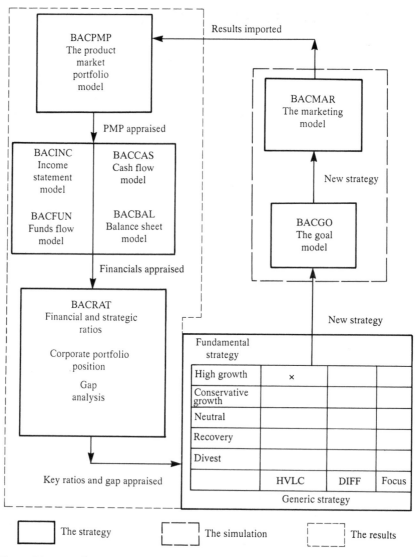

Figure 55   Developing new strategies for Bacchus

comprise a series of scenarios in which the strategies, the goals, the strategy variables and the environmental influences are varied until an optimal scenario is achieved.

In passing, it should be noted that this is one of the major contributions that computer modelling confers on strategic management: it enables the simulation of many alternative scenarios before a final strategy is selected.

THE STRUCTURE OF THE MODELS

Only the goal model, Bacgo, and the marketing model, Bacmar, have input data. All the other models work on the basis of imported data. It should be noted, however, that after some experience in running the models, the user ought to be able to alter various relationships in the income statement model, Bacinc.

A NOTE ON RUNNING THE MODELS

You should now set up alternative scenarios by running the complete suite of models a number of times. To do this proceed as follows:

Place the disk in drive A and close the drive. Then
Type A:
Type Bacgo

This loads the goal model, Bacgo. You should now alter the goals and then proceed to the marketing model, Bacmar. Alter the strategy variables and the environmental influences, and then run the suite of models as far as Bacrat. You should then return to the goal model, Bacgo, and go through the same procedure until an optimal scenario is developed.

14 Strategy implementation

INTRODUCTION

Although for effective strategic management implementation is essential, it is not always easy. Frequently there can exist an unbridgeable gap between the aspiration (the strategy) and its fulfilment (the implementation). Thus although the UK automobile manufacturer Rover has often *formulated* apparently winning strategies, it has yet to successfully *implement* them.

Implementation is defined as the process through which the aspirations of the fundamental/generic strategies developed in Chapter 12 are transformed into operating realities, i.e. where goals are refined into day-to-day procedures. Although in the implementation of a strategy the focus will be within the company, the emphasis will be on ensuring that there is congruence between the strategy and the goals, leadership, culture, functional policies, resources, and structure of the company. A broad cognizance of the external environment should always be present to ensure that the strategy being implemented retains its original external validity.

AN OVERVIEW OF IMPLEMENTATION

The effective implementation of any strategy poses a fundamental dilemma for strategic planners, for it requires the accommodation of two fundamentally opposing forces: those leading to *integration* and those leading to *segmentation*. Thus, implementation is usually most effective if, somehow, the strategy can be communicated throughout the company so that at every level and in all departments:

- There is a clear recognition of what the strategy actually is.
- Each department understands the role that it ought to play in implementation.
- There is consensus at all levels and in all departments about the wisdom of pursuing the strategy.

In contrast to this policy, effective implementation usually requires the segmentation of a fundamental strategy into relatively small and simple constituent elements so that each department, especially those at the lowest levels in the company, have clear targets or budgets to which they can relate. This will tend to have a segmenting influence.

Therefore effective implementation requires, on the part of planners, a recognition of this 'integration–segmentation' dilemma, and subsequent provision for the fruitful accommodation of these frequently opposing forces. This can be achieved through sensitive communication (which recognizes the fears and hopes at every level and in every department) of the strategy and appropriate use of the company power structure.

The process of implementation is complex, and Figure 56 provides a flowchart showing it in skeleton form. The figure assumes that a new strategy has been adopted and that the only issue is effective implementation. It is suggested that this should be done through matching a number of key elements in the company with the given strategy, the key elements being:

1 Leadership.
2 Culture.
3 Organization structure.
4 Functional policies.
5 Resources.
6 Control and evaluation procedures.

How well each element fits with the given strategy is ascertained, and then the process of implementation proceeds.

In interpreting the flowchart it is important to bear in mind that in practice it is unlikely that the implementation process will 'flow' smoothly in the sequence indicated. The process is essentially evolutionary and many of the constituent activities may take place simultaneously or in a different order; however, the flow of 'key elements' and decisions given in the flow chart is logical and generally approximates practice. The role of each of these 'key elements' in the strategy implementation process is now considered.

THE BEHAVIOURAL DIMENSIONS OF IMPLEMENTATION

Leadership

The quality of the leadership (individual or collective) and its commitment to a new strategy are perhaps the most crucial elements in determining successful implementation. If the leadership does not have the requisite qualities, *or if it is not fully committed to the strategy*, then it is extremely unlikely that implementation will be successful. Consequently a fundamental question

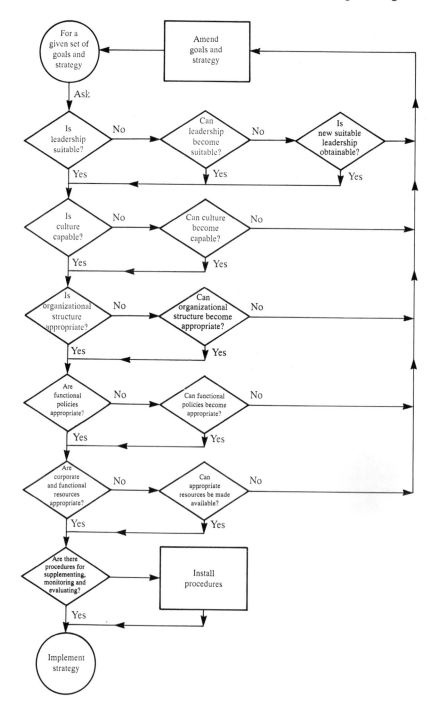

Figure 56   A flowchart showing schematically how a strategy may be implemented

Aberconway Library

Items on loan 25/10/2007 15:12
XXXXXX4849

Item Title	Due Date
Strategic management : a P	08/11/2007
Strategy implementation : st	08/11/2007
Strategy implementation : th	08/11/2007
* CRM : redefining customer	08/11/2007

* Indicates items borrowed today

O   e items will incur charges.

R   ems at: http://library.cf.ac.uk

Aberconway Library

Items on loan 25/10/2007 15:10
XXXXXX4849

em Title	Due Date
Strategic management : a	08/11/2007
Strategy implementation : s	08/11/2007
Strategy implementation : t	08/11/2007

Indicates items borrowed today
Overdue items will incur charges.
Renew items at: http://library.cf.ac.uk

Items on loan 25/10/2007 15:10
XXXXXX4849

Strategic management : a	08/11/2007
Strategy implementation :	08/11/2007
Strategy implementation : t	08/11/2007

Indicates items borrowed today
Overdue items will incur charges.
Renew items at: http://library.cf.ac.uk

that must be raised at the start of the implementation process is: 'Can the incumbent leader lead?' Three answers are possible:

1   'Yes', and the incumbent leader continues as a leader.
2   'Yes', if leadership development takes place. The incumbent leader continues but changes, or develops, certain facets of his leadership.
3   'No', and a new leader is brought in.

The incumbent leader continues

This situation is most likely to occur if the incumbent leader is generally regarded as having successfully led the company in the past and the new strategy is not significantly different from past strategy.

The incumbent leader continues, with leadership development

This situation is most likely to occur if the incumbent leader is generally regarded as having led the company successfully in the past but the new strategy is a major break with history. When such discontinuity occurs, even though there may be general respect for the incumbent's past achievements, there may also be a question of his ability to implement the new strategy. When this occurs, it may be possible for the leader to develop his claim to continued leadership through the development in himself of those skills considered necessary to implement the new strategy, or by expanding the leadership through recruiting to it suitably qualified personnel. When there is doubt about an incumbent's future potential as the leader, this doubt will frequently pivot around the following issues.

Leader's intellectual knowledge and skills

If the new strategy requires a new set of intellectual knowledge or skills, this may cause doubts to arise about the leadership. For example, if a company were to plan to diversify on a relatively large scale into an unrelated technology, then there may be a question of the incumbent's ability to provide the required technical leadership in this new area.

Leader's vision

One aspect of leadership that is worthy of special mention is that of vision. For effective implementation it is often necessary for the leader to have width and depth of vision – width to see the strategic challenges facing the company

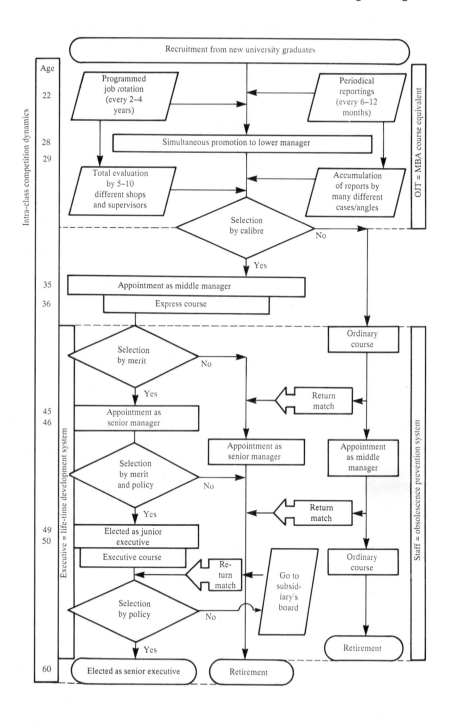

Figure 57   Generic career paths for Japanese managers in large Japanese companies[1]

in a distinctive and informed light, and depth to see and attend to those small details that must be considered if implementation is to be effective.

Japanese companies are extremely adroit at strategy implementation, and one aspect of their management practice that contributes significantly to the visionary powers of senior Japanese managers in implementation is their use of job rotation. Thus, in contrast to the usual practice in Western companies, many large Japanese companies place great emphasis on developing managers who are generalists, with skills in all the functions, rather than specialists, with the bulk of their skills in just one area (usually finance in the West). Senior Japanese managers develop this broad view of management by having career structures that are characterized by job rotation, i.e. when a new manager enters a company, he will spend a number of years in, say, production, then he will move to, say, marketing, then to finance, etc. A consequence of this job rotation is that when such a manager has reached a senior level, he has a balanced knowledge of all the functional areas of management, and this contributes greatly to his width of vision in strategic decision-making and implementation. Figure 57 shows generic career paths for Japanese managers in large Japanese companies.

Leader's behavioural or attitudinal skills

If the new strategy requires a different behavioural attitude from the leader, this may cause problems. For example, if in the past a company has always had a production/engineering orientation, i.e. good knowledge of and en-thusiasm for excellence in engineering has been synonymous with good leadership – and it proposes a new strategy in which marketing is predomi-nant, then there may be doubts whether the incumbent can implement this new orientation.

In passing, it is not unusual to find that a leader who has been instrumental in inventing or developing a successful product line may, in the process, have developed such an emotional attachment to it that it prevents him from taking a wider and more commercially rational view of the product's poten-tial and the appropriate strategies for its commercial development.

The age of the leader

The age problem tends to occur very often in family-owned businesses, where the leader, 'father or grandfather', is unwilling to 'surrender' the leadership to a later generation. When the leader's age is considered to be an issue, it usually means that he is considered to be too old for the arduous tasks of implementation. However, this is not always so. A relatively youthful in-cumbent may be the wrong man because his goals, interests or ambitions are inappropriate to the strategy or he does not have the experience for effective implementation.

Staying power of incumbent leader

In all the above situations it is postulated that whether the incumbent continues as leader or ought to be replaced depends upon whether he has the necessary attributes or is capable of developing them. If they are present or will be developed, then he should continue; if not he should be removed. In practice, however, this frequently does not happen, for a variety of reasons, including the following:

- The leader has erected around himself a power structure (a managerial palisade of supporters) that protects him.
- There is often a cultural impediment to leadership change – if the incumbent has been a leader for a considerable time, it conditions others to regard him as the leader irrespective of his suitability.
- There are no other suitable potential leaders available.
- The rewards for leadership are not sufficient.

A new leader is brought in

There are two main circumstances under which a new leader is brought in. The first is when the existing leader departs voluntarily, a new leader takes over, and there is no major strategic or operational change. In this situation the new leadership is new largely in name only, and the organizational effects of the change tend to be relatively minor.

Of course a 'voluntary' departure does not always mean a willing departure. For example, when in a family firm the leader, it is generally agreed, is at the retirement stage, it is not always the case that he will retire without protest. Similarly when an organization has been achieving results that are not entirely satisfactory (but are still not severely damaging to the organization), a power struggle will often be necessary in order to remove such a leader.

The second circumstance in which a new leader may be brought in occurs when the company faces a crisis that is so severe that its existence is threatened. In this situation the existing leader is often forcibly removed, and a new leader, or saviour, is installed.

Motivation to implement

In the above consideration of the role of leadership in implementation it was assumed that the leader actually does wish to implement the strategy. For various reasons this may not always be so. Leaders may be unenthusiastic about implementing a given strategy for a number of reasons, including:

1 They disagree with the wisdom of pursuing the strategy, i.e. they feel that whole-hearted pursuit of the strategy is not in the best interests of the company or their SBU.

2   They feel that they are not going to receive adequate compensation for the additional tasks that implementation is going to impose.
3   They feel they do not have the skills or resources to implement the strategy.
4   They feel that the benefits of implementation will accrue to others and not themselves.

Therefore, in the implementation stage it is important for planners to be aware of potential motivational impediments.

Culture

Because the culture of a company is not usually stated explicitly, it may not appear to be important in the implementation process. This is not so. When implementation is being considered, there should be a recognition that its ultimate success will be related to the degree of cultural acceptance and support it receives. Success in implementation is often directly related to the magnitude and the speed of the proposed strategic change, where 'change' can be divided into two main types: minor strategic change and major strategic change.

Minor strategic change

When the new strategy is a minor break with the past, e.g. a quantitative adjustment in goals, relatively minor additions or deletions to products and markets, or other relatively minor functional adjustments, then it is likely that implementation will be readily accepted. Normally the existing leadership and the existing power groups will see the new strategy as confirmation of the correctness of their previous performance and will not feel threatened by it: the existing status quo is likely to continue. Additionally, people at all levels will tend to feel 'comfortable' with the new strategy, as they will be familiar with similar operations in the past.

Major strategic change

However, when the new strategy is a major break with the past, implementation (irrespective of how worthwhile it is) is likely to encounter severe cultural resistance. This resistance will be especially strong if the change is to be implemented rapidly and there is little time for adjustment.

Natural resistance

In most companies' view those strategies and practices that have worked in the past will continue to work in the future: in other words there is a natural disinclination to change, which must be overcome. This disinclination to change is not a fault or an organizational vice; rather it is a natural phenomenon, and, in planning implementation, provision should be made for it.

Cultural resistance

Normally major strategic change will threaten existing power relationships and preferences, and those most threatened will tend to resist most fiercely. This resistance can occur at many levels: company-wide, in the hierarchy, or in departments.

Company-wide resistance

This may occur when there is general agreement about the historical correctness of the strategic direction in which the company has been going, and the new strategy is at variance with this direction. For example, when an SBU that has historically pursued a strategy of high growth is then required by corporate headquarters to engage in consolidation or reduction, strong cultural resistance throughout the SBU is likely to be engendered.

Hierarchical resistance

Hierarchical resistance may occur when implementation means a change in the status, the power, or the influence of the different levels in the hierarchy. For example, a new strategy may require a company-wide commitment to quality improvement, and in order to achieve this there must be an enhancement of the communication links between management and 'the shop floor'. If to effect this it is proposed that shop floor and management have common dining and washroom facilities, then there is likely to be managerial resistance to what managers may see as an erosion of their status.

Departmental resistance

Implementation that changes inter-departmental power relationships is likely to be resisted by those departments that perceive their power to be diminished. For example, it is often the case[2] that potentially successful businesses develop difficulties during periods of rapid growth because minimal attention is given to financial control. Frequently, in order to return such companies to health, it is necessary to impose 'control', by the appointment of additional financial staff to senior positions. In such circumstances it is not unusual to find that this change of direction is strongly opposed by personnel in the marketing function.

Promoting cultural change

Although there are no rigid rules for promoting cultural change Baker[3] has suggested that among the more important stimuli are the following.

Role-modelling by leaders

When cultural change is required, leaders themselves reflect it. For example, if the new strategy calls for financial restraint, this restraint should be seen in the behaviour of the leaders.

Positive reinforcement

There should be positive reinforcement of those individuals and those departments that are seen to be adopting the new strategy and its new culture. The most potent method of reinforcement is the allocation of resources, i.e. those departments that are most successful in following the new strategy receive the greatest rewards.

Promotion

Linked to the lever of positive reinforcement is that of promotion. Change can be effected through ensuring that those individuals who are most strongly embracing the new culture should be promoted most rapidly, and their influence extended.

Negative reinforcement

Negative reinforcement may be used as an instrument of change where the stimulus to change is the threat of the consequences of not changing. For example, those who do not comply with the new culture will not be promoted, and indeed, ultimately, will be dismissed. It should be pointed out, however, that the use of this approach tends to develop a much lower level of commitment than the positive reinforcement approach; and for this approach to be feasible there must be a power structure capable of enforcing it.

Communication

Effective communication, both explicit and implicit, is essential for cultural change. Explicit communication can take the form of verbal and written directives, targets, budgets, etc. Implicit communication is more subtle, and can take many forms. It is displayed through the actions rather than the words of the leaders. For example, a directive from the managing director emphasizing the importance of good company-wide communication issued through his remote office by an assistant will probably have less effect than if he were regularly to meet personnel at all levels.

Recruitment

Careful recruitment of new staff who have the attributes necessary for the implementation of the new strategy can be an effective method of effecting cultural change. Indeed in some cases it may be the only way.

Organizational design

Organizational structure can have significant cultural effects. For example, a company that has a pyramidal hierarchial structure, in which all important decisions are scrutinized by the top management, is likely to restrict individual flair and risk-taking.

Physical design

The physical design and layout of an organization can have cultural effects. This can be seen in the case of one of the UK's more successful companies, JCB, the UK excavator manufacturing company. Under the guidance of its chairman, J. Bamford, this company has very open offices, populated in places by stuffed jungle animals. One of the reasons is to encourage a culture of creativity.

Conclusion

Effecting cultural change is never easy and may, even in the face of imminent failure, prove to be impossible to achieve. This difficulty is well illustrated by the case of the prestigious UK luxury automobile manufacturer, Rolls-Royce Motors, which in 1983, for the first time in 23 years, suffered a bitter 5-week strike:

> What struck observers most was not that the 2,800 shopfloor workers downed tools for five weeks. It was the sullenness outside the factory gates and the animosity towards the company bubbling to the surface in every conversation.
>
> Something was very wrong in an enterprise where resentment sought such expression and where the management had conspicuously failed to carry the workforce with it during a very difficult period of the Company's life.[4]

STRUCTURE

The most common types of organizational structure have already been discussed in Chapter 2. Consequently only the role of structure in implementation is considered below.

The particular structure that a company has at any particular moment should not be thought of as static, but rather as something that can be changed, and which evolves and develops in response to strategic challenges that the company faces.

The relationship between strategy and structure

Chandler[5] investigated the relationship between strategy and structure in seventy large American corporations, and found that the structure that an organization had was a reflection of its strategy. In other words, it tends to be the case that structure develops as a result of strategy, i.e. structure follows strategy. If this is so, then it follows that at the implementation stage a company's structure should be examined to see if it is synchronized with its strategy.

A clear example of the importance that is attached to effecting a match between strategy and structure is provided by the structural changes that were announced in the German 'vehicle manufacturer' Daimler Benz in July 1986. Between 1984 and 1986 there was a fundamental change in the strategy of the company. During this period the company, which had previously been engaged almost exclusively in vehicle manufacture, rapidly diversified, through a series of major acquisitions, into engines (MTU), aerospace (Dornier), and electricals (AEG), to become West Germany's largest industrial concern. The total spent on these acquisitions was approximately DM 2.6 bn, and in the process Daimler Benz changed from being a 'vehicle manufacturer' to being a highly diversified high technology company. In order to implement its new strategies the company changed its structure. Perhaps the most significant change was in the composition and responsibilities of the executive board. The previous board, which comprised nine people who had mainly functional responsibilities, was expanded in July 1986, and the responsibilities of members changed from a functional orientation to a product-grouping orientation, i.e. instead of having responsibility for areas such as sales, production, etc., board members had responsibility for product groupings such as cars, engines, and aerospace. This was a significant structural change carried out in order to implement a new strategy.

There is no one structure that is best. Rather the structure adopted should be that which will enable the strategy to be implemented most successfully, will enable the company to achieve its goals, and will ensure that resources are directed to those areas most in need of them.

THE HIERARCHICAL NATURE OF STRATEGY IMPLEMENTATION

In this book implementation is assumed to take place in the context of a company whose structure is shown schematically in Figure 58. This is assumed to be a holding company in which the relationships between the corporate level and the SBU level are mainly financial, and there is minimal corporate control and guidance of individual SBUs. Consequently the exposition below will concentrate on how strategy is implemented at the SBU and the functional levels, i.e. it will be assumed that corporate goals and strategies and SBU goals and strategies have been largely determined, and the major concern is with the translation of the given corporate goals into effective functional operations.

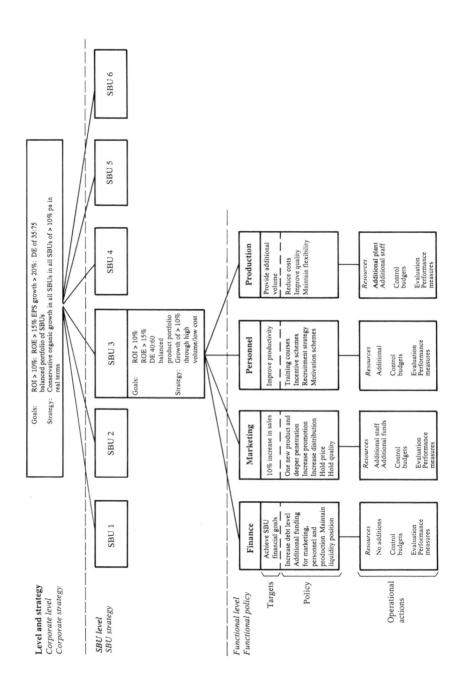

Figure 58 Schematic representation of the organizational structure in which implementation is assumed to take place

The flow of the implementation process

The company's corporate strategy is implemented in a hierarchical fashion, i.e. the top level goals and strategies are progressively refined and made more operational as they are communicated throughout the company and cascade downwards. The implementation process is assumed to take place at three levels: the corporate, the SBU, and the functional. The hierarchical nature and the flow of the process are shown in Figure 58.

As Figure 59 shows, implementation is an iterative process in which strategies from the top of the company are progressively refined and checked as they flow through the company. Irrespective of the level in the organizational hierarchy, the implementation process will have the following common sequence of activities:

- Goals or targets are set.
- Strategies or policies are formulated, and they will enable the goals or targets to be achieved.
- Projections to see the effects of following alternative strategies are made, and then those strategies most closely meeting the formulated goals are chosen.
- Resources are allocated to enable the chosen strategies to be followed.
- Evaluation and control systems are set up to provide *feedback* so that progress in the implementation of the chosen strategies can be monitored.

Although, for the purposes of exposition the above elements in the implementation process are separated out and considered independently, in practice they all interact with and impact upon each other, and therefore an iterative approach to implementation is necessary. Consequently the precise quantitative consequences of following alternative strategies should evolve only after projection, review, discussion and amendment of their impacts upon each other. This mutual dependence of the elements is portrayed graphically in Figure 60.

Implementation at the corporate level

At the top level in the hierarchy, the corporate, the goals and strategies tend to be couched in mainly financial terms and to a lesser extent in marketing terms. Typical corporate goals and strategies could include the following:

1 *Corporate goals: financial and marketing*
   (a) Achieve a return on investment of at least 10 per cent each year.
   (b) Achieve a return on equity of at least 15 per cent each year.

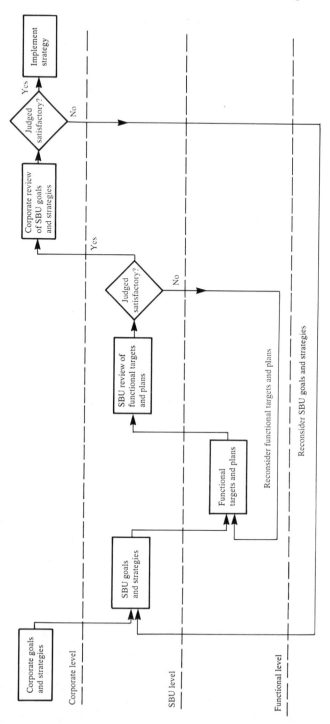

Figure 59   The hierarchical process of strategy implementation

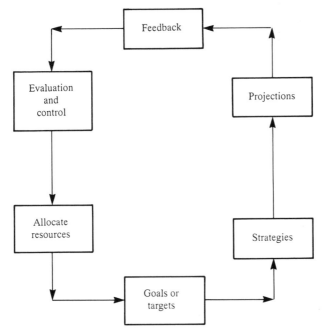

Figure 60 How elements of the implementation process interact

(c) Achieve a growth in earnings per share of at least 15 per cent each year.
(d) Maintain a debt to equity ratio of 30:70.
(e) Achieve a growth in sales of at least 10 per cent in real terms each year.
(f) Continue environmental surveillance for acquisitions that will strengthen the portfolio of SBUs.
2 *Corporate goals: portfolio.* Maximize the returns from the portfolio of SBUs while keeping the cash flows in balance and minimizing the risk profile of the portfolio. The corporate portfolio to be (1) augmented by acquisitions that have the potential to contribute to financial and marketing goals and (2) reduced through the disposal of those SBUs which are failing to meet corporate financial goals and show no prospect of doing so.
3 *Corporate strategy.* Conservative organic growth in sales of at least 10 per cent, in all SBUs, in real terms, for each of the next three years.
4 *Corporate projections.* At this level it is suggested that projections should be based upon consolidations of individual SBU-projected income statements, cash flow statements, product market portfolios and ratio statement balance sheets, and that the wisdom of pursuing particular strategies should be determined by measuring how well alternative consolidations meet corporate goals.

Corporate resources

In this model it is assumed that the only resource corporate management uses for implementation and control is finance. It therefore has the task of determining which SBUs should receive additional funding, perhaps to support anticipated growth; which should be allowed to remain cash neutral i.e. SBUs neither contribute to corporate funds nor do they receive any; and which SBUs ought to contribute to corporate funds.

Although in theory corporate resource allocation decisions ought to be made on the basis of quantitative assessments, in practice the judgement and experience of the top corporate management will often be of extreme importance and may override the quantitative dimensions of the decision.

Control and evaluation

Ensure that devices to enable the finally agreed strategies to be monitored are in place. These were shown in Chapters 8 and 10.

Implementation at the SBU level

At this level each SBU will formulate a set of goals and strategies that will enable it to comply with or exceed the higher level corporate goals. Typical SBU goals and strategies could include the following:

1   SBU goals: financial and marketing
    (a)   Achieve a return on investment of at least 10 per cent each year.
    (b)   Achieve a return on equity of at least 15 per cent each year.
    (c)   Maintain a debt to equity ratio of 30:70.
    (d)   Achieve a growth in sales of 25 per cent in real terms each year for each existing product.
    (e)   Introduce two new, related products into existing markets.
2   SBU goals: portfolio. Maximize the returns from the portfolio of products while keeping the cash flows in balance and minimizing the risk profile. Ensure the future viability of the portfolio by introducing two major new, related products in the forthcoming year. Monitor the performance of existing products to ensure that their current and future contributions are satisfactory.
3   SBU strategy. Exceed corporate goals through a strategy of conservative organic growth in sales of 15 per cent in real terms for the next 3 years. This growth is to be achieved by continuing to follow the generic strategy of high volume/low cost with the same product lines, introducing two new, related products, using the same channel of distribution in the same markets.

4   SBU projections. Implementation decisions should be based upon projected SBU income statements, cash flow statements, balance sheets,
portfolios and strategic ratios statements.

SBU resources

It is assumed that financial resources are provided by corporate management,
and the SBU top managers are free to use these resources to achieve SBU
goals.

Control and evaluation

Ensure that devices to enable the finally agreed strategies to be monitored are
in place. These were shown in Chapters 8 and 10.

Implementation at the functional level

The objective of functional implementation is to refine the corporate and SBU
goals and strategies into targets, policies and actions that will guide and
control each functional area in ways that will ensure implementation actually
takes place.

A general approach to implementation in each functional area is set out
below and a specific case study example is given in Chapter 16. Typical
implementation issues for each functional area are now presented.

Implementation in the marketing function

Targets

To achieve the given growth rate what are the sales targets in terms of the
following:
- Total sales volumes and values?
- Return on sales?
- Sales volumes and values broken down by product line, channel of
distribution, location of sales, and customer type?
- Contribution margins by product line, channel of distribution, location
of sales, and customer type?

Policies

To achieve the marketing targets that have been set above, the following
policy issues must be resolved:

- What are the markets for the products – new markets or existing ones?
- How should the markets be segmented?
- What are the desired product positions in each market segment?
- What are the necessary marketing mix policies?

Projections

When the marketing policies have been decided, then, together with other relevant information from the other functional areas, the effects of implementing particular policies can be projected, using standard financial statements and the consequences appraised. On the basis of these projections, if the initial policies are considered to be unsatisfactory, they can be amended, and then, using the amended policies, further projections can be made in order to try to 'steer' the company towards its desired goals. This process can be continued until an optimal set of policies has been devised.

Resources

On the basis of the policies selected, determine the resources necessary to implement them and establish budgets that will then allocate such resources.

Control and evaluation

Ensure that devices to enable the finally agreed policies to be monitored and evaluated are in place. These were shown in Chapters 8 and 10.

Implementation in the finance function

Targets

In order to achieve its given growth goal and its given financial goals the financial targets could be set in terms of the following:

- The target ROI.
- The target ROCE.
- The target debt to equity ratio.
- The target debt structure.
- Target levels of equity.
- The target ROE.
- Target levels of dividends.
- Target levels of liquidity.

Financing policies

Assuming that additional finance will be required to support the growth, will these additional funds come from external or internal sources? If external sources are used, then:

- Debt or equity or a combination?
- What capital structure ought the company to have?
- What are the ownership implications?

If internal sources are used, then:

- Should it be retained earnings?
- Should it be more stringent control of such elements as working capital, debtors, creditors or stock?

What should be the balance between long-term sources of finance and short-term? Irrespective of the source of finance, at what time(s) of the forthcoming year should it be sought?

Dividend policies

What is the level of dividend payout that will satisfy shareholders and also achieve financial targets?

Liquidity policies

What cash balances should be maintained?

Projections

The proposed financial policies should be included in the 'marketing projection' and the financial consequences ascertained. As with the marketing policies, if the results are deemed to be unsatisfactory, then the financial variables can be changed to try to achieve more satisfactory results.

Resources

On the basis of the policies decided upon determine the resources necessary to implement these policies and draw up budgets to allocate these resources.

Control and evaluation

Ensure that devices to enable the finally agreed policies to be monitored and evaluated are in place. These were shown in Chapters 8 and 10.

Implementation in the production function

Production requirements are dependent variables directly determined by the proposed sales schedules.

Targets

For the forthcoming year what are the production targets in terms of:

- Total volume of production according to product types?
- Capacity utilization?
- Costs?
- Quality?
- Stock levels?

Policies

The following policy issues must be resolved to meet the above production targets:

- What is the production capacity necessary for the given volumes of sales?
- How should the production capacity be increased – by new factories, additional plant, additional personnel, or longer working with existing plant?
- What proportion of the production should be made and what proportion should be bought in?
- What policies are being adopted to meet cost targets: automation, special purchasing arrangements, value engineering, product and process redesign, or minimizing stock levels?
- With regard to policies towards suppliers, how can the relationships with suppliers be enhanced so that both parties benefit economically?

Projections

The production data are integrated with data from the other functional areas, and projections are made to calculate break-even and safety stock levels and to see the broader consequences of the proposed policies. After projection, policies may be amended if necessary.

Resources

On the basis of the policies decided upon, determine the resources necessary to implement them, and draw up budgets to allocate these resources.

Control and evaluation

Ensure that devices to enable the finally agreed policies to be monitored and evaluated are in place. These were shown in Chapters 8 and 10.

Implementation in the personnel function

The personnel requirements are dependent variables directly determined by the proposed sales and production schedules.

Targets

What are the personnel targets in terms of:

- Numbers of personnel broken down according to functions?
- Skills, motivation, days lost, productivity?
- Total labour costs and unit labour costs?

Policies

In order to meet the sales and production schedules:

- Is the labour force adequate in terms of numbers, skills, and location?
- What recruitment and training programmes will be necessary to provide the required labour force?
- What is the level of motivation or commitment and what policies should be adopted to maintain or improve it – training, incentives, salaries and wages, conditions, etc?
- Is compensation linked to results?
- What is the current level of absenteeism?

Projections

The personnel data are combined with other functional data to help provide integrated projections for the SBU.

Resources

On the basis of the policies decided upon determine the resources necessary to implement these policies and draw up budgets to allocate these resources.

Control and evaluation

Ensure that devices which will enable the finally agreed policies to be monitored and evaluated are in place. These were shown in Chapters 8 and 10.

Conclusion on functional implementation

This chapter has provided a framework through which strategy a company's can be implemented. The framework is multi-dimensional, in that it explicitly

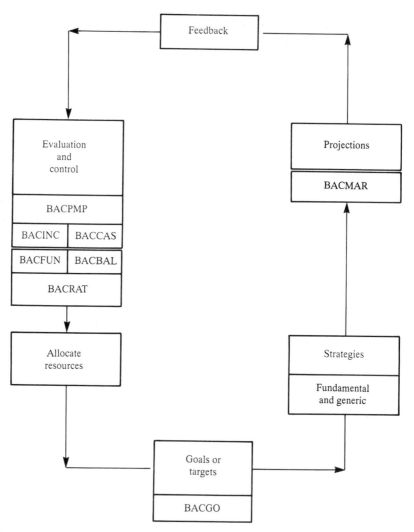

Figure 61   How elements of the implementation process interact in the Bacchus model

recognizes the need for a broader range of concerns than simply the refining of corporate goals into functional targets. In addition cognizance must also be taken of the behavioural elements of the process.

MODELLING THE PROCESS OF IMPLEMENTATION

A separate chapter has not been devoted to this topic, because the modelling process set out in previous chapters implies that the informational, as opposed to the behavioural, requirements for implementation have been set in place. However, Figure 61 shows how implementation in Bacchus is indeed directly related to the general process of implementation, as shown in Figure 60.

References

1 Yamada, E., *Ethos of Japan with Regard to the Post War Economy*, Oka Shobo Publishing Co. Ltd, Tokyo, 1985.
2 Murray, J., 'Strategic Behaviour in the New Venture', *IBAR*, Vol. 6, No. 1, 1984.
3 Baker, E. L., 'Managing Organizational Culture', *Management Review*, July 1980, pp. 9–13.
4 Garnett, A. D., 'Pulling slowly Out of a Patrician Past', *Financial Times*, 9 June 1986, p. 20.
5 Chandler, A. D., *Strategy and Structure*, MIT Press, 1972.

15 Evaluation and control

INTRODUCTION

The final element in the strategic planning model is that of evaluation and control. It is concerned with appraising how well the chosen strategy is being implemented, with the basis of the appraisal being how well the actual results achieved during its operation compare with the forecast results. The evaluation stage thus provides management with the opportunity to examine how well goals and objectives are being achieved, to monitor the progress of implementation, and to take corrective action should the level of achievement be considered unsatisfactory.

Evaluation and control are particularly important at the corporate or strategic level, as the operations evaluated at this level tend to be long-run, important ones. It is at this level that the composition of the company's fixed assets may be changed, through, for example, the acquisition of a new company or the disposal of an SBU. Consequently the success or failure of corporate or strategic plans is a fundamental determinant of future success.

The contributions that evaluation and control can make

Some form of evaluation and control is generally essential for the economic well-being of all companies, and when it is effectively employed, it is a mechanism for helping to keep the company strategically and operationally healthy through the contributions it can make in the following areas.

Tracking the environment

A comprehensive approach to evaluation is not confined to internal issues; rather it also tracks the environment, so that the company can shift its strategy and its structure in response to significant environmental changes. The importance of environmental surveillance in evaluation is a function of the nature of the industry. For example, successful companies in the computer industry must constantly sift the technological developments for significant change: failure to do so will lead to extinction. This sensitivity to environmental change is less important in more stable industries, such as the legal profession.

Tracking company performance

Performance at all levels in the company hierarchy will not normally conform to the targets that have been set. Deviations from pre-ordained standards or goals will naturally occur as different departments either fail to meet, or exceed, targets. Control and evaluation mechanisms are necessary to monitor and appraise the impact of deviations and to ensure that actions taken will ensure company-wide compliance with the strategies that have been adopted.

Providing feedback

In most companies feedback about the effectiveness of strategies is an important ingredient in ensuring that adherence to an approved strategy continues. Evaluation and control provide a mechanism for doing this.

Acting as a motivator

The process of control and evaluation can be a strongly motivating force (either as a negative reinforcer, where failure to meet targets results in some form of sanctions, or as a positive reinforcer, where success in achieving targets results in some form of rewards). Individuals at all levels who are aware of the criteria by which they will be judged will have clear personal targets that should help motivate them to achieve company objectives.

Acting as a sensitizer

An effective control and evaluation system should be sensitive to internal and external stimuli and should enable the company to respond quickly and appropriately.

Impediments to effective control and evaluation

Although the necessity for having mechanisms for control and evaluation is widely accepted, the power of such mechanisms can be greatly diminished if they have the following characteristics.

Coerciveness

Coercive control and evaluation mechanisms, which cause personnel to have the feeling of constant threatening appraisal, normally have demotivating effects that are ultimately harmful to the company. Personnel seek to avoid sanctions rather than strive to achieve company goals.

Systems that encourage cheating

Related to coercion is the element of cheating. In companies in which there are severe penalties for failing to meet targets, there may be an inclination for personnel to submit false figures of achievement in order to avoid the penalties associated with failure. Such an attitude can corrupt the company's data and consequently greatly reduce the value of monitoring procedures.

Timeliness

A fundamental determinant of the effectiveness of control and evaluation is the timeliness of the information provided. This timeliness can be considered to have two related aspects:

1   If information is provided only after significant landmarks in the implementation process have been passed, then it does not provide the feedback to guide subsequent implementation. This type of information provision merely records such landmarks and contributes little to control. For example, should the sales department of a company experience a sudden and significant decline in its sales, the more speedily this information is communicated through the company, the more speedily can a recovery strategy be planned and implemented.
2   If the control and evaluation process is merely mechanical, i.e. it takes place at regularly pre-ordained intervals rather than continuously and dynamically, then adherence to the timetable for evaluation may destroy its diagnostic and prescriptive powers. This is not to say that control and evaluation should take place at random intervals. Rather, in addition to regular reports, there should also be a complementary continuous control and evaluation process, so that deviations from planned goals or targets are spotted as speedily as possible.

Costliness

The costliness of providing information can be measured in terms of two major resources: personnel time and money. Thus relatively large amounts of time spent on control and evaluation may be less fruitful than if the time were spent on more creative activities. Similarly, if the monetary cost of providing information for control and evaluation is high, then the benefits derived from the process may not justify the expenditure.

A GENERAL FRAMEWORK FOR EVALUATION AND CONTROL

Irrespective of the level in the company at which evaluation and control is being carried out the process has some common features. These include the following:

The objectives of control and evaluation

In general the objectives of control and evaluation will be:

- To set standards for achievement: these are the goals or targets for the strategy.
- To measure company performance, i.e. how well the goals or targets are being achieved.
- To make comparisons between the set standards and the actual performance achieved: this is the evaluation of the performance.
- To take action when appropriate: this is the dynamic aspect of the process, which attempts to ensure that the strategy being followed continues to meet company goals.

Types of measure

Generally two types of measures – qualitative and quantitative – may be used. The qualitative measures describe the quality of company performance and how well goals are being achieved, e.g. 'the company's sales growth has been satisfactory'. Quantitative measures attempt to give a precise numerical measure of performance and goal achievement, e.g. 'the company's sales revenue grew by 11.1 per cent last year'. Because of the subjective nature of qualitative measures of performance, it is normally considered that the quality and utility of such measures are greatly enhanced if they can be complemented by quantitative ones. For example, if in evaluating the performance of a product in a market against competing products the qualitative assessment is that 'the product has performed better than competitors' products in terms of sales and consumer acceptance', then this assessment would be greatly enhanced if it were to be accompanied by quantitative assessments such as 'the product's relative market share changed from 0.10 at the start of the year to 0.20 at the end of the year. This increase in relative market share of 100 per cent was much superior to next best performing competitor which was only able to increase its relative market share by 25 per cent'.

The dual focus

In most evaluations a dual focus will be necessary, i.e. there must be a consideration of internal and external factors that may be influencing the level of performance and goal achievement.

Information quality

The quality of control and evaluation process will be directly determined by the quality of information upon which the assessments are based:

poor information will generally lead to poor control and evaluation, and vice versa. Generally information should be correct, timely, concise, and relevant.

Assignment of responsibility

Effective control and evaluation requires that the responsibility for activities should be assigned unambiguously to particular individuals. Therefore the system should be based on the existing set of responsibility centres and should reflect the type of responsibility that is vested in each centre, i.e. a cost centre should be evaluated on its 'cost performance', an investment centre on its 'investment performance' and a profit centre on its 'profit performance'.

Action orientation

Control and evaluation procedures that do not lead to action being taken when necessary are merely paper exercises.

Future or historical orientation

Although control and evaluation are usually considered from a historical perspective, i.e. the process is concerned with appraising the effectiveness of a past strategy, they can also have a future orientation. Thus the techniques outlined on pp. 215–217, which may be employed in control and evaluation, can be used both as devices for assessing the anticipated future impact of different strategic options *before* implementation and as devices for reviewing the *historical performance* of a company *after* a strategy has been followed. How the techniques are applied is identical in each case: the projected or the historical performance is judged against the goals or targets set and, depending upon the degree of congruence between the projected or achieved performance, action is taken. How the process of control and evaluation is affected is now considered.

THE GENERAL RESULTS OF CONTROL AND EVALUATION

When the operation of any strategy is being evaluated just two results are possible.

The goals are being achieved

In this circumstance the strategy is being implemented successfully, i.e. pre-ordained goals and targets are being met, and therefore, assuming that the original strategy is still optimal, it should continue to be implemented as before.

The goals are not being achieved

If an organization is failing to achieve its goals or targets, it may be due to one or both of the following reasons:

1   The external environment has changed and the original strategy is no longer appropriate. In this case it is likely that a change of strategy will be required, so that the company can adapt to the changed environmental circumstances. For example, a significant environmental change could be the entry of new and aggressive competitors into the market. Such an event would usually require a strategic realignment that explicitly considers changes necessary to meet this increase in competitive pressure. Drucker[1] has suggested that in this type of situation, i.e. where the environment has changed, the company's current strategy is lacking in *effectiveness* and a change of *strategy* is required.
2   The other possible cause of a company failing to achieve its goals is that its internal operations are being carried out unsatisfactorily. Here it is likely that, rather than a change of strategy, a change in operations or procedures is required. For example, if a company was experiencing unsatisfactory levels of sales because of a lack of communication between the marketing department and the production department, then the appropriate change would be action to improve communication between the two departments, with the original strategy continuing to be implemented. Drucker has suggested that in this type of situation the strategy is lacking in *efficiency* and a change in *operations* is needed.

The nature of evaluation and control

Thus in the evaluation and control of strategy there is a spectrum of possible actions that ranges from 'doing nothing' other than fine-tuning the existing strategy (the strategy is working satisfactorily and little change is required) to fundamental changes in the strategy (the strategy is failing, and unless action is taken corporate failure will occur). The degree of strategy change will be determined by the size of the variances from strategic goals, and whether the cause of the variances is ineffectiveness or inefficiency.

EVALUATION AND CONTROL AT THE FUNCTIONAL, SBU AND CORPORATE LEVELS

For evaluation and control it is suggested that it is more appropriate to 'invert' the company hierarchy outlined on p. 230 in Chapter 14 and consider the process from a 'bottom-up' rather than a 'top-down' approach. This is suggested because:

1 It is the results at the lowest levels of the hierarchy that ultimately determine SBU results.
2 It is the consolidations of the SBU results that determine corporate results.
3 The time horizons in which lower level targets or goals must be achieved are shorter, and therefore results are available sooner.
4 Lower level results are more easily measured, in that they tend to be expressed in figures, e.g. 'Have total sales of Product 1 of £250,000 in 1991'.

It is assumed that in any company evaluation and control always take place in the same fashion, irrespective of whether the level is functional, SBU or corporate. The process is as follows.

The process of evaluation and control

This can be considered under three main headings:

- Evaluation of the degree of achievement of goals or targets.
- Evaluation of the strategies.
- Evaluation of the balance.

The detail of evaluation and control

The detail of how evaluation and control is carried out is provided in Chapter 8, and how it is modelled is provided in Chapter 9.

Reference

Drucker, P., *Management*, Heinemann, 1974.

16 Developing and writing a strategic plan

INTRODUCTION

It is often the case that when managers are required to develop and write a strategic plan, they feel in need of guidance. Questions they often seem to ask include:

1 Just what is a strategic plan?
2 In what way is it different from a normal planning exercise?
3 What is its structure?
4 What are the topics?
5 How do I start?

With this apparent need for guidance in mind this chapter sets out an approach the author has used successfully with many managers who were writing their first strategic plan.

The approach sets out a generic structure – called the Skeleton Strategic Plan – which, after they have read the other chapters in this book, should enable managers to write their own strategic plan. The Skeleton Strategic Plan is 'the bones' of a strategic plan that managers should be able to flesh out so that it becomes an effective planning document for their own company. It should be noted that the strategic plan can be developed with or without the computer modelling elements of the book.

THE SKELETON STRATEGIC PLAN

The Skeleton Strategic Plan assumes that there is an SBU called XXX and its managing director is required by corporate headquarters to develop a strategic plan for his SBU. The Skeleton, which is presented below, sets out the headings that ought to appear in a strategic plan, and each heading makes reference to the relevant chapter or chapters in this book. The skeleton ought to 'flesh out' to a plan of between 13 and 18 pages. Consequently it is hoped that after reading the book, managers should be well prepared to undertake this task.

**THE SKELETON OF THE STRATEGIC PLAN
FOR
XXX STRATEGIC BUSINESS UNIT**

199X to 199Z

Prepared by...

Date

THE STRATEGIC DIRECTION OF SBU XX LTD, 199X–199Z

SECTION
1 *EXECUTIVE SUMMARY*
   A summary of the main issues to be covered in the report.
2 *INTRODUCTION*
   (a) The recent history and performance of Strategic Business Unit XXX.
   (b) The substance of this report: a distillation of the views of the decision makers of the group.

   Reading: Chapter 2.
3 *DEFINING BUSINESS UNIT XXX's BUSINESS*
   Defining Business Unit XXX's current business and its likely future businesses, in terms of products, markets, customers, technology and competitors.

   Reading: Chapter 4.
4 *BUSINESS UNIT XXX's MISSIONS AND GOALS*
   Business Unit XXX's mission, goals, objectives and targets: current and in the next 3 years. Qualitative and quantitative measurement. How they relate to the main board's mission, goals, and objectives.

   Reading: Chapter 8, p. 140.
5 *BUSINESS UNIT XXX's PORTFOLIO POSITION*
   Business Unit XXX's corporate portfolio position.

   Reading: Chapter 4.
6 *BUSINESS UNIT XXX's STRENGTHS AND WEAKNESSES*
   A strategic view of the areas in which Business Unit XXX excels, and the areas in which it needs to be strengthened.

Reading: Chapter 6.

7 *BUSINESS UNIT XXX's ENVIRONMENT*
An assessment of the competitive environment in which Business Unit XXX operates today, and how that environment is likely to change in the next 3 years.

Reading: Chapters 8 and 10.

8 *BUSINESS UNIT XXX's CURRENT STRATEGIC POSITION*
   (a) An assessment of Business Unit XXX's current strategic position.
   (b) A financial analysis of Business Unit XXX's current strategic position.
   (c) Key financial and strategic ratios to show Business Unit XXX's current strategic position.
   (d) An assessment of Business Unit XXX from a product market portfolio perspective.

Reading: Chapter 12.

9 *A GAP ANALYSIS FOR BUSINESS UNIT XXX*
This gap analysis to be carried out at the following levels:
   (a) Individual product lines.
   (b) The business unit.

Reading: Chapter 12.

10 *BUSINESS UNIT XXX's STRATEGIES FOR THE FUTURE*
   (a) The fundamental and generic strategies that Business Unit XXX will follow over the next 3 years.
   (b) Alternative Business Unit XXX portfolios over the next 5 years, together with their cash consequences.

11 *BUSINESS UNIT XXX's RESOURCES*
The resource implications of following the strategies set out under 10.

Index